The Shabbat Elevator and Other Sabbath Subterfuges

The Shabbat Elevator and Other Sabbath Subterfuges

An Unorthodox Essay on Circumventing Custom and Jewish Character

Alan Dundes

ROWMAN & LITTLEFIELD PUBLISHERS, INC.
Lanham • Boulder • New York • Oxford

ROWMAN & LITTLEFIELD PUBLISHERS, INC.

Published in the United States of America
by Rowman & Littlefield Publishers, Inc.
4720 Boston Way, Lanham, Maryland 20706
www.rowmanlittlefield.com

12 Hid's Copse Road, Cumnor Hill, Oxford OX2 9JJ, England

British Library Cataloguing in Publication Information Available

Library of Congress Cataloging-in-Publication Data

Dundes, Alan.
The Shabbat elevator and other Sabbath subterfuges : an unorthodox essay on circumventing custom and Jewish character / Alan Dundes.
p. cm.
Includes bibliographical references and index.
ISBN 0-7425-1670-9 (alk. paper)—ISBN 0-7425-1671-7 (alk. paper)
1. Sabbath (Jewish law). 2. Prohibited work (Jewish law). 3. Jews—Psychology. 4. Judaism and psychoanalysis. I. Title.
BM685.D86 2002
296.4'12—dc21 2001041927

Printed in the United States of America

∞ ™ The paper used in this publication meets the minimum requirements of American National Standard for Information Sciences—Permanence of Paper for Printed Library Materials, ANSI/NISO Z39.48–1992.

Dedication

This extended essay is dedicated to a former student who wishes to remain anonymous. This student took my courses in anthropology and folklore at Berkeley in the early 1960s. In March 2000, he kindly chose to honor me by sending me a check (made out to the university, but indicating that the allocation of it was up to me). The check was for the amount of one million dollars. It was the thrill of a lifetime to receive such a letter with such a remarkable gift. The extraordinary generosity of this student will ensure that the study of folklore will continue at Berkeley after my retirement. And for this, I shall always be grateful.

Contents

Acknowledgments

I am indebted to those friends, colleagues, and students who were kind enough to recommend sources for the present study and to those who generously shared personal anecdotes, a number of which I have gratefully incorporated into this essay. Among those helpful individuals are: Robert Alter, Jody Ames, Haya and Zeev Bar-Itzhak, Dan Ben-Amos, Stanley Brandes, William and Lisa Brinner, Frances Cattermole-Tally, Michael Chyet, Erika K. Clowes, Marvin Cohen, Lauren Dundes, Marc Galanter, Tova Gazit, Michele Goldwasser, Yehuda Goodman, Ilana Harlow, Galit Hasan-Rokem, Misha Klein, Rachel Lewis, Sabina Magliocco, Rosalyn McGillivray, Wolfgang Mieder, Elissa Mondschein, Rodney Needham, William Propp, Alison Renteln, Ron Rosenberg, Marlo Seidel, Eric Silverman, Ira Steingroot, Allan Stone, and Emily Zaiden. It goes without saying that none of the above mentioned individuals are in any way responsible for my general thesis or for any of my conclusions. I take full responsibility for what I have written.

For a close reading of an early draft of this manuscript, I thank my daughter Lauren Dundes, Professor of Sociology at Western Maryland College, and for a helpful set of suggestions and bibliographical recommendations based on a meticulous review of the completed manuscript, I express my gratitude to anthropologist Eric Silverman of De Pauw University. Professor Silverman's extensive expertise in Judaica and his unusual openness to Freudian thought made it possible for him to consider this unabashedly psychoanalytic essay on Jewish character sympathetically.

My thanks too goes to Rowman & Littlefield editor Dean Birkenkamp who has proven more than once that he is willing to take intellectual risks by encouraging my various research projects—including this one.

Prologue

Just in case anyone is curious how this research project came about, I should indicate that it all started in June 1999 in the lobby of the Hotel Dan-Panorama in Haifa, Israel. Having been invited to address the Israeli Folklore Society at their annual meeting, my host, Professor Haya Bar-Itzhak, chair of the Department of Hebrew and Comparative Literature and head of folklore studies at the University of Haifa, and her convivial husband, Ze'ev, were kind enough to lodge my wife, Carolyn, and me at that fine hotel.

One morning, my wife noticed a small sign placed over the left-hand elevator of a bank of three elevators. The plaque read simply "Shabbat Elevator." She asked me what that meant. I said I had no idea. Her response was, "Let's go to the desk and ask." I protested as most American males would under the circumstances, being culturally programmed never to admit ignorance by asking for directions or for other presumably elementary information. So naturally we proceeded to ask the clerk at the desk for the meaning of the sign "Shabbat Elevator."

"That's for our Orthodox patrons," we were told. "They are not allowed to push elevator buttons on the Sabbath and so we always assign Orthodox visitors who are here over the Sabbath to rooms on one of the first three floors because the Shabbat elevator is set to stop automatically at each of these floors. This means that an Orthodox Jew would not need to push the button to get to his or her floor. The sign also alerts non-Orthodox Jews so that they can avoid stopping at floors one through three enroute to their higher destination." I regret to say that I laughed out loud upon hearing this explanation, so loud in fact that I embarrassed my wife by my unrestrained outburst of laughter in the hotel lobby. I later learned that there were other variations of the Shabbat elevator in Israel and in the United States. In Israel, for example, there are hotel Shabbat elevators that stop only at odd-numbered floors or at even-numbered floors. But the underlying rationale remains constant.

The ongoing importance of Shabbat elevators is signaled by the fact that in July of 2001, the Israeli Knesset passed a law stating that every new multi-storied building, public or private, built with more than one elevator must have at least one Shabbat elevator. Observant occupants of the building who wish to use the Shabbat elevator will be obliged to pay a fee to cover the expenses of operating it.

My discovery of the Shabbat elevator gradually led me to investigate other Sabbath traditions observed by some (though by no means all) contemporary (mostly Orthodox) Jews. In some way, this odyssey of discovery has been a very personal one. My parents were both Jewish. I remember that my maternal grandfather, David Rothschild, was given a sort of loving cup from the temple to which he belonged to thank him for his years of faithful attendance and service. My father, Maurice Dundes, was, I believe, the president of his (Jewish) fraternity Zeta Beta Tau, at City College of New York in the 1920s. But I gathered from numerous conversations that both my parents had felt somewhat suffocated by the close Jewish atmosphere in which they lived in New York City and so when I was just one year old, they fled to a rural area near Patterson, New York, about sixty miles north of the city. And it was on a former farm there that I spent my childhood. Although almost all of our family friends were Jewish, I did not have much exposure to formal Jewish religious practices. As a result, although I was always proud of my heritage, I felt quite ignorant of the religious elements in Judaism. Even after I became a professional folklorist, earning my doctorate in folklore in 1962, I did little to fill in this gap in my education. Instead, I studied the folklore of various groups: Native Americans, African Americans, and the peoples of India, among others. It was not until the Shabbat elevator incident that I set about learning about Jewish religious ritual in earnest.

Because of my ignorance, I was forced to rely on the vast numbers of scholarly writings on Jewish religion. Since I was concentrating on the Sabbath, I found Yehoshua Y. Neuwirth's two volume *Shemirath Shabbath: A Guide to the Practical Observance of Shabbath* (1989) and the various books written by Simcha Bunim Cohen especially valuable. Equally helpful was Hyman E. Goldin's translation of Rabbi Solomon Ganzfried's *Code of Jewish Law* (1961). These four volumes in one containing "A Compilation of Jewish Laws and Customs" provided data not easily available elsewhere. Alfred J. Kolatch's *The Jewish Book of Why* (1995), first published in 1981, and the sequel *The Second Jewish Book of Why* (1985) furnished up-to-date coverage of many traditional ritual practices. I have also consulted many of the classic Jewish religious texts including the Mishnah and the Babylonian Talmud among others. All quotations from the Old and New Testament come from my family Bible, which happens to be the King James Version. I am well aware of other translations of the Bible, specifically the Old Testament, but as my intended audience includes non-Jews, I decided to utilize the King James Version, first published in 1611. In addition to reading contemporary popular how-to-be-a-good-Jewish-home manuals, I have not hesitated to cite Jewish jokes and proverbs where I thought they were appropriate. The great advantage of jokes and proverbs is that they, like all forms of folklore, provide an unequalled, often succinct and concise, picture of a people, their foibles and follies, their anxieties and apprehensions, in a relatively uncensored fashion. Jokes not specifically attributed come from my own personal repertoire.

There are even Jewish jokes about Jews who study Jewish culture. For example, the doyen of Jewish folkloristics is Professor Dov Noy, who established the modern study of Jewish folklore at Hebrew University in Jerusalem. A peripatetic scholar, he is constantly flying around the world giving lectures on Jewish subjects. A well-known joke about him, circulating among Israeli folklorists, goes as follows: "Did you hear about the two planes that crashed over Indonesia? Dov Noy was on both of them."

Among scholars devoted to Jewish religious studies, none is more prominent or more prolific than Jacob Neusner. He seems to have published more books than the number of articles written by most scholars. By his own count, he has written or edited more than three hundred books, all but one of them devoted to Judaism (1991, 13). It is his earthy American translation of the multivolume *Babylonian Talmud* that I have relied upon in this research. And it is his remarkable productivity that provides the basis for the following joke circulating among students of Jewish studies in the United States: A student calls the Neusner home asking to speak to Professor Neusner. His wife answers the caller by saying "Professor Neusner is busy right now writing a book." The student responds, "That's okay, I'll hold."

No doubt my own training as a folklorist and my avowed Freudian bias have very much colored my selection of source materials as well as my perception of Jewish religious ritual connected with Sabbath observance. But at the same time, these influences have given me a different perspective from that normally encountered in literature devoted to Jewish studies. It is for the reader to decide whether this new perspective illuminates our understanding of the character of one of the oldest known human groups on the face of the earth.

The Shabbat Elevator and Other Sabbath Subterfuges

THE CONCEPT OF CUSTOM

Folklorists study many different genres or types of folklore. These include myth, folktale, legend, proverb, riddle, ballad, curse, charm, and superstition among others. There are dozens of folklore genres. Some are major such as epic; others are minor such as tongue twisters. Of all the hundreds of folklore genres, none is more basic and fundamental than custom. Sometimes the term used to refer to this form of folklore is "custom and belief" and this is appropriate because a given routinized and even ritual behavioral pattern is often intimately connected to belief of some kind. In some instances, the custom may be related to religious conviction. For example, a dietary custom of either eating a particular item (or not eating that same item) may be proscribed by a formal religious rule.

Custom is also known under a great variety of names: folkways, mores, usages, traditions, to mention a few. Anthropologist Ruth Benedict (1887–1948) in her 1929 essay "The Science of Custom," an essay that eventually became the first chapter of her landmark book *Patterns of Culture* in 1934, speaks of custom as "behavior at its most commonplace" but pays tribute to the "predominant role that custom plays in experience and in belief." Custom, Benedict argues, structures the way man perceives his world. In her words, "There is no social problem it is more incumbent upon us to understand than that of the role of custom in our total life. Until we are intelligent as to the laws and the varieties of customs, the main complicating facts of human life will remain to us an unintelligible book. The first concern of the anthropologist is always for this affair of custom."

A few years earlier, in 1926, anthropologist Bronislaw Malinowski (1884–1942) devoted one chapter of his *Crime and Custom in Savage Society*, titled "The Rules of Custom Defined and Classified," to a discussion of the nature of custom. Malinowski's notion was that "the sum total of rules, conventions, and patterns of behaviour" could be designated as "the body of custom" (1967, 51). Both Benedict's and Malinowski's conceptions of custom come perilously close to equating custom with culture. The same goes for anthropological linguist Edward Sapir's definition of custom, which appeared in his entry on the subject in the first edition of the *Encyclopaedia of the Social Sciences* in 1931. "The word custom is used to apply to the totality of behavior patterns which are carried by tradition and lodged in the group, as contrasted with the more random personal activities of the individual. It is not properly applicable to those aspects of communal activity which are obviously determined by biological considerations" (658).

A more judicious position might be to consider custom as one component, albeit a major one, of the broader notion of the totality of culture. (For further considerations of the concept of custom, see Hultkrantz 1960; Leiser 1971; Wolfram 1972; Kelley 1990; and Thompson 1991, 1–15.) The Jewish equivalent of the concept of custom seems to be called *minhag* (Kalir 1965; Pollack 1973, 1980; Jacobs 1984b, 221–235; A. Cohen 1995; Rabinowitz 1996, 160–161).

One of the most problematic issues in custom research is the distinction or difference, if any, between custom and law. Some scholars have argued that custom is orally transmitted, whereas law is written and essentially codified. But others have argued that custom was either the original source of law or if not, that custom was the equivalent of law (Kelley 1990, 145). The notion of *Lex non scriptum*, or customary law, further confuses the question of the separation of custom and law (Renteln and Dundes 1995). The position taken here is that custom and law in the present context are essentially synonymous, and accordingly, the idea of circumventing custom could certainly legitimately be construed as circumventing law, especially folk law. The Hebrew terms, however, do reflect a difference based on the presumed source of the behavioral norm with "Halacha" (law), which comes from the Torah and the Talmud in contrast to "minhag" (custom), which comes from "popular practice" (Kolatch 1985, 253). When they are in conflict, sometimes custom takes precedence (Kolatch 1985, 256–257; 1995, 3).

In any event, the influence of custom upon behavior and thought is so great that it rivals "nature" as a determining factor in human experience. Indeed, Plutarch (46–120) in the course of discussing how difficult it was to give up eating meat in his "Advice About Keeping Well" (1956a, 265) described custom as being "almost second nature," a comparison earlier articulated by Cicero (106–43 B.C.E.) in his essay *De Finibus Bonorum et Malorum*. Cicero's version (1951, 476–477) was "Consuetudine quasi alteram quandam naturam effici" ("Custom produces a kind of second nature"). The modern proverbial form is: "Custom is second nature" (Kelley 1990, 131; for a Yiddish version of this proverb, see Kumove 1985, 62). One rabbi contended that the concept of "Habitual behavior becomes second nature" is the most significant construct responsible for Jewish patterns of thought and behavior (Amsel 1970, 64). In terms of the conventional nature versus nurture debate, custom clearly belongs to nurture. But the point is that once custom is acquired through the process that anthropologists call enculturation, it might as well be "nature." It is extremely difficult to reject the customs of one's culture and to avoid their often pervasive influence.

One of the major subcategories of custom falls under the rubric of "calendar customs." These customs are closely associated with particular days of the year, however a year may be defined differently in a particular culture. Calendar customs in the Western tradition would include traditions associated with the first day of April, the first day of May, and of course, the first day of January (New Year's Day). The year in any given culture is marked by a series of calendar customs, which may range from behavior lasting for a day, a week, or a month. Easter, Halloween, and Christmas celebrations would qualify as calendar customs. In the Jewish calendar, Yom Kippur, Passover, and Purim would be examples of calendar customs. Many holy days or holidays are marked by customary behavior reserved exclusively for those occasions.

It would not be wrong to categorize Sabbath observance as a form of calendar custom. Although the origins of the Sabbath are obscure, there can be no question that it is defined as the final day of a seven-day week (Negretti 1973). In the Jewish calendar, the Sabbath occurs on Saturday, although the beginning of the Sabbath coincides with the end of the previous day, that is to say, Friday. In theory, the end of Friday or the beginning of Saturday could be said to be midnight on Friday, but conception of "day" in this case depends instead on sunset. Accordingly, Jewish Sabbath begins with sunset on Friday and lasts until sunset on Saturday. Again, the arbitrariness of the definition of when day begins is apparent. For example, one could argue that a day logically begins with sunrise. In that case, the Sabbath would begin with sunrise on Saturday. Supposedly the Jewish rationale for their definition of a day comes from Genesis (Kertzer 1993, 205). "And God called the light Day, and the darkness he called Night. And the evening and the morning were the first day" (Gen. 1:5). It clearly does not say "And the morning and the evening were the first day." Moreover, this same sequence of "evening and morning" in that order is used to define the second, third, fourth, fifth, and sixth days (Gen. 1:8, 13, 19, 23, 31). Leviticus confirms this definition with specific reference to the Sabbath: "At even, from even unto even, shall ye celebrate your Sabbath" (23:32). So it would appear evident that God's concept of day unquestionably begins with the evening and ends with the day. (For a representative discussion of the relative merits of the "evening theory" versus the "morning theory" of the time when the biblical day begins, see Stroes 1966.)

Actually, the Sabbath, for all intents and purposes, begins shortly before sunset on Friday and ends shortly after sunset on Saturday. According to one account "Shabbat begins eighteen minutes before sunset on Friday and ends forty-two minutes after sunset on Saturday" (Greenberg 1983, 58). The choice of "eighteen minutes before sunset" seems to be the most common agreed-upon time to begin the Sabbath celebration, possibly because the numerical value of the letters in the Hebrew word for "life," *chai*, is eighteen (Steingroot 1995, 203), but the custom in Jerusalem, according to several sources, favors "forty minutes" before sunset (S. Cohen 1995, 14; Pick 1998, 18). Actually, many shops and businesses in Israel close at noon on Fridays so as to give people some time to leave the mundane world and prepare for the onset of Sabbath (Peli 1988, 101). One reason for having a fixed time for the beginning of Sabbath has to do with the candle-lighting ceremony that signals the onset of the Sabbath. Since one of the Sabbath rules prohibits lighting a fire, the candles must be lighted prior to the beginning of the Sabbath. Accordingly, "If, for example, one forgets to light the candles and suddenly realizes that the sun has set, one must celebrate the Sabbath without candles, because to light them would be a flagrant dishonoring of the very holiday, the Sabbath, that one is intending to honor" (Asheri 1978, 101).

THE SABBATH IN THE OLD TESTAMENT

Of all the hundreds upon hundreds of calendar customs celebrated around the world, the Sabbath may be unique insofar as it seems to be the only one directly mandated by God himself. For the command to celebrate the Sabbath is one of the Ten Commandments, supposedly communicated directly to Moses by God. As one writer phrased it, "The Sabbath is ordained by God Himself and is actually built into nature from its very beginning" (Peli 1988, 109). According to another, "Of all the rituals of Judaism, Shabbos is the only one included among the Ten Commandments" (Finkelman 1991, 34). Apparently, observing the Sabbath is of comparable importance to the

Supreme Being as "Thou shalt not kill" and "Thou shalt not steal." Moreover, if the actual order of the Commandments has any significance in terms of any hierarchy of importance, then it may be worth recalling that the Sabbath injunction is either the fourth or fifth Commandment, depending upon which version of the Ten Commandments is considered (Goldman 1956, 28–32), which would hint that it may rank higher than half of the Commandments including "Thou shalt not kill" and "Thou shalt not steal."

Also it should be noted that the Commandment concerning the Sabbath is much more detailed than any of the other Commandments. Most of the Commandments consist of a single sentential injunction. In contrast, the Sabbath imperative is extended over several sentences. Indeed, it has been pointed out (Caplan 1996, 11) that the so-called Sabbath Commandment actually consists of two separate commandments: a positive commandment to "Remember the Sabbath day" and a negative commandment "Thou shalt not do any work." (For a discussion of the different versions of the Sabbath Commandment, see Biggs 1975; for a discussion of the Ten Commandments as evidence of the original orality of the Old Testament, see Dundes 1999.) Whatever the Sabbath's ranking may be, it is surely the case that no other calendar custom on the face of the earth can claim its authority on the basis of its being one of the Ten Commandments. That much is certain.

One version of the Ten Commandments includes the following (Exod. 20:8–11):

> Remember the Sabbath day, to keep it holy. Six days shalt thou labor, and do all thy work: But the seventh day is the Sabbath of the Lord thy God: in it thou shalt not do any work, thou, nor thy son, nor thy daughter, thy manservant, nor thy maidservant, nor thy cattle, nor thy stranger that is within thy gates: For in six days, the Lord made heaven and earth, the sea, and all that in them is, and rested the seventh day: wherefore the Lord blessed the Sabbath day, and hallowed it.

Part of this definition of Sabbath is echoed later in Exodus (34:21): "Six days thou shalt work, but on the seventh day thou shalt rest: in earing time and in harvest time thou shalt rest." In Leviticus, the regulation prohibiting work on the Sabbath is repeated: "Six days shall work be done: but the seventh day is the Sabbath of rest, a holy convocation; ye shall do no work therein: it is the Sabbath of the Lord in all your dwellings" (23:3), but in Leviticus (19:3, 30), the divine instruction varies slightly. Here it is not a question of "remembering" the Sabbath, but rather "keeping the Sabbath." Some Jews, troubled by the apparent discrepancy between "remembering" and "keeping," attempt to finesse the issue by citing a line from Psalm 62:11:

"God hath spoken once; twice have I heard this" (Peli 1988, 49). "Keeping" is also the term of choice in another full version of the Ten Commandments, namely, that found in Deuteronomy. In this version, the celebration of the Sabbath is linked to the exodus from Egypt, a somewhat puzzling linkage (Jastrow 1898, 340), rather than the original creation of the world (Deut. 5:12–15):

> Keep the Sabbath day to sanctify it as the Lord they God hath commanded thee. Six days thou shalt labor, and do all thy work: But the seventh day is the Sabbath day of the Lord thy God: in it thou shalt not do any work, thou, nor thy son, nor thy daughter, nor thy manservant, nor thy maidservant, nor thine ox, nor thine ass, nor any of thy cattle, nor thy stranger that is within thy gates; that thy manservant and thy maidservant may rest as well as thou. And remember that thou wast a servant in the land of Egypt, and that the Lord thy God brought thee out thence through a mighty hand and by a stretched out arm: therefore the Lord thy God commanded thee to keep the Sabbath day.

There are several interesting differences in these versions of the Sabbath portion of the Ten Commandments (Eder 1997). An ox and an ass are specifically mentioned in Deuteronomy as being required to be allowed to rest on the Sabbath; they are not mentioned at all in the Exodus version. (It is quite remarkable that there is any variation at all inasmuch as the Ten Commandments were supposed to have been inscribed on stone tablets by either Moses or God himself!) But whether the command is to "Remember" the Sabbath or "Keep" the Sabbath, it would appear that by the time God got around to issuing the Ten Commandments, the Sabbath tradition was already known to the Jews, and that it was already in effect (Budde 1928, 5). One cannot, logically speaking, possibly "remember" or "keep" a tradition that is being enunciated or created for the first time. So it is safe to assume that the Sabbath must be older than the Ten Commandments. As Lauterbach remarks: "It was first instituted at the very beginning of creation and God Himself observed it" (1973, 439). In other words, either God created the Sabbath at the time of Creation or it antedated the act of creation, in effect obliging God himself to obey its mandate.

How much older than the Ten Commandments or the Old Testament might the Sabbath be? It is difficult to say. In 1883, Wilhelm Lotz in his *Questiones de historia Sabbati* suggested a Babylonian origin for the Hebrew Sabbath (Andreasen 1972, 1; Kimball 1978, 307). This theory was later championed by Friedrich Delitzsch, professor of Assyriology at the University of Berlin in 1903, in his book *Babel and Bible*, where he declared with some certainty that the Sabbath custom had indeed been borrowed from Babylonian culture.

> The Babylonians also had their Sabbath day (*shabattu*), and a calendar of feasts and sacrifices has been unearthed according to which the 7th, 14th, 21st and 28th days of every month were set apart as days on which no work should be done, on which the king should not change his robes, nor mount his chariot, nor offer sacrifices, nor render legal decisions, nor eat of boiled or roasted meats, on which not even a physician should lay hands on the sick. Now this setting apart of the seventh day for the propitiation of the gods is really understood from the Babylonian point of view, and there can therefore be scarcely the shadow of a doubt that in the last resort we are indebted to this ancient nation on the banks of the Euphrates and the Tigris for the plenitude of blessings that flows from our day of Sabbath or Sunday rest. (1903, 38–39)

Certainly the linguistic parallel is persuasive: *shabattu* and Sabbath (Shabat) (Budde 1928, 7). Even now the word for "Saturday" in several Indo-European languages would appear to be cognate: Italian *sabato*, Spanish *sabado*, Serbo-Croatian *subota*, and Russian *subbota*. In this connection, it is interesting, linguistically speaking, that the Arabic word for the number seven is *sab* (Somogyi 1958, 246). The specifics of prohibiting work on each of the series of seventh days of the Babylonian month even to the point of not permitting physicians to treat the sick are certainly convincing evidence that the Sabbath custom did not begin in ancient Israel. Delitzsch in his rebuttal to a host of critics of his argument added further details to his discussion of the Sabbath: "The mooted words in the calendar of festivals run, according to our present knowledge, thus: 'The shepherd of the great nations shall not eat roasted or smoked (?) meat (variant: anything touched by fire), not change his garment, not put on white raiment, not offer sacrifice" (1903, 156; cf. Pinches 1904, 52). We shall return later to the taboo of not eating "anything touched by fire."

The case for a Babylonian connection to the Jewish Sabbath is also strengthened by the existence of a tradition of number symbolism in both cultures, namely, of the number seven (Hehn 1907, 1925). Part of this notion referred to astronomical data, for example, the understanding at that time that there were only seven planets or only seven stars in the Pleiades (Celada 1948; Colson 1926). However, the symbolic significance attributed to the number seven extended far beyond Babylonia (Andrian 1901). In any event, this Babylonian origin theory has not been popular, partly, I suspect, for reasons that have to do with the understandable resistance among both Jews and Christians to the notion that any part of their precious religious heritage could have derived from earlier "pagan" sources. Jastrow notes (1898, 317) that even before the Jewish exile in Babylonia, there was a "hostile spirit" on the part of the Hebrew leaders "towards anything Babylonian—a hostility which grew to still larger proportions during the exile." Lauterbach insists that the Sabbath "is a unique institution, conceived and developed by the Jewish genius, without any equivalent among the similar institutions of other people" (1973, 437), and this is a view held by many (Peli 1988, 18).

One should keep in mind that the negative image of Babylon has scriptural precedent. In the startling book of Revelation, the last book of the New Testament, we find a graphic account of the whore of Babylon:

> I saw a woman sit upon a scarlet-colored beast full of names of blasphemy, having seven heads and ten horns. And the woman was arrayed in purple and scarlet color, and decked with gold and precious stones and pearls, having a golden cup in her hand full of abominations and filthiness of her fornication: And upon her forehead was a name written, MYSTERY, "BABYLON THE GREAT, THE MOTHER OF HARLOTS AND ABOMINATIONS OF THE EARTH." (Rev. 17:3–5)

Babylon, the incarnation of evil, is later described by an angel who came to earth from heaven:

> "Babylon the great is fallen, is fallen, and is become the habitation of devils, and the hold of every foul spirit, and a cage of every unclean and hateful bird. For all nations have drunk of the wine of the wrath of her fornication, and the kings of the earth have committed fornication with her, and the merchants of the earth are waxed rich through the abundance of her delicacies." (Rev. 18:2–3)

With this kind of highly negative image, it is no wonder that Christians, at any rate, have no wish to rejoice in a possible Babylonian origin of the Sabbath. There are also Jews who utterly reject a Babylonian origin of their beloved Sabbath. Hayyim Schauss's book, *The Jewish Festivals: History & Observance*, first published in 1938, opens with a substantial discussion of the Sabbath (1962, 3–37): "The origin of the Sabbath is obscure, as are the beginnings of all other festivals. Only this much is certain, that the Jewish Sabbath did not originate in Babylonia, as some Assyriologists asserted." Others insist that the biblical conception of the Sabbath is unique and not to be found in surrounding ancient Near Eastern cultures (Hallo 1977, 15).

There is a huge mass of scholarship devoted to ascertaining the origin of the Sabbath (cf. North 1955; Andreasen 1974; for a representative sample of the voluminous scholarship devoted to the Sabbath, see the "Special Bibliography on the Sabbath" in Negretti 1973, 20–24), but whether it derives from an earlier Babylonian custom bearing a cognate name or is related to the possible numerological significance of "seven" or is a sign of a lunar calendar with the moon's waning construed as a type of "rest" or "cessation" (cf. Meinhold 1909; Meek 1914; McKay 1991, 1992, 1994) or is simply a form of "rest day" (Webster 1916, 242–271), or is a combination of two or more of these hypotheses is not our concern in this essay. (For helpful surveys of Sabbath origin theories, see Mahler 1908; Kraeling 1933; Dressler 1982; and especially Andreasen 1972.) Whatever the ultimate origin of the Sabbath may be, we are primarily interested in describing aspects of the celebration of the Sabbath as observed by Jews, specifically Orthodox Jews, in modern times.

According to one source, Orthodox Jews constitute approximately ten percent of American Jewry (Frank et al. 1997, 199) or to put it another way, the number of Orthodox Jews in the United States is approximately a half million with the figure in Israel probably slightly under a million. Calculating that there are about another half million elsewhere (e.g., in France, England, Russia, South Africa, Argentina, and Brazil) we can reasonably estimate that of the world's total Jewish population of some thirteen million, Orthodox Jews number a little more than two million. Sociobiologist Edward O. Wilson calls Orthodox Jews the "most resilient of all groups" (1978, 170), referring no doubt to their ability to persist in the face of an often hostile or at any rate an alien environment. This is not to say that these two million Orthodox Jews are united in their religious beliefs and practices. There are degrees of orthodoxy such that even among Orthodox Jews one can distinguish what are usually referred to as "ultra-Orthodox" Jewish sects from slightly less strict Orthodox Jewish groups (Wouk 1959, 235). Sabbath observance may be found, however, among all Orthodox Jews and for that matter, some form of Sabbath practice, if less stringent, is part of both Conservative and Reform Judaism.

From the very beginning, the Sabbath was far more than simply a day of rest, a day when no work was to be done. Indeed, some scholars have argued that the original concept of the Sabbath had little or nothing to do with the idea of "rest" (Jastrow 1898, 353; Robinson 1980). Rather the Sabbath was a day filled with specific do's and don'ts. For example, it was forbidden to leave one's home on the Sabbath, say, to go into the fields to gather the manna provided by God to the starving people of Israel being led out of bondage in Egypt by Moses. Initially, Moses had instructed his charges to gather the manna and not wait until morning to do so. A few disobeyed him and waited until morning, but by then the manna had "bred worms, and stank" (Exod. 16:20).

> And it came to pass, that on the sixth day they gathered twice as much bread, two omers for one man: and all the rulers of the congregation came and told Moses. And he said unto them, "This is that which the Lord hath said, 'To-morrow is the rest of the holy Sabbath unto the Lord: bake that which ye will bake today, and seethe that ye will seethe; and that which remaineth over lay up for you to be kept until the morning.' " And they laid it up till the morning, as Moses bade: and it did not stink, neither was there any worm therein. And Moses said, "Eat that to-day; for to-day is a Sabbath unto the Lord: to-day ye shall not find it in the field. Six days ye shall gather it; but on the seventh day, which is the Sabbath, in it there shall be none." And it came to pass that there went out some of the people on the seventh day for to gather, and they found none. And the Lord said unto Moses, "How long refuse ye to keep my commandments and my laws? See, for that the Lord hath given you the Sabbath, therefore he giveth you on the sixth day the bread of two days: abide ye every man in his place, *let no man go out of his place on the seventh day*." So the people rested on the seventh day. (Exod. 16:22–30, my emphasis)

Here we find a charter for several features of the contemporary Jewish Sabbath. One is forbidden to leave one's home on the Sabbath and furthermore, one is not permitted to bake or cook on the Sabbath. Food preparation must be carried out well before the Sabbath. In the passage cited, two days of manna or bread are gathered on the sixth day to avoid having to gather any on the Sabbath.

One reason why baking and cooking were interdicted had to do with the taboo against kindling a fire of any kind, another proscription still observed by religious Jews. Lest anyone doubt the seriousness of behaving properly on the Sabbath, consider the following instruction given by Moses:

> And Moses gathered all the congregation of the children of Israel together, and said unto them, "These are the words which the Lord hath commanded, that ye should do them. Six days shall work be done, but on the seventh day there shall be to you a holy day, a Sabbath of rest to the Lord: *whosoever doeth work therein shall be put to death. Ye shall kindle no fire throughout your habitations upon the Sabbath day*." (Exod. 35:1–3, my emphasis)

There are other versions of the threat of death for Sabbath violation:

> And the Lord spake unto Moses, saying, "Speak thou also unto the children of Israel, saying, 'Verily my Sabbaths ye shall keep: for it is a sign between me and

> you throughout your generations that ye may know that I am the Lord that doth sanctify you. Ye shall keep the Sabbath therefore for it is holy unto you. *Every one that defileth it shall surely be put to death*: for whosoever doeth any work therein, that soul shall be cut off from among his people. Six days may work be done; but in the seventh is the Sabbath of rest, holy to the Lord: *whosoever doeth any work in the Sabbath day, he shall surely be put to death.* Wherefore the children of Israel shall keep the Sabbath, to observe the Sabbath throughout their generations for a perpetual covenant. It is a sign between me and the children of Israel for ever: for in six days the Lord made heaven and earth, and on the seventh day he rested, and was refreshed.' " (Exod. 31:12–17, my emphasis)

I am not aware of many individuals that were actually put to death for violating Sabbath rules, but the very fact that this extreme threat was articulated is itself prima facie evidence of the importance placed upon the Sabbath by Moses and God himself. But there are instances of the death penalty imposed for Sabbath violations contained in the Old Testament. Consider the following account:

> And while the children of Israel were in the wilderness, they found a man that gathered sticks upon the Sabbath day. And they that found him gathering sticks brought him unto Moses and Aaron, and unto all the congregation. And they put him in ward, because it was not declared what should be done to him. And the Lord said unto Moses, "The man shall be surely put to death: all the congregation shall stone him with stones without the camp." And all the congregation brought him without the camp, and stoned him with stones, and he died; as the Lord commanded Moses. (Num. 15:32–36)

This passage confirms God's own involvement in seeing that the Sabbath is not violated as it is God himself who imposes the death penalty for the offense of gathering sticks on the Sabbath. The sticks are presumably gathered for the purpose of making a fire, which was also prohibited on the Sabbath (Budde 1928, 14; Weingreen 1966, 362), although it has been suggested that the gathering of sticks constituted a form of work and that this act in and of itself was sufficient to be considered an infringement of Sabbath restrictions (Phillips 1969, 127), and in any case "carrying" the sticks would also constitute a transgression (Pick 1998, 43). Incidentally, the likely reason why all members of the congregation were asked to throw stones at the Sabbath violator was to spread the blame so to speak for killing him. No one individual is thus responsible for the death of the "criminal." It is the same basic principle underlying the custom of "firing squads" charged with carrying out executions. No one knows which bullet actually kills the individual executed. It is a collective effort that also makes it difficult if not impossible for relatives of the deceased, or the deceased himself returning as a revenant, to take revenge on any one single individual. The death penalty for Sabbath violations certainly seems to be extreme and it is clearly not practiced today. But as we shall later see, the prohibition against kindling a fire on the Sabbath continues today unabated in contemporary Orthodox Jewish practice.

Another Sabbath restriction articulated in the Old Testament concerned "carrying objects either out of one's house or in through the gates of the city." We find a clear statement of this injunction in Jeremiah:

> Thus saith the Lord: "Take heed to yourselves, and *bear no burden on the Sabbath day*, nor bring it in by the gates of Jerusalem. *Neither carry forth a burden out of your houses on the Sabbath day*, neither do ye any work, but hallow ye the Sabbath day, as I commanded your fathers. . . . And it shall come to pass, if ye diligently hearken unto me, saith the Lord, *to bring in no burden through the gates of this city on the Sabbath day*, but hallow the Sabbath day, to do no work therein." (17:21–22, 24, my emphasis)

As no work was permitted on the Sabbath, it made sense to forbid conducting business as usual and this entailed the cessation of the transport of goods as well as any transaction involving buying and selling. Nehemiah bears witness to the fact that this Sabbath rule was not always obeyed:

> In those days saw I in Judah some treading winepresses on the Sabbath, and bringing in sheaves, and lading asses; as also wine, grapes, and figs and all manner of burdens, which they brought into Jerusalem on the Sabbath day: and I testified against them in the day wherein they sold victuals. There dwelt men of Tyre also therein, which brought fish, and all manner of ware, and sold on the Sabbath unto the children of Judah and in Jerusalem. Then I contended with the nobles of Judah, and said unto them, "What evil thing is this that ye do, and profane the Sabbath day? Did not your fathers thus, and did not our God bring all this evil upon us, and upon this city? Yet ye bring more wrath upon Israel by profaning the Sabbath." (13:15–18)

It should perhaps be noted that the Old Testament conception of the Sabbath referred to more than just the seventh day of the week. There are strong indications that in accordance with the significance of the number seven it also encompassed the seventh month and the seventh year. In Leviticus 23, there is a long list of rules governing what should be done in the seventh month. For example, "And the Lord spake unto Moses, saying, 'Speak unto the children of Israel, saying, In the seventh month, in the first day of the month, shall ye have a Sabbath, a memorial of blowing of trumpets, a holy convocation. Ye shall do no servile work therein' " (23:23–25). In the seventh month, the Feast of Tabernacles was to be celebrated for "seven days" (23:34) and in this festival of Sukkoth, intended to honor the events of the Exodus, observant Jews were supposed to construct huts or booths in which they were supposed to dwell for seven days (23:42). The seventh and last day of Sukkoth is called Hoshana Rabba, and on that day, a procession in the Temple makes its way around the altar seven times (Kolatch 1995, 255). The same emphasis on "sevenness" holds for the year.

> And the Lord spake unto Moses in mount Sinai, saying, "Speak unto the children of Israel and say unto them, 'When ye come into the land which I give you, then shall the land keep a Sabbath unto the Lord. Six years thou shalt sow thy field and six years thou shalt prune thy vineyard, and gather in the fruit thereof; But in the seventh year shall be a Sabbath of rest unto the land, a Sabbath for the Lord: thou shalt neither sow thy field, nor prune thy vineyard. That which groweth of its own accord of thy harvest thou shalt not reap, neither gather the grapes of thy vine undressed: for it is a year of rest unto the land. And the Sabbath of the land shall be meat for you; for thee, and for thy servant, and for thy maid, and for thy hired servant, and for thy stranger that sojourneth with thee." (Lev. 25:1–6)

Allowing fields to fall fallow after six years might possibly be an early folk form of crop rotation. The idea of having a seventh year of rest after six years of work survives today in the academy with the custom of earning a sabbatical leave after six years of teaching, at some universities and colleges. This custom was introduced at American institutions of higher learning in the late nineteenth century beginning with Harvard University in 1880 (Kimball 1978).

While on the subject of seeming secular parallels to the Sabbath, one is tempted to identify as such a common custom practiced at American professional baseball games. To the extent that the Sabbath represents a time of rest or a break from or interruption of routine activity, one could conceivably consider the so-called seventh-inning stretch as a kind of Sabbath reflex. Home team baseball fans in the middle of the seventh inning stand up and "stretch" to exercise their limbs after sitting for an extended length of time but also to exhort their team particularly if they are behind the other team in terms of score. The point is that this "stretch" could in theory come in any inning, but the fact is that it occurs in the seventh inning. In terms of urging a team to rally, it would seem to make more sense for the stretch to take place in the ninth and final inning.

There are many other indications of the importance of the seven-year period of time. For example, Jacob had to serve his prospective father-in-law, Laban, for seven years to earn his bride. Jacob thought his bride would be Rachel (Gen. 29:20), but when Laban, following the custom that a younger daughter could not be married before an older one, conspired to substitute Leah, his firstborn daughter, for Rachel, a deceit that Jacob discovered only the morning after the wedding night, Jacob was obliged to serve yet another seven years to earn his beloved Rachel (Gen. 29:27–28).

Another striking instance of an occurrence of "sevens" is found in the puzzling dreams of Pharaoh, which were brilliantly interpreted by Joseph. The first dream involved seven fat cows and seven lean cows; the second dream contained images of seven full ears of corn and seven thin ears of corn (Gen. 41:2–7). The lean cows devoured the fat cows and the seven thin ears of corn did likewise to the full ears of corn. Joseph interpreted the dreams as omens of a forthcoming time of famine: "The seven good kine are seven years; and the seven good ears are seven years: the dream is one. And the seven thin and ill-favored kine that came up after them are seven years; and the seven empty ears blasted with the east wind shall be seven years of famine" (Gen. 41:26–27).

In the story of Samson, his Philistine wife's kinsmen had seven days within which to solve his famous riddle, and it was on the seventh day that Samson finally revealed to his wife the answer to that riddle (Judg. 14:17) and for that matter, Samson's extraordinary strength was contained in the "seven locks" of hair on his head (Judg. 16:13). Another Old Testament instance of the number seven adduced to demonstrate its spiritual significance (Finkelman 1991, 145) is the sevenfold listing in the commandment of those for whom work is forbidden: "Thou, nor thy son, nor thy daughter, thy manservant, nor thy maidservant, nor thy cattle, nor thy stranger that is within thy gates" (Exod. 20:10).

The seeming obsession with the number seven did not stop with weeks, months, and years. After seven periods of seven-year intervals, there was to be a fiftieth jubilee year of rest. Here are the relevant instructions:

> "And thou shalt number seven Sabbaths of years unto thee, seven times seven years; and the space of the seven Sabbaths of years shall be unto thee forty and nine years. Then shalt thou cause the trumpet of the jubilee to sound on the tenth day of the seventh month, in the day of atonement shall ye make the trumpet sound throughout all your land. And ye shall hallow the fiftieth year. . . . A jubilee shall that fiftieth year be unto you: ye shall not sow, neither reap that which groweth of itself in it, nor gather the grapes in it of thy vine undressed." (Lev. 25:8–10, 11)

One practical problem posed by the Jubilee year resulted from the fact that the same rules that governed the forty-ninth year, a seventh year, were in effect. Consequently, this meant that there would be a cessation of work on the land for two consecutive years (Marchant 1986, 20), both the forty-ninth and fiftieth years, a serious matter for observant Jews whose livelihood was based upon agricultural produce. As Carmichael phrases it, "If these rules were actually observed, how, then, would the people eat?" (1999, 224). (For a detailed consideration of the concept of Jubilee in the Old Testament, see North 1954.)

The detail of sounding the trumpet to celebrate the Jubilee reminds us of the passage in Leviticus cited above: "And the Lord spake to Moses, saying, 'Speak unto the children of Israel saying, In the seventh month, in the first day of the month, shall ye have a Sabbath, a memorial of blowing of trumpets, a holy convocation' " (Lev. 23:23–24). This in turn cannot help but bring to mind perhaps the most obsessive example of sevenfold repetition in the Old Testament, namely, the destruction of the wall surrounding the city of Jericho. Keeping the idea of the Sabbath firmly in mind, consider the following dramatic account:

> And the Lord said unto Joshua, "See I have given into thine hand Jericho and the king thereof, and the mighty men of valor. And ye shall compass the city, all ye men of war and go round the city once. Thus shalt thou do six days. And seven priests shall bear before the ark seven trumpets of rams' horns and the seventh day ye shall compass the city seven times, and the priests shall blow with the trumpets. And it shall come to pass that when they make a long blast with the rams' horn, and when ye hear the sound of the trumpet, all the people shall shout with a great shout; and the wall of the city shall fall down flat." (Josh. 6:2–5)

It is striking that Joshua and his men circumambulate Jericho once a day for six days and then on the seventh day they do so seven times. "And it came to pass on the seventh day, that they rose early about the dawning of the day, and compassed the city after the same manner seven times: only on that day they compassed the city seven times. And it came to pass at the seventh time, when the priests blew with the trumpets, Joshua said unto the people, 'Shout; for the Lord hath given you the city' " (Josh. 6:15–16).

Another striking illustration of the seven pattern is found in Deuteronomy 15. There in essence we are told that completion of the sixth or seventh year provides an occasion for "release." For example, "At the end of every seven years thou shalt make a release" (Deut. 15:1), and this is followed by an instruction to forgive a loan or debt: "And this is the manner of the release: Every creditor that lendeth aught unto his neighbor shall release it; he shall not exact it of his neighbor, or of his brother; because it is called the Lord's release" (15:2). The seventh year, in modern times, often referred to as *Shmittoh* (Marchant 1986, 17) or *shemita* (Kolatch 1985, 320), is specifically called "the year of release" (15:9) and even slaves should be released in the seventh year following six years of service: "And if thy brother, a Hebrew man, or a Hebrew woman, be sold unto thee, and serve thee six years; then in the seventh year thou shalt let him go free from thee" (15:12). The release of a slave is linked to God's freeing the Hebrews from Egyptian bondage: "And thou shalt remember that thou wast a bondman in the land of Egypt and the Lord thy God redeemed thee: therefore I command thee this thing to-day" (15:15). It should be recalled that the Deuteronomy version of the Sabbath Commandment was also tied to the exodus from Egypt (5:15).

The presence of "seven" as a pattern number in the Old Testament cannot be denied. It has been suggested that "seven" connotes a sense of completeness and perfection (Hehn 1925, 130–131; Kapelrud 1968, 495; Negretti 1973, 57). A glance at the "seven" entry in any standard concordance to the Bible will reveal the frequent occurrence of "seven" and "seventh" in the Old Testament. In one version of the "flood myth" for example, Noah is instructed by God to bring seven of every clean beast and seven of all the fowls of the air. "And the Lord said unto Noah, Come thou and all thy house into the ark . . . of every clean beast thou shalt take to thee *by sevens*, the male and his female. . . . Of fowls also of the air *by sevens*, the male and the female; to keep seed alive upon the face of all the earth" (Gen. 7:1–3, my emphasis). Even earlier in Genesis, after Cain has slain his brother Abel, he complains to God that he will be a fugitive and that every one who finds him will try to kill him. God's response is to mark Cain so that no one will kill him: "And the Lord said unto him, 'Therefore whosoever slayeth Cain, vengeance shall be taken on him *sevenfold*.' And the Lord set a mark upon Cain, lest any finding him should kill him" (Gen. 4:15, my emphasis). In purification sacrificial offerings, a priest was supposed to "dip his finger in the blood and sprinkle of the blood seven times before the Lord" (Lev. 4:6, 17; 16:14, 19; Num. 19:4). When King Hezekiah wanted to make a purification offering at the temple, he did so as follows: "Then Hezekiah the king rose early, and gathered the rulers of the city, and went up to the house of the Lord. And they brought seven bullocks and seven rams, and seven lambs, and seven he goats, for a sin offering for the kingdom, and for the sanctuary, and for Judah" (2 Chron. 29:20–21).

A similar numerical pattern is also to be found in the Talmud. For example, there is a folk medical cure contained in the Shabbat tractate of the Babylonian Talmud that seems a bit overly formulaic:

> For a tertian fever, bring seven barbs from seven palm trees, seven chips from seven beams, seven pegs from seven bridges, seven piles of ashes from seven ovens, seven piles of dirt from under seven door sockets, seven bits of pitch from seven ships, seven handfuls of cumin, seven hairs from the beard of an old dog; tie them in the nape of the neck with a white twisted thread. (Neusner 1992–1993, IIb, 122)

Another interesting example of the importance of seven in the Old Testament is found in the particular definition of the human life span. Not only is it seventy years, according to one of the psalms, but the way seventy is defined divides the seventh decade from the first six. "The days of our years are threescore years and ten" (Ps. 90:10). The lumping together of the first six decades under the rubric of "threescore" separates it from the seventh and final decade, a pattern surely reminiscent of the distinction between the first six days of the week and the seventh day or Sabbath. Incidentally, the "threescore and ten" formula recurs repeatedly in the Old Testament, for example, "all the souls of the house of Jacob, which came into Egypt, were threescore and ten" (Gen. 46:27), a figure echoed in Deuteronomy, "Thy fathers went down into Egypt with threescore and ten persons" (10:22). Gideon also "had threescore and ten sons of his body begotten: for he had many wives" (Judg. 8:30), as did Jerubbaal whose sons "are threescore and ten persons" (Judg. 9:2).

The separation of six and seven, as signaled by the distinction between the sixth and seventh decades of life expectancy, calls to mind a truly strange speculation on the part of Freud. In a letter of August 22, 1924, written to his colleague, Berlin psychoanalyst Karl Abraham, Freud expressed his belief "that the significance of the number 7 originated in a period when men counted in sixes" (Abraham and Freud 1965, 365). This was in response to an earlier letter by Abraham in which he indicated his intention of studying the significance of the number seven in custom and myth. Unfortunately, Abraham's early death in December 1925, at age forty-eight, precluded the completion of the planned monograph. Abraham did note, however, that Freud's idea, though interesting, was not sufficient to explain why dangerous things were seven in number or why "Seven is the number of abstinence (Sabbath, etc.)" (367, 370, 378). Freud then answered that "The problem of 7 still interests me greatly. I have not got any further with it" (376).

Seven and seventy are also prominent in the New Testament. A question Peter poses to Jesus may serve as a representative example: "Then came Peter to him and said, 'Lord, how oft shall my brother sin against me, and I forgive him? Till seven times?' Jesus saith unto him, 'I say not unto thee, Until seven times: but, Until seventy times seven' " (Matt. 18:21–22). But in this essay we are primarily concerned with seven in the Old Testament.

One could reasonably say that the most important seven in the Old Testament involved the seven-day week, with the Sabbath being defined as the seventh day. It is also worth remarking that Pesach or Passover, arguably the principal festival of the Jewish calendar even up to modern times, was originally "a feast of seven days" (Ezek. 45:21). In Israel, it continues to last seven days (Rosten 1970, 289). The original menorah was a seven-branched candelabrum made of gold and placed in the Tabernacle (Exod. 37:17–18, 23).

In contemporary Jewish practice, the number seven continues to be prominent in wedding ritual. There is "an ancient custom that the bride circles her groom seven times" upon entering the ceremonial canopy called a *chuppah* (Linke 1999, 157; Jacobs 1999, 185). Furthermore, the *sheva b'rachot*, or seven blessings "comprise the bulk of the wedding liturgy. . . . The Talmud mentions only six wedding blessings, but since the sixth century, Jews have made a universal practice of adding *kiddush*—the sanctification of God's name over wine—to round the number up to the much more mystically satisfying seven. Seven is the number of completion, the number of days it took God to create the universe" (Diamant 1985, 179–180). One of several different explanations offered as to why arm phylactery straps are conventionally wound around the arm seven times (Donin 1980, 35) is that it symbolizes the seven benedictions recited at weddings (Sperling 1968, 27–28; Donin 1980, 310).

It should be noted that seven is not always a positive number. For example, "He that toucheth the dead body of any man shall be unclean seven days" and "This is the law, when a man dieth in a tent: all that come into the tent, and all that is in the tent, shall be unclean seven days" (Num. 19:11, 14). Also polluting is menstrual blood and that too involves periods of seven days: "And if a woman have an issue and her issue in her flesh be blood, she shall be put apart seven days. . . . But if she be cleansed of her issue then she shall number to herself seven days, and after that she shall be clean" (Lev. 15:19, 28).

The traditional period of mourning is also seven days and the deceased is usually dressed in seven garments (Kolatch 1995, 53). After the funeral, which requires the cortege to halt seven times enroute to the grave site (Ganzfried 1961, 4:102; Kolatch 1995, 61–62; Isaacs 1998, 119), religious Jews "sit *shivah*" for seven days in the house of the deceased. "*Shivah*" is the Hebrew word for seven (Rosten 1970, 347), and the preferred period of mourning may be inspired in part by the fact that Joseph mourned his father Jacob for seven days (Gen. 50:10). According to one tradition, Shivah was supposed to be observed in the home of the deceased because it was believed that "for seven days after death the soul hovers about the house in which the deceased lived" (Kolatch 1985, 195) and the prayers of the mourners helped console the unhappy spirit. It has also been suggested that "the passage of seven days is an essential part of the restoration of the unclean and a means of achieving holiness" in Old Testament times (Meier 1991, 6). Whether the seven-day purification period is derived from the Sabbath tradition or whether the Sabbath tradition of rest and restoration after six days is a vestige of the ritually favored seven-day interval is difficult to ascertain. It would appear, however, that both the preferred duration of purification and the Sabbath are somehow connected to the ascribed numerological significance of seven.

Seven continues to be a magic number, one of several, in Western culture. One thinks of the Seven Wonders of the Ancient World, the Seven Deadly Sins, Seventh Heaven, the Seven Seas, and even Snow White and the Seven Dwarfs among other examples. (For representative discussions of the significance of the number seven in connection with the Sabbath, see Hirschfeld 1896; Hehn 1907, 1925; Williams 1945; Celada 1948; Janssens 1958; Nádor 1962; Negretti 1973. For the importance of seven in the Arab world, see Somogyi 1958.)

THE SABBATH IN THE NEW TESTAMENT

Jesus was born a Jew and was undoubtedly familiar with the Old Testament concept of the Sabbath. While specifics of Sabbath restrictions are somewhat scanty in the New Testament, we can get some idea of how strict Sabbath regulations in the times of Jesus were by consulting a section of one of the documents contained in the Dead Sea Scrolls. In the Damascus Document, which dates from approximately 100 B.C.E., there is a section devoted to Sabbath rules. These are a few pertinent excerpts:

> No man shall work on the sixth day from the moment when the sun's orb is distant by its own fulness from the gate (wherein it sinks). . . . No man shall speak any vain or idle word on the Sabbath day. He shall make no loan to his companion. He shall make no decision in matters of money and gain. He shall say nothing

> about work or labour to be done on the morrow. No man shall walk abroad to do business on the Sabbath. He shall not walk more than one thousand cubits beyond his town. No man shall eat on the Sabbath day except that which is already prepared. . . . No man shall walk more than two thousand cubits after a beast to pasture it outside his town. . . . No man shall take anything out of the house or bring anything in. And if he is in a booth, let him neither take anything out nor bring anything in. He shall not open a sealed vessel on the Sabbath. . . . No man minding a child shall carry it whilst going and coming on the Sabbath. . . . No man shall assist a beast to give birth on the Sabbath day. And if it should fall into a cistern or pit, he shall not lift it out on the Sabbath. (Vermes 1998, 139–140; Kimbrough 1966)

More than two thousand years later, many of these regulations and prohibitions remain in effect (e.g., beginning Sabbath at sunset, the proscriptions against doing business and carrying objects into or out of one's domicile. Not even small children can be carried [Spirn 1992]).

We cannot be certain whether all of these rules were known to Jesus. It has been suggested that the twenty-eight Sabbath prohibitions listed in the Damascus Document may indicate that the particular Jewish group involved may have been more stringent than other Jewish groups of the same time period (Sharvit 1979, 47). Nevertheless, it is pretty clear that Jesus chafed under what he considered to be the overly oppressive restrictions of the traditional Sabbath. When he consistently violated Sabbath rules (e.g., by plucking ears of corn on the Sabbath and more importantly by healing the sick on the Sabbath), he enraged the Pharisees.

The Jews have long held that it is permissible to violate the Sabbath rules in the case of a life-threatening situation (Cohen 1988, 108). The doctrine is sometimes referred to as *pikuah nefesh*, which according to one translation means "an opening for a life" (Mirsky 2000, 50). It comes from a passage indicating that if a person is buried under a rock slide on the Sabbath, we should make an opening in the heap of stones covering him in order to save his life (cf. Neusner 1988, 278). For example, in present-day Israel, if a man's pregnant wife is about to deliver and it is the Sabbath, it is considered acceptable behavior to drive her to the hospital. (Normally, one cannot drive on the Sabbath.) However, in that instance, the husband, if Orthodox, would be obliged to leave his car at the hospital and walk back to his home, unless the distance involved is greater than the limit he would normally be permitted to walk, that is, two thousand cubits (Neuwirth 1989, 662). For that matter, if the pregnant woman arrives at the hospital too early because of "false labor" and the hospital refuses her admission or discharges her, she is not allowed to return home in a vehicle driven by a Jew (587). Similar rules were proposed for Orthodox Jews serving in the police force. It was permitted for an Orthodox Jew to use a vehicle to reach the scene of a crime (e.g., of a homicide), but one was not permitted to return from the scene by car until the end of the Sabbath and for that matter, thieves apprehended far from a police station could not be transported by vehicle to a place of detention until Sabbath concluded (Abramov 1972, 3). Similarly, "A dentist should not drive his own car home from the scene of a dental emergency (office, hospital, etc.) but should take a taxi or have his car driven by a non-Jewish driver to minimize the Sabbath prohibitions involved" (Tendler and Rosner 1987, 60). But life-threatening illness is one thing; a non–life-threatening illness is quite another.

Jesus' decision to heal the sick on the Sabbath in cases where the illness was not life-threatening was a direct contravention of Sabbath protocol. And he chose to do this on more than one occasion. A passage from the Gospel of Matthew may give a sample of Jesus' anti-Sabbath behavior:

> At that time Jesus went on the Sabbath day through the corn; and his disciples were ahungered, and began to pluck the ears of corn, and to eat. But when the Pharisees saw it, they said unto him, "Behold, thy disciples do that which is not lawful to do upon the Sabbath day." (Matt. 12:1–2)

Jesus reminds the Pharisees that when King David and his men were similarly "ahungered" they entered into a temple and ate the "showbread," which was reserved for priests only, and that "on Sabbath days the priests in the temple profane the Sabbath, and are blameless" (12:5), and he concludes, "For the Son of man is Lord even of the Sabbath day" (12:8), a line repeated in Luke (6:5).

Immediately after this corn-plucking episode, Jesus encounters a man with a withered hand. "And, behold, there was a man which had his hand withered. And they asked him, saying, Is it lawful to heal on the Sabbath days? That they might accuse him" (Matt. 12:10). Jesus responded with one of his famous parables:

> And he said unto them, "What man shall there be among you, that shall have one sheep, and if it fall into a pit on the Sabbath day, will he not lay hold on it, and lift it out? How much then is a man better than a sheep? Wherefore it is lawful to do well on the Sabbath days." Then saith he to the man, "Stretch forth thine hand." And he stretched it forth; and it was restored whole, like as the other. Then the Pharisees, went out, and held a council against him, how they might destroy him. (Matt. 12:11–14)

The version of these incidents in Mark is equally graphic. In Mark's account, Jesus' response to the corn-plucking criticism includes an additional line that has become almost proverbial: "And he said unto them, 'The Sabbath was made for man, and not man for the Sabbath' " (cf. Beare 1960; Gils 1962) followed by the familiar: "Therefore the Son of man is Lord also of the Sabbath" (Mark 2:27–28). Mark's version of the man with the withered hand also varies slightly from that of Matthew:

> And he entered again into the synagogue; and there was a man there which had a withered hand. And they watched him, whether he would heal him on the Sabbath day; that they might accuse him. And he saith unto the man which had the withered hand, "Stand forth." And he saith unto them, "Is it lawful to do good on the Sabbath days, or to do evil? To save life, or to kill?" But they held their peace. And when he had looked round about on them with anger, being grieved for the hardness of their hearts, he saith unto the man, "Stretch forth thine hand." And he stretched it out: and his hand was restored whole as the other. And the Pharisees went forth, and straightway took counsel with the Herodians against him, how they might destroy him. (Mark 3:1–6, cf. Luke 6:5–11)

From these accounts, we can see, first of all, that the Sabbath continued to be of great importance to devout Jews during the time of Jesus, but also that the observance of the Sabbath or the violation thereof was one of the principal points of contention between Jesus and the strictest segment of the Jewish community.

The curing of the man with the withered hand on the Sabbath was not an isolated instance. In the very first chapter of the Gospel of Mark, Jesus entered a synagogue on the Sabbath where he exorcised an "unclean spirit" from a man possessed, and on the same day he also cured the fever of Simon (Peter)'s mother-in-law (Mark 1:21–26, 30–31; cf. Luke 4:31–39). In an incident reported by Luke, Jesus again rebukes the Pharisees, using the animal-in-the-pit exemplum, but this time with an ass or an ox rather than a sheep:

> And it came to pass, as he went into the house of one of the chief Pharisees to eat bread on the Sabbath day, that they watched him. And, behold, there was a certain man before him which had the dropsy. And Jesus answering spake unto the lawyers and Pharisees, saying, "Is it lawful to heal on the Sabbath day?" And they held their peace. And he took him, and healed him, and let him go; And answered them, saying, "Which of you shall have an ass or an ox fallen into a pit, and will not straightway pull him out on the Sabbath day?" And they could not answer him again to these things. (Luke 14:1–6)

Jesus used a similar ox-and-ass argument in the case of a crippled woman.

> And he was teaching in one of the synagogues on the Sabbath. And, behold, there was a woman which had a spirit of infirmity eighteen years, and was bowed together, and could in no wise lift up herself. And when Jesus saw her, he called her to him, and said unto her, "Woman, thou are loosed from thine infirmity." And he laid his hands on her: and immediately she was made straight and glorified God. And the ruler of the synagogue answered with indignation, because that Jesus had healed on the Sabbath day, and said unto the people, "There are six days in which men ought to work: in them therefore come and be healed, and not on the Sabbath day." The Lord then answered him, and said, "Thou hypocrite, doth not each one of you on the Sabbath loose his ox or his ass from the stall, and lead him away to watering?" And when he had said these things, all his adversaries were ashamed: and all the people rejoiced for all the glorious things that were done by him. (Luke 13:10–17)

The Gospel of John gives two reports of Jesus violating the Jewish Sabbath. In one case, Jesus came upon a man who had been blind from birth. Jesus "spat on the ground, and made clay of the spittle, and he anointed the eyes of the blind man with the clay. And said unto him, 'Go, wash in the pool of Si-loam.' . . . He went his way therefore, and washed, and came seeing. . . . And it was the Sabbath day when Jesus made the clay, and opened his eyes" (John 9:6–7, 14). The Pharisees questioned the man, even doubting that he had actually been blind from birth. " 'Therefore' said some of the Pharisees. 'This man is not of God, because he keepeth not the Sabbath day.' Others said, 'How can man that is a sinner do such miracles?' And there was a division among them" (John 9:16).

The instance of the cure of the invalid at the pool at Bethesda is an even more striking example. In this case, the alleged violation was not so much the miraculous cure, but rather that Jesus instructed the man to carry his bed and walk to the pool, thereby violating the injunction against carrying anything on the Sabbath. The Bethesda pool attracted a "great multitude of impotent folk, of blind, halt, withered" waiting for an angel to descend to stir the water. "Whosoever then first after the troubling of the water stepped in was made whole of whatsoever disease he had" (John 5:3–4). The issue was that it was critical to be the first to enter the pool after the angel's action.

> And a certain man was there, which had an infirmity thirty and eight years. When Jesus saw him lie, and knew that he had been now a long time in that case, he saith unto him, "Wilt thou be made whole?" The impotent man answered him,

> "Sir, I have no man, when the water is troubled, to put me into the pool: but while I am coming, another steppeth down before me." And Jesus saith unto him, "Rise, take up thy bed, and walk." And immediately the man was made whole, and took up his bed, and walked: and on the same day was the Sabbath. The Jews therefore said unto him that was cured, "It is the Sabbath day: it is not lawful for thee to carry thy bed." He answered them, "He that made me whole, the same said unto me, 'Take up thy bed, and walk.' " Then asked they him, "What man is that which said unto thee, Take up thy bed, and walk?". . . The man departed, and told the Jews that it was Jesus which had made him whole. And therefore did the Jews persecute Jesus, and sought to slay him, because he had done these things on the Sabbath day. But Jesus answered them, "My Father worketh hitherto, and I work." Therefore the Jews sought the more to kill him, because he not only had broken the Sabbath, but said also that God was his Father, making himself equal with God. (John 5:12, 15–18)

In reading these passages, one should keep in mind that the ultimate penalty for violating the Sabbath, according to the Old Testament, was death. In the New Testament, we have Jesus flagrantly and unrepentantly violating the Jewish Sabbath. It is almost as though Jesus intended to deliberately provoke the Pharisees, the strict constructionist precursors of modern Orthodox Jews, by choosing to heal the sick on the Sabbath. It is certainly not in the least surprising, therefore, that some religious Jews were truly offended and upset by Jesus' actions. There were a number of different factors that led to the crucifixion of Jesus, but there can be no doubt that Jesus' resolute refusal to obey the Old Testament Sabbath regulations played some part in incurring the Pharisees' wrath toward him.

On the other hand, some scholars have argued that Jesus did not really violate the Sabbath but rather that he redefined or reinterpreted it (Weiss 1990, 15). Evidence supporting the idea that Jesus respected the Sabbath Commandment includes, "And he came to Nazareth where he had been brought up: and, as his custom was, he went into the synagogue on the Sabbath day, and stood up for to read" (Luke 4:16). Similarly, members of Jesus' coterie also apparently observed the Sabbath. After the crucified body of Jesus was claimed, allegedly by Joseph of Arimathea, the women devoted to Jesus began to make certain preparations. "And that day was the preparation, and the Sabbath drew on. And the women also, which came with him from Galilee, followed after, and beheld the sepulchre, and how his body was laid. And they returned, and prepared spices and ointments; and rested the Sabbath day according to the commandment" (Luke 23:54–56). From this, one might logically assume that the basic legitimacy of the Jewish Sabbath was not in question, but only the issue of what sorts of activities were to be permitted on that day (Weiss 1990, 223).

Nevertheless, it seems plausible to think that Jesus' resistance to the strict enforcement of the Jewish Sabbath rules and regulations might have been one factor in the Christian revamping of Sabbath. In what could be termed "The great Sabbath divide," Christians over time with only a few exceptions (e.g., Seventh-Day Adventists) changed the day of the Sabbath from Saturday to Sunday, beginning perhaps as early as 150 C.E. (Bishai 1963, 30), thus distancing themselves from the Jews. Generally speaking, it is fair to say that Christianity retained the Old Testament as the original basis of their religious belief and practice, but at the same time they modified and revised it to produce a new religion. The shift from Sabbath to Lord's Day has been much discussed and debated (Cotton 1933; Bacchiocchi 1977, 1977, 1998; Strand 1978, 1979; Carson 1982).

The term Lord's Day almost certainly refers to the Christian assumption that Jesus was resurrected on the "first day of the week," which if the Sabbath is considered the seventh and last day of the week would make the day of Resurrection, one day after the Sabbath, that is, Sunday. According to Matthew (28:1), "In the end of the Sabbath, as it began to dawn toward the first day of the week, came Mary Magdalene and the other Mary to see the sepulchre." At the sepulchre, an angel announced, "He is not here: for he is risen" (28:6). Mark confirms that the women came to the sepulchre "When the Sabbath was past" and "Very early in the morning, the first day of the week, they came unto the sepulchre at the rising of the sun" (Mark 16:1, 2). Luke says much the same: "Now upon the first day of the week, very early in the morning, they came unto the sepulcher" (24:1)—and so does John: "The first day of the week cometh Mary Magdalene early, when it was yet dark" (20:1). So if the Resurrection occurred on the first day of the week, it made sense to celebrate the first day of the week, that is, Sunday or the Lord's Day.

The evolution of the names of the days of the week is a whole different research problem. The Anglo-American names are a combination of at least two different systems. One is based on the names of the planets, but specifically the planets as identified in Ptolemaic or geocentric terms. In ancient times, both the sun and moon were considered to be planets. (For a detailed discussion of the seven planetary origin of the week, see Gandz 1948–1949.) Hence the days of the week derived from the planetary basis were (in Latin): *Dies Solis* (day of the sun or Sunday); *Dies Lunae* (day of the moon or Monday); *Dies Martis* [Mars] (Tuesday, but in French *Mardi*, Italian *Martedi*, Spanish *Martes*, Romanian *Marti*); *Dies Mercurii* (Wednesday, but in French *Mercredi*, Italian *Mercoledi*, Spanish *Miercoles*, Romanian *Miercuri*); *Dies Jovis*

[Jove or Jupiter] (Thursday, but in French *Jeudi*, Italian *Giovedi*, Spanish *Jueves*, and Romanian *Jovi*); *Dies Veneris* (Friday, but in French *Vendredi*, Italian *Venerdi*, Spanish *Viernes*, Romanian *Veneri*), and *Dies Saturni* or *Sabbatum* (Saturday, but in French *Samedi*, Italian *Sabato*, Spanish *Sabado*, Romanian *Simbata*). There is also an ancient tradition of the hours of the day being perceived in cycles of seven with the hours designated by the names of the seven planets (Gandz 1948–1949, 218).

The Anglo-American names of Tuesday, Wednesday, Thursday, and Friday come from the names of Scandinavian rather than Roman deities. Thus Wodan's Day became Wednesday, Thor's day became Thursday, and Freia's day became Friday. The Anglo-American Sunday is a continuation of the Roman *Dies Solis*, but many European languages reflect the shift from *Dies Solis* to *Dies Domini*, or day of our Lord or Lord's Day. One thinks of French *Dimanche*, Italian *Domenica*, Spanish *Domingo*, and Romanian *Duminica*.

One cannot help wondering how conscious people are about the significance of the names of days or months. While an English speaker might well make the connection between the name Sunday and the fact that it was in times past a day named for the sun, that same individual might not realize that Monday is a form of "moon day." In similar fashion, most individuals who could easily identify December as the twelfth month of the year might not realize that the word is derived from the Latin word for "ten," not twelve. November, the eleventh month, comes from "nine," October, the tenth month, from "eight," and September, the ninth month, from "seven." What this indicates is that our year did not always begin in January, but rather in March or April, which upon reflection makes much more sense as the season of spring is metaphorically much more appropriate, at least in the Northern Hemisphere, as a time of rebirth or as a time to begin again, than the dead of winter in January.

No matter how intriguing or fascinating the question of the origin of Sabbath might be or how complex the evolutionary shift from Jewish Sabbath to Christian Lord's Day appears to be, neither of these issues is relevant to matter of the nature of contemporary Orthodox Jewish Sabbath customs, which constitute the subject of this essay.

THE SABBATH IN RABBINICAL TRADITION

It is true that the roots of contemporary Orthodox Jewish Sabbath practice are to be found in the Old Testament, but this source (e.g., the Pentateuch or first five books of the Old Testament, known as the Torah in Judaism) does not nearly cover all of the dozens upon dozens of Sabbath rules and regulations. Supposedly there are some 613 commandments contained in the Torah (Caplan 1996), but these divine instructions have been elaborated and refined over the centuries. The instructions cover many aspects of life, not just the Sabbath. They refer, for example, to rules governing ritual purity and to dietary restrictions. Two of these 613 instructions are contained in one version of the Ten Commandments (Exod. 20:8, 10): "Remember the Sabbath day to keep it holy" and "Thou shalt not do any work" (Asheri 1978, 99).

Orthodox Jews revere what is known as the "Oral Torah," a set of regulations and explanations that were believed to have been given to Moses by God in addition to the Ten Commandments. The Oral Torah is said to have remained in oral tradition until the destruction of the Temple in 70 C.E., which led to the dispersal of Jews. Rabbis then feared that the Oral Torah might be lost if it were not written down. Eventually much of this Oral Torah was written down and became part of the Talmud. There are two principal versions of the Talmud: The so-called Palestinian Talmud and the Babylonian Talmud. The Talmud consists of the Mishnah and the subsequent rabbinical discussions of the Mishnah which are called the Gemara.

The Mishnah, first formulated near the end of the second century C.E., contains a series of six tracts dealing with agricultural rules, seasonal regulations, laws governing the transfer of women and property from a father to a husband, principles of both civil and criminal law, rules for the conduct of cult and behavior in the Temple, and finally regulations pertaining to ritual purity in the home and at the Temple (Neusner 1988, xv).

The first section of the second tract, which is concerned with a code of conduct required for various appointed seasons including festivals, gives a detailed list of regulations governing the Sabbath (Neusner 1988, 179–208). In the Shabbat chapter of the Mishnah, we find a list of the thirty-nine types of work (*Melachos*) that are forbidden on the Sabbath. Many of the activities are ones no longer commonly found in the majority of urban Jewish households. Nevertheless, they have been constantly updated and reinterpreted by various rabbis, sometimes in response to questions posed by Jews in doubt about the appropriateness of some particular activity, and so they are still regarded as being in effect. One broad definition of "work" for Sabbath purposes is any act that results "in a significant increase in the utility of some object" (Rosenfeld 1966, 60). Here is a list of the thirty-nine proscribed forms of work:

> The main classes of [prohibited] work are forty save one: sowing, ploughing, reaping, binding sheaves, threshing, winnowing, cleansing crops, grinding, sifting, kneading, baking, shearing wool, washing or beating or dyeing it, spinning, weaving, making two loops, weaving two threads, separating two threads, tying [a knot], loosening [a knot], sewing two stitches, tearing in order to sew two stitches, hunting a gazelle, slaughtering or flaying or salting it or curing its skin, scraping it or cutting it up, writing two letters, erasing in order to write two letters, building, pulling down, putting out a fire, lighting a fire, striking with a hammer and taking out aught from one domain into another. These are the main classes of [prohibited] work: forty save one. (Danby 1958, 106)

In theory, all of the thirty-nine prohibited forms of work were forbidden because all of them were understood to have been involved in the construction of the Tabernacle (*Mishkan*) (Halperin 1986, 63–64; Ginsburg 1989, 64; S. Cohen 1995, 1). The construction of this part of the Temple was thought to be man's equivalent of God's acts of creation (Finkelman 1991, 36). And just as God rested after these acts, so man was obliged to rest or desist from any regular everyday work activity. So it is not the degree of physical exertion that defines a given activity as work, but rather its assumed "similarity to those activities needed in constructing the *Mishkan*" (Marchant 1986, 27). At this point in time, however, it is not always obvious how a particular proscribed form of work was connected with Tabernacle construction. Writing, for example, is deemed to refer to the craftsmen marking or writing a number on planks used in construction so that if and when it was disassembled, the planks could be reassembled correctly (S. Cohen 1995, 1).

Once the Talmud (Mishnah and Gemara) was written down, the evolution of Jewish belief and practice continued. There were further commentaries on the Torah and the Talmud; there were various attempts to codify Jewish "religious" custom—one of the most famous was the authoritative *Shulchan Aruch* (Set Table) written in 1565 by Rabbi Joseph Caro (often spelled Karo) (1488–1575)—and there were also what are known as *responsa*, the answers of individual rabbis to inquiries seeking clarification about a particular issue or problem (Zeplowitz 1997, 388). The totality of Jewish law or Jewish religious law resulting from the conglomeration of these diverse sources is called *Halakha* from the Hebrew meaning "to walk." Orthodox Jews are constantly concerned with evaluating prospective technological innovations and ascertaining whether they can legitimately be utilized on the Sabbath on the basis of *Halachic* principles. It should be understood that rabbis did not always agree on the proper interpretation of a Sabbath restriction and on what was or was not permitted. (For a sample of rabbinical debate on Sabbath regulations, see Neusner 1992.) Often, *Halakhic* discussions distinguish between those Sabbath prohibitions that are "scriptural" and those that emanate from rabbis (Gilat 1963, xxiv; for a helpful extensive chart listing of Torah and rabbinical prohibitions relevant to the practice of medicine on the Sabbath, see Sokol 1986, 155–269). For example, "if one has to bring a person to the hospital on Shabbat, it is unquestionably preferable to call a taxi (for a gentile driver) by telephone which most consider only a rabbinical violation than to drive there oneself (which is unquestionably a biblical violation)" (Broyde and Jachter 1991, 23). Sometimes there are extremely fine lines between the two. For instance, "turning on a light is considered to be a Biblical prohibition. . . . However, turning a light *off* is only Rabinically prohibited" (Cohen 1993, 69).

There has been some discussion of the possible significance of there being thirty-nine types of *melakha* or work prohibited on the Sabbath (Hoenig 1978). Why thirty-nine and not thirty-eight or forty? It seems likely that we have once again a connection with number symbolism. Specifically, it may have to do with the notion of perfection or completion. Seven, for example, is a number with that connotation and that may be why the seventh day is reserved for the service of God, a seventh day whose holiness should not be infringed by everyday human activity. Just as "seven" is reserved for God's worship, so also does "forty" fall into the same category. In the ancient, and for that matter, the modern Middle East, forty is a number of completeness. In this connection, it may be of interest that the root "sbt" (underlying Shabat) according to one authority signifies "coming to an end or being brought to an end of" (Robinson 1980, 37). Forty could be roughly translated as meaning "a lot of" or "a great number of," or "finally getting to the end of." That may be why one version of the flood myth records that it was at the end of "forty days" that Noah opened the windows of the ark (Gen. 8:6) and that may be why Jesus remained in the wilderness for forty days tempted by Satan (Mark 1:13), and why he "fasted forty days and forty nights" (Matt. 4:2). That may also be why in secular life we have the Arabic folktale of "Ali Baba and the Forty Thieves" or the Franz Werfel (1890–1945) novel, *The Forty Days of Musa Dag* (1935) among many other examples (cf. Brandes 1985; Pinker 1994). In that context, we may better understand why it would have been presumptuous for a man-made list to have included forty proscribed acts, even if the list were thought to be derived from God's commands. Accordingly, we have a list of "forty less one" generative acts of labor. The "forty less one" formula does not occur often in the Bible. Paul does, however, comment that he was beaten by Jews as punishment for being a minister of Christ: "Of the Jews five times received I forty stripes save one"

(2 Cor. 11:24). It is also possible that there was some taboo connected with the number thirty-nine, either because it was a multiple of the ritual number three or because it was three times "thirteen," a number with definite negative connotations. Morgenstern comments on the "Semitic practice of avoiding unlucky numbers by speaking of one more or one less than that number" (1966, 25). In any case, there are thirty-nine forms of work prohibitions governing behavior on the Sabbath. These include eleven concerning food, thirteen to do with clothing, three for shelter, four for tanning, five for writing, two for the use of fire, and one for carrying (Hoenig 1978, 198–199).

The evolution of Sabbath restrictions includes no handling of objects labeled *Muktzeh*, which are basically work tools and other implements used in routine daily chores. *Muktzeh* objects include "all tools, writing instruments, money, matches, cigarettes" (Asheri 1978, 104). Also there is a ban on any discussion of normal weekday matters. This second restriction interdicts discussion of business. There can be no reference to buying or selling. Money cannot be touched. In addition, there are other forbidden acts. For example, it is not permitted on the Sabbath to ask a non-Jew or Gentile to carry out a proscribed task such as turning on or off one's stove or lights, if one has forgotten to do so oneself before the start of the Sabbath.

Here is a typical listing of Sabbath off-limits activities:

> Today, we observe a variety of restrictions on Shabbat: no turning on electricity (which is considered a form of kindling fire), no use of television, radio, telephone, vacuum cleaner, food processor, public transportation, or automobile; no cutting paper or fabric, sewing, mending, laundry, writing, playing a musical instrument, no home repair jobs, arts and crafts, sports activities of a certain type, or business activity of any sort, no cooking, baking, squeezing a sponge, opening sealed mail, pushing electric buttons such as doorbell or elevator; no shopping. (Greenberg 1983, 32)

These sorts of restrictions are not just theoretical. Four young couples in Los Angeles were studied in the mid-1990s to see how the practice of Orthodox Judaism affected their daily lives. Sabbath observance was one of the topics investigated. "The participants reported that they refrained from such occupations on the Sabbath as (a) cooking, cleaning, showering, and doing laundry; (b) using electrical appliances, machines, and equipment; (c) writing or erasing; (d) switching lights on or off; (e) driving a vehicle; and (f) carrying, pushing, or moving an object or even carrying a child more than 6 feet in public" (Frank et al. 1997, 201).

For a reader unfamiliar with rabbinical reasoning, it may seem odd to equate turning on a device run by electricity with the act of lighting a fire. The late Raphael Patai explained the reasoning very clearly:

> When electricity was introduced, the Orthodox rabbis decided that it was forbidden to operate an electric switch on the Sabbath. Their argument ran as follows: There is a Biblical-Talmudic prohibition against lighting fire on the Sabbath; hence it had for long been forbidden to light a candle on the Sabbath, even if it could be done as effortlessly as by striking a match. To turn on an electric light was declared essentially the same act as lighting a candle—therefore it was forbidden. By the same token, the turning off of an electric light was equated with the putting out of fire—another forbidden act. (1977, 254)

So, for example, "When a dentist has completed the treatment of a dental emergency on the Sabbath, he should close his office but not turn off the lights" (Tendler and Rosner 1987, 59).

Patai continues, "A further extension of this prohibition was the inclusion of the switching on and off of all appliances, which worked with electricity. What the rabbis did allow was the use of automatic electric timing devices, which can be set on Friday afternoon to turn on lights or appliances at a pre-set hour on the Sabbath and to turn them off thereafter, or vice versa. Modern Orthodox Jewish households are equipped with such time-clocks" (1977, 254). It is permitted, for example, to use electric blankets if they are connected to a time switch (Jacobs 1999, 106). "Religious kibbutzim in Israel use timing devices to activate the electric milking machines early Saturday morning and to turn them off after the milking is completed" (Patai 1977, 254). In the present context, one could argue that the use of timing devices to turn on electric appliances on the Sabbath is a perfect example of circumventing custom. Although it is forbidden to turn on an electric appliance such as an ordinary light on the Sabbath, it is permitted to have the light go on automatically (so long as the timing device was set before the onset of Sabbath) or if a helpful non-Jew, known as the *Shabbes Goy* (Katz 1989) does so. Such a helpful individual cannot be asked on the Sabbath itself to do so, but could legitimately be asked prior to the Sabbath. In other words, the light can be turned on, but not by an observant Orthodox Jew him- or herself. This is what I mean by the idea of "circumventing custom."

THE SHABBAT ELEVATOR

With the dozens upon dozens of regulations prohibiting various forms of behavior on the Sabbath, it might seem that the most ordinary of acts risks violating these negative injunctions. The Jews have always been a resourceful people and in this instance, they have had to be in order to function on the Sabbath. The trick was to find an acceptable way around the regulations, a loophole so to speak, or what has been aptly termed a Sabbath subterfuge (Jacobs 1981, 28). It is precisely these various forms of the circumvention of Sabbath regulations that are the subject of this extended essay. Sometimes the means of circumvention reflect the letter of the law in question but not the spirit. In other words, the Orthodox Jew is technically not guilty of violating the injunction, but at the same time, he or she is only able to avoid committing a technical violation by means of a highly ingenious form of casuistic reasoning, or some cleverly designed technological innovation.

Let us begin our consideration of custom circumvention with the Shabbat elevator. The problem lies in the proscription against using electricity (deemed a form of fire, hence pushing an electrical switch or completing an electrical circuit counts as starting a fire). At the time these regulations were formulated, there were no skyscrapers, nor were there any elevators. But with the construction of high-rise buildings, the invention of elevators was a godsend. Otherwise, individuals living or working on the fifteenth floor would be forced to walk up numerous flights of stairs in order to reach their apartment or office.

Here is an example of a way of using an elevator without pushing the elevator call button. "There's an elderly lady who lives on the 15th floor of a New York hotel. At ten o'clock on Saturday mornings, she stands by the elevator, but she won't ring the bell. She has to wait until someone else on her floor comes along, or the cleaning man who knows she needs help shows up. Then the bell is pushed, and she takes the elevator to the lobby and walks to the synagogue" (Kaye 1987, 195). This is one technique: wait until someone else, presumably not a Jew, comes along to summon the elevator by pushing the call button. In this case, the cleaning man is functioning as a *Shabbes Goy*, a critical role that will be discussed in depth later in this essay. If, on the Sabbath, an observant Jew wants to take an elevator from the ground floor up to his or her apartment, he or she may enter the elevator, but may not push the appropriate floor button. Instead, the individual must wait until someone else enters the elevator and hope that the newcomer pushes the button. Ideally, the newcomer is going to the same desired floor, but if not, the Jew will have to exit at the newcomer's floor and walk up or down the stairs to his or her own floor. In the case where a Jew enters an elevator that has a Gentile on it and the Jew intends merely to exit at the Gentile's floor, even if the Gentile asks the Jew which floor he or she wants, the Jew is not supposed to reply by asking the Gentile to press the button of the Jew's floor (Broyde and Jachter 1995, 85). If a Jew enters an empty nonautomatic elevator, he or she must simply wait until the elevator is summoned, presumably by a non-Jew and just trust that the floor of the summoner might be reasonably close to his or her destination (Broyde and Jachter 1995, 81–82).

There is another acceptable means of circumvention besides depending upon the good offices of a *Shabbes Goy*. This technique is based upon the principle of performing an everyday routine act in a completely different or unorthodox way. This principle is known as *shinui*, which literally means "change" or "modification" in Hebrew. One authority defines *shinui* as "a deviation from the manner in which it [an action] is usually done (Cohen 1993, 76). Another authority speaks about the same concept but calls it *Kil'achar Yad* defining it as "the performance of a prohibited action in a non-normal (irregular) manner" (Halperin 1986, 133). Still another authority suggests that the principle derives from rabbinical interpretation of a passage in Isaiah (58:13) in which God instructs Jews to "turn away" from doing their pleasure on the Sabbath and to honor Him by not doing their [usual] ways (Neuwirth 1989, 427).

A good illustration of *shinui* is contained in the Shabbat tract of the Mishnah with reference to the prohibition against carrying an object from a private to a public domain:

> He who takes something out (1) whether in his right hand or in his left, (2) in his lap, or (3) on his shoulder, is liable. . . . If he takes something out (1) on the back of his hand, (2) on his foot, (3) in his mouth, (4) in his elbow, (5) in his ear, or (6) in his hair . . . he is exempt from liability to a sin offering. For he has not carried the object out the way people generally carry out objects (Neusner 1988, 191–192; 1992–1993, IIc, 100, 103).

In the case of the elevator, one informant reported that while it was forbidden to push the elevator button with one's finger, one could push the button with one's elbow or even one's nose. However, the more usual circumventory technique consists of waiting patiently for a non-Jew to push the button.

The Sabbath rules regarding elevator usage are quite specific on these points. "A Jew may ascend in an electric elevator operated by a non-Jewish attendant for both Jews and non-Jews, as long as the attendant does not set it in motion especially for the Jew. . . . It follows that the Jew should enter and leave the elevator only at floors where it is also being entered or left by non-Jews" (Neuwirth 1989, 479–480). An elevator without an operator may be used by a Jew on the Sabbath only if it functions automatically, that is goes up and down by itself at fixed intervals or continuously, and if the elevator stops by itself at the various floors without the need of any human intervention (342).

An analogous situation occurs with respect to buildings that have automatic doors activated by a motion detector or a switch under the doormat. "Both of these are electrical devices whose use is forbidden to us, so we must either find a conventional door or wait until someone else goes into the building and run in quickly behind them so we do not activate the device" (Schlossberg 1996, 19). This is often the case at modern hotels that have electronic doors. "When we encounter one on Shabbos we have to wait until another guest activates the door. Then we politely dash inside after the surprised door-opener" (83). Such a door-opener is in effect functioning as a *Shabbes Goy*. It is not only the front door of hotels that causes a problem, but the rooms themselves. Many modern hotels utilize electronic pass cards in place of keys (Oratz 1993, 141–149). Orthodox Jews staying at such hotels are obliged to ask for standard "old-fashioned" keys to their assigned rooms (Schlossberg 1996, 83). One college girl who returned to her dormitory late on a Friday evening (after the evening had commenced) was forced to remain outside all night. The door to her dormitory was opened by passing a card through a groove. She had the proper card but felt too guilty about using it on the Sabbath to open the door to return to her room.

Hotel stays over the Sabbath also cause other difficulties. If a bellman carries an Orthodox Jew's suitcases up to a room, the Jew cannot tip him as handling money on the Sabbath is forbidden. Also if the same bellman needs a signature, say, for delivering a package or food from room service, the Jew cannot provide such as writing too is forbidden on the Sabbath (Schlossberg 1996, 83). Police handing out tickets (e.g., to a jaywalking pedestrian Jew), have a problem inasmuch as they are required to obtain the offender's signature, and a truly Orthodox Jew is not permitted to write on the Sabbath. Not all police understand why their jaywalker adamantly refuses to sign the ticket.

It may come as something a surprise to the reader to learn that there is an entire book devoted to the Shabbat elevator. *Maaliot B'Shabat* (*Elevators on the Sabbath*) was written by Rabbi Yitzhak Halperin, director of the Department of Halacha at the Institute for Science and Halacha located in Jerusalem, which was founded in 1963. Rabbi Halperin has devoted more than sixteen years of his life to the problem of just how to construct a type of elevator that would allow observant Orthodox Jews to use it on the Sabbath without their violating the Sabbath regulations (Broyde and Jachter 1995, 68n20).

In the early 1960s, several rabbinical *responsa* were published regarding the use of elevators on the Sabbath. One ruling was that it was "forbidden to use all elevators on Shabbat, even automatic elevators" while another stated that "one is permitted to ride on an elevator on Shabbat so long as one does not push any buttons" (Broyde and Jachter 1995, 64). Rabbi Halperin, the acknowledged authority on the Shabbat elevator, has an intermediate position, namely, that "it is always forbidden to ride on a descending elevator (unless special modifications have been made to the elevator) and that it is permitted to ride on an ascending elevator" (Broyde and Jachter 1995, 68). The rationale for this distinction involves some fairly technical discussion (Oratz 1993, 170–249), but at the risk of oversimplifying the issue, it seems to be a matter of the passenger's body weight being a critical factor in causing an elevator to descend whereas it is not so in the case of an ascending elevator (Neumann 1983; Broyde and Jachter 1995, 68–70). Halperin's argument is that an Orthodox Jew's stepping into a down elevator on the Sabbath directly contributes to the creation of energy that may be turning on lights or operating machines, both of which are forbidden (Broyde and Jachter 1995, 71). Elevators certified as permissible for Shabbat usage by Halperin have had their circuitry modified so that when they descend, the electricity generated is totally dissipated and the modifications are such as to neutralize the effect of the passenger's weight (88). Not all authorities agree with Halperin, and several have proposed detailed criticisms of his reasoning (72–76).

As early as the 1950s, some rabbis, usually Conservative or more likely Reform, have argued against the elevator taboo. Neulander, for example, declared the "identification between electricity and fire to be wrong both on Halachic and on scientific grounds." His reasoning was that the Halachic definition of fire included the idea that a combustible substance was consumed in the process and "is turned to charcoal or ashes" and further that a fire in Halachic terms "must produce a flame" (1950, 167). He concludes "It, therefore, follows that by both tests, electricity does not qualify as fire from the standpoint of the Halachah: (a) a filament of an electric light, when it becomes incandescent and gives off light, is undergoing no combustion, and (b) it gives off no flame" (1950, 168). The incandescence issue is an important one in Orthodox Judaism inasmuch as it is held that turning on an incandescent electric light on the Sabbath violates a biblical prohibition, whereas turning on a nonincandescent light such as a fluorescent one is permitted (Broyde and Jachter 1991, 8, 10; Sokol 1986, 275n26). In any case, Neulander's position is that using electricity on the Sabbath to ride an elevator does not properly fall under the category of fire and that furthermore some additional use of electricity on that day is permissible. So "we may permit turning on electric lights, telephoning, refrigeration, using a radio and television. But we cannot countenance the use of electricity for work prohibited on the Sabbath, such as cooking and baking, shaving with an electric razor, using the washing machine or an electric iron. The prohibition is here derived not from the use of electricity but from the nature of the work itself" (1950, 170–171). So the telephone can be used to "strengthen family ties . . . to convey a message of cheer to the sick. . . . But the telephone should not be used for shopping purposes or for making a business appointment, much less a business transaction" (1950, 171). The members of the Institute for Science and Halacha in Jerusalem have attempted to solve the problem of the telephone much as they have done for the elevator. They have invented a "Shabbos telephone" the use of which does not violate the Sabbath (Greenberg 1983, 41–42); for a discussion of the use of telephones on the Sabbath, see Broyde and Jachter (1991, 31–35) and Oratz (1993, 35–53). Among other ingenious inventions is the Shabbat Scooter, which is advertised as "The only electrically driven mobility product permitted for use by the disabled and elderly to be driven on Shabbat and Holidays."

In the case of a medical emergency, say with a newborn baby, one can use a normal telephone to speak to a doctor. The life-threatening rule that takes precedence over any Halachic principle would obviously be in effect. Still, even in this instance, it is preferable to employ some form of *shinui*. "The receiver of the telephone should be lifted off with one's elbow or with another object. The number should be dialed with the end of a spoon, one's little finger, the joint of a finger, etc." (Cohen 1993, 79–80). Such *shinui* is also critical in the practice of medicine on the Sabbath so that if a telephone cannot be dialed by a non-Jew, it can be done by a Jew with elbows or two hands (Sokol 1986, 159). When the telephone rings in a doctor's house on the Sabbath, he should lift up the receiver in an unusual manner (e.g., removing it with his elbow or wrist, or lift it up together with another person) (Neuwirth 1989, 635). Similarly, the all-important doctor's pager's button can be pressed with one's knuckles or with a spoon (Sokol 1986, 160).

It should be pointed out, however, that these devices are not acceptable to all Orthodox Jews. Strict Orthodox Jews persist in not using electricity and for that matter, not using elevators or telephones at all, not even Shabbat elevators, or Shabbos telephones. The extreme measures devised to avoid generating electricity may be illustrated by the expressed concern not to wear any clothing on the Sabbath that might produce "static electricity" (Broyde and Jachter 1991, 37). It is hard to keep track of all the various prohibitions and restrictions connected with the Sabbath. For example, individuals using hearing aids that depend upon electrical current should switch them on before the onset of the Sabbath and also set them so that they will need no adjustment, as it is forbidden to increase or decrease the volume (Levi 1966, 47; Abramov 1972, 5). On the other hand, "One may not go out in a place where there is no eruv wearing a hearing aid if part of it (such as the battery) is in one's pocket" (Neuwirth 1989, 569). (An *eruv*, or sanctioned extension of domestic space, will be discussed later in this essay.) With respect to hearing aids, there has been considerable debate over whether or not microphones can be used in synagogues so that rabbis and others will not have to strain their voices (Jacobs 1999, 155). One solution has been to use battery-operated microphones, which somehow are thought not to utilize electric current of the sort produced by inserting a plug into an electric outlet.

The debate about whether or not it is permissible to use electricity on the Sabbath has spawned a vast literature. One authority refers to a 1975 bibliographical survey, which lists more than two hundred pages of sources on the subject (Rabinowitz 1996, 26n1).

THE LIGHT IN THE REFRIGERATOR

There are at least two reasons not to open a refrigerator door on the Sabbath. One has to do with the refrigerator motor and the other with the refrigerator light. Opening the refrigerator door, according to one discussion, "allows warm air to enter, thus causing a drop in temperature which causes the motor to go on" (Broyde and Jachter 1991, 28). This is because there is a thermostat controlling or regulating the starting and stopping of a compressor motor. When the temperature at the thermostat rises above a set level, the compressor motor becomes activated in order to lower the temperature. Once the temperature has dropped sufficiently, the thermostat switch causes the motor to stop. The point is that "Opening the door admits warmer air and therefore raises the temperature inside the refrigerator more rapidly; consequently it causes the motor to be switched on earlier than it would have started had the door remained closed" (Levi 1966, 44). To the extent that this door-opening action results in the flow of electric current, it could be construed as a violation of Sabbath rules (Broyde and Jachter 1991, 30). But the more common concern has to do with the light in the refrigerator.

Most refrigerators have a light inside that goes on automatically whenever the doors are opened. Since opening the refrigerator door results in the light going on, which is deemed a form of "lighting a fire," it would appear to be impossible to open one's refrigerator without violating a fundamental Sabbath law. One might wonder just how a refrigerator lightbulb's being on could constitute a "fire" and the answer depends upon whether one considers that the bulb's filament is "burning" when the power goes into it (Siegel 1982, 50; Jacobs 1984b, 169). In any case, the practical solution to this problem turns out to be quite simple. One either unscrews or removes the lightbulb or bulbs prior to the Sabbath (Schlossberg 1996, 19). This is explicitly permitted: "Before Shabbath, one should disconnect, or remove, the internal light of a refrigerator one is going to use on Shabbath, so as to prevent its being automatically turned on by the opening of the door. . . . One should not close the door of a refrigerator whose internal light will thereby be extinguished" (Neuwirth 1989, 533–534). If one fails to do this, there are still other alternative courses of action. "If one has forgotten to remove or disconnect the internal light, one should, where the possibility exists, prevent the bulb from being turned on when the door is opened, by carefully inserting the blade of a knife through the hinge side of the door while it is still closed and holding the switch in a depressed position" (101). Still another alternative technique is to "tape the switch that controls the light, so that the light will not go on when the door is opened" (Cohen 1988, 48; Halperin 1986, 161). In other cases, one needs to consult an expert on such matters. "If, upon opening an electric refrigerator on Shabbath . . . one finds that the internal light has automatically been switched on, . . . one should consult a qualified rabbinical authority about what to do with regard to closing the door of the refrigerator again" (Neuwirth 1989, 103). One difficulty here, however, is how to reach a qualified authority in such an "emergency." An Orthodox rabbi, after all, is not permitted to answer his telephone on the Sabbath. One could presumably walk to the synagogue to speak to a rabbi about the refrigerator light fiasco, but during all that time, someone would in theory have to hold the refrigerator door ajar to prevent it from closing without the necessary benefit of the counsel of a "qualified rabbinical authority." Perhaps the easiest solution to the whole refrigerator light difficulty is simply to ask a non-Jew to open or close a refrigerator (486).

The quandary of what to do if the light in the refrigerator goes on when the door is opened on the Sabbath has analogues. For example, a woman relates an anecdote about her uncle: "On a trip once, he went to the toilet somewhere; when he locked the door, a light went on automatically—and just so he won't desecrate the Sabbath a second time, what does he do?—he sits there for fourteen hours" (Jungk 1985, 51). There are many such anecdotes concerning the prohibition against turning lights on or off. A Jewish American family living in an apartment building in Zurich in 1974 was invited upstairs for dinner one Friday evening. The hosts were observant Jews. After dinner, the two families sat talking when suddenly the lights went out. They were obviously on a timer and were presumably set to go off at bedtime. The two families sat in the dark for some time with no one referring to the absence of light. The Jewish Americans who were not Orthodox were quite surprised that neither of their hosts made any effort to turn the lights back on. Finally, the hosts' youngest son got up and turned on the lights.

There are even jokes about the problem arising from the taboo against turning out a light or in the old days, snuffing out a candle. One such joke that describes an unusual but effective circumventory technique goes as follows: Froyim Greidinger, the Galician prankster, was on his way home one Friday night. It was past midnight when he passed the house of his pious grandparents. To his surprise he saw that they were still up, the Sabbath candles burning brightly, so he went in. "Why aren't you asleep?" he asked. "It's past midnight." His grandparents looked dejected. "We can't go to sleep on account of the candles," his grandfather explained. "If we let them burn themselves out, the house may catch fire, and we can't snuff them out because it's the holy Sabbath. Nor is there a peasant around to blow them out." For a moment Froyim was lost in thought. "Tell me grandpa, when is *Purim*?" asked Froyim standing in front of one of the candles. He spoke in a very loud voice and, when he came to the letter P in *Purim*, he puffed out his cheeked and bellowed. The candle went out instantly. Then, standing in front of the second candle, Froyim asked, "And when is Passover?" When he came to the letter P in Passover, he again puffed out his cheeks and bellowed. The second candle also went out. Then turning with a grin to his grandparents, Froyim said, "Now you can go to bed. Thank God none of us had to violate the Sabbath!" (Ausubel 1948, 303–304). This clever use of the aspirate allophone of the /p/ phoneme—there is an inaspirate allophone of the phoneme found when "p" occurs in medial or final position in a word—shows remarkable linguistic mettle. "P" in initial position in English is always aspirate, which means that air is expelled when it is pronounced (as opposed to initial "p" in French, which is inaspirate). Fortunately, both Purim and Passover feature an initial aspirate "p."

In modern times, of course, the issue concerns turning on or off an electric light rather than blowing out a candle. One clever form of circumvention devised by the Institute for Science and Halacha to allow individuals to read on the Sabbath without turning on a light consists of turning on a florescent light before the Sabbath and then placing a special cover on it so that it can burn all day and be blocked out when unwanted (Precker 1981, 73). Then there are occasions when "One leaves a light on in the living room so that one can read on the Sabbath, only to find that someone else has forgotten and switched the light off—and Halachah forbids asking anyone to turn it on again" (Danzger 1989, 257).

Another striking example of the degree to which observant Jews will go to avoid pushing a button to turn a light on or off on the Sabbath is provided by the case of certain stoplights located in the Fairfax district of Los Angeles, a district with a large Jewish population. In many cosmopolitan areas, traffic lights remain on green (to facilitate automobile traffic) until a pedestrian pushes a button on a street corner, which thereby causes the green light to change to red, causing the traffic to come to a full stop. Typically, the pushed button also causes a "walk" sign to appear, indicating that it is now safe for the pedestrian to proceed to cross the street. Since observant Orthodox Jews are not permitted to push "electrical" buttons on the Sabbath, a number of key traffic lights have been programmed so that the walk sign goes on automatically when a person reaches the corner (working presumably on a principle similar to that employed with the Shabbat elevator). These lights are located at the junctions of La Brea Avenue and Second Street, Oakwood Avenue and La Brea, and the intersection of Beverly Boulevard and Poinsettia Place, among other locations. Of course, these automatic lights also work just as well for non-Jews, as the lights are obviously nondiscriminatory. Still, the installation of these specially programmed traffic lights in a predominantly Jewish neighborhood shows how the requirements of circumvention impact upon the design of public city streets.

The Sabbath prohibition against switching lights on or off can be circumvented in the case of a refrigerator by essentially disarming the light fixture, that is, by unscrewing the lightbulb. However, the situation of the light in an elevator demands a different procedure. In some elevators, a light goes on when the door is opened and is extinguished when the elevator passenger exits (and the door closes). The solution here is to arrange for the elevator lighting to remain on continuously (Oratz 1993, 240). By this means, a passenger's entrance or exit does not cause a light to go on or off.

The more general problem of having lights turned on during the Sabbath has been partly solved through the use of timing devices. But even here there is a potential problem of appearances. This is referred to as *marit ayyin* "for the sake of appearances" (Jacobs 1999, 109; Kolatch 1985, 13–14), or *Maris Ayin* which translates literally as "the way the eye sees" (Cohen 1988, 69). The issue here is not one of wrongdoing but rather the mere appearance of wrongdoing. According to one source, one of the best-known examples of this principle found in the Talmud is "that if a man has been drenched in a shower or downpour or through falling into a river, he should not hang out his garments to dry on the washing-line because it might give the impression that he has washed the clothes on Shabbat. When people hang out washing on the line, it is usually because they have just washed the clothes they hang out" (Jacobs 1999, 109; Neusner 1992–1993, IIb, 116; S. Cohen 1995, 188–189; Pick 1998, 132). In the discussion of this in the Babylonian Talmud, we are told "In any case in which sages have imposed a prohibition for appearance's sake, then even if one is in the innermost chambers, such an action still is forbidden" (Neusner 1992–1993, IIe, 93). On the subject of the prohibition against doing laundry on the Sabbath, as well as the issue of appearances, it is noteworthy that "If mud or moist dirt adhered to a garment and it is still wet, one is permitted to scrape it off before it dries, provided that it will leave behind a stain. Since the garment will remain soiled, removing the dirt cannot be considered an act of laundering" (S. Cohen 1995, 180).

If neighbors see the lights go on in a house occupied by supposedly observant Jews after sundown on Friday night, they might assume, wrongly, if they don't know about the timing devices, that the occupants have turned on the lights themselves thereby violating the Sabbath rules (Broyde and Jachter 1995, 82n73). The same matter of appearances also applies to the use of a telephone wake-up call. Assuming the request for the wake-up call was properly made before the Sabbath, the difficulty lies in the fact that if other people hear the telephone ring on the Sabbath in a given house, those people might suspect the individuals in that house of using a telephone on the Sabbath (Oratz 1993, 51). Similarly, if an automatic dishwasher is set by a timer (before the onset of the Sabbath) to go on during the Sabbath, people might logically come to the conclusion that prohibited work was being done on the Sabbath (163). This matter of appearances is also germane in the case of a Jewish family asking a Gentile maid to work on the Sabbath. On the one hand, the way around the prohibition against asking a Gentile, in effect, a *Shabbes Goy*, to do forbidden work on the Sabbath is to tell her that she does not have to any such work on the Sabbath if she would prefer to do it on another day of the week. "If she, herself then chooses to do it on Shabbat, that is her business" (Katz 1991, 18). On the other hand, if a Gentile is seen working for a Jew on the Sabbath by passersby, they might (wrongly) assume that the Jew had directed the Gentile to the work on that day (19). Accordingly a live-in maid is not permitted to shop, garden, or take out a baby in a carriage on the Sabbath because of the appearance of wrongdoing, and because activities that make a loud noise are considered to be disrespectful of the Sabbath, the live-in maid should not use a vacuum cleaner or run a dishwasher, washing machine, or dryer on the Sabbath (Cohen 1988, 89).

The prohibition against lighting a fire also has repercussions with respect to bathing. One cannot use hot water in a bathtub or shower because in most modern water-heating systems, if one draws hot water from the water heater, the heater automatically begins to heat a new incoming supply of cold water. If, say, a gas heater came on, that would bring about a clear violation of the "fire-lighting" injunction. It is best, then, to bathe before the Sabbath unless one is willing to do so using cold water. In a strict Orthodox environment, even cold water may not be available as it is forbidden to turn any faucet on or off. Turning a faucet is construed as work. There is, however, an optional circumvention. One can simply leave the water running for the duration of the Sabbath thereby getting around the prohibition against turning a faucet on or off. The prohibition against turning on a hot water faucet causes real difficulty for Orthodox physicians who must wash their hands before examining or touching a patient. One solution to reduce the infraction in such an instance to a rabbinical rather than a scriptural matter consists of turning on the faucet using one's knuckles or elbows rather than one's fingers (Sokol 1986, 190). These techniques, examples of *shinui*, are similar to those allowed to relieve a seriously ill patient on a hot summer's day by turning on a fan or air conditioner using one's elbows or wrists instead of one's hands (Neuwirth 1989, 543).

The hot water taboo also impinges on infant care. Cloth diapers, for example, "must not be 'flushed' or rinsed on Shabbos . . . nor may they be discarded into a water or detergent-filled pail, since this initiates the laundering process," which is forbidden on the Sabbath. The solution: use disposable paper diapers (Tendler 1988, 52). But even this solution turns out to be the subject of heated debate. Apparently, the issue concerns whether the act of attaching the self-adhering tabs on the diaper constitutes a form of sewing (a forbidden act on the Sabbath) and whether the act of breaking the adhesion to remove the soiled diaper constitutes a form of tearing (also a forbidden act on the Sabbath). (For the incredible intricacies of this debate, see Bleich [1986].)

With regard to infant care, there is a problem caused by the prohibition against "smoothing." If, on the Sabbath, one wishes to comfort a baby suffering from diaper rash or sunburn, one should apply a liquid medication using a type of *shinui*, that is, carrying out an action in an unusual manner (e.g., using the little finger or the back of one's hand). If the ointment or cream is in a jar, one should similarly remove it in an unusual manner (e.g., with the handle of a spoon or fork) (Cohen 1993, 92).

While it may be relatively easy to see the linkage between the "fire-lighting" restriction and the refrigerator light issue, the connection between the prohibition against driving and the ban against lighting a fire may not be quite so obvious. According to one source, a person's pushing his foot down on the gas pedal of an automobile is equivalent to making or stoking a fire, and by analogous reasoning pushing down on the brake pedal is the equivalent of damping a fire, which is also forbidden. "Thus, driving a car on the Sabbath is forbidden by Torah law" (Himelstein 1990, 60). Just in case the underlying logic is still not entirely clear, it is supposedly the "igniting of the gasoline" that is deemed a form of "making a fire" (22).

The driving prohibition in some instances works to promote Jewish religiosity. The reason is that it effectively forces observant Jews to live close to their synagogue (Weinberger 1991, 16). One could even contend that such a Sabbath rule ensures the continuity and solidarity of a Jewish community. "By virtue of the Sabbath, it is given that one will live within walking distance of the synagogue and, invariably, within walking distance of at least some, if not most or all, of the other members of the synagogue-community" (Waxman 1982, 41). As one source phrases it, "A Sabbath observer to whom the entire Sabbath day is precious would in the first place not consider establishing his permanent residence in an area where there is no synagogue within reasonable walking distance" (Donin 1972, 94). However, the reality is that whereas in centuries past in Europe, Jews usually lived in close proximity to their synagogues, in modern America, many Jews may live miles away from their place of worship. This is presumably why "the Conservative movement has permitted Jews to drive to the synagogue on the Sabbath seeing the need for synagogue attendance as overriding the prohibition of driving" (Himelstein 1990, 22; Kahn 1968, 7). Some Conservative Jews make the distinction between riding in a vehicle and driving it. Riding in order to attend services might be acceptable, but driving the car would not (Kolatch 1985, 269). Presumably, the vehicle could be driven by a non-Jew, that is, a *Shabbes Goy*. But the Orthodox Jews remain steadfastly opposed to driving. The answer to the inevitable question "Isn't it better to drive to *shul* than not to go at all?" is an emphatic "No, it is not better!" (Donin 1972, 95–96). In contrast to the intractable Orthodox position of banning driving altogether, except in the case of a life-threatening emergency, one Jew writes, "I do not consider it inconsistent to keep a kosher home yet to ride on the Sabbath" (Eisenstein 1970, 235). What he does object to is the hypocrisy that results by pretending to conform to the Orthodox principle. He gives the example of the man who drives his car to the synagogue on the Sabbath but parks it two blocks away. He reports an incident when such a man told him in the process of preparing to go to the synagogue on a rainy Friday night, "All right, we'll drive over. But we are going to walk the last two blocks. The one thing we have got to be sure of is that our umbrellas are wet when we come in" (235). This is surely a blatant example of circumventing custom. One does wonder, however, about the umbrellas, wet to demonstrate that their owners had walked in the rain. In theory, the umbrellas should not even have been carried from one's private home into a public arena (Sigal 1982, 77). For that matter, opening an umbrella on the Sabbath is also forbidden because it supposedly violates the prohibition against providing shelter (Trepp 1980, 71).

There have been occasions when Orthodox Jews were caught driving on the Sabbath or on other "high holidays" while in the act of exceeding the speed limit. According to a captain in the Central Traffic Division of the Los Angeles Police Department, these Jews often plead with the officers not to give them tickets. It was not so much a matter of the possible fine, but rather the disgrace of having written documentation of the fact that they had been driving on the Sabbath.

An illustration of the seriousness of violating the driving prohibition is provided by an incident in Israel in October 1966. A Bar Mitzvah ceremony was scheduled to begin but at the very last minute, the local officiating rabbi ordered the boy and his father to leave the synagogue because "some members of the family and their friends had driven to the synagogue in cars." There was considerable public protest over the rabbi's action, which essentially punished the boy for the actions of others, but the rabbi remained unrepentant. He even issued an open letter stating, "I hereby declare that I do not repent of my deed, and I am still of the opinion that what I did was just and necessary." The Bar Mitzvah ceremony was, however, celebrated a week later in a different synagogue (Abramov 1976, 355).

Still another example of circumvention involving the prohibition against driving on the Sabbath consists of the following dodge: One drives to the synagogue the night before, that is, well before sunset on Friday. One has supper there and sleeps on a cot. The next day one participates in services and socializes. When the sun sets, one then drives home, and the driving prohibition is successfully circumvented.

Even the obvious alternatives to driving one's own car to get to the synagogue for Sabbath services present problems. For instance, if one took a taxi (driven presumably by a Gentile) or took a bus or subway, one would have to handle money to pay the fare and that is forbidden (Jacobs 1984b, 172). In theory, one could pay a taxi driver in advance for his services, but it would be hard to arrange this in the case of a bus or subway train.

Sometimes the Sabbath rules conflict and thereby cause seemingly insuperable difficulties. For example, it is typically the woman of the household's task to light the Sabbath candles on Friday evening, and this has to be done before sunset, as it is not permitted to light a fire on the Sabbath. One traditional sexist explanation for Jewish women's Sabbath candle-lighting duties is that they are thereby atoning for Eve's original transgression in the Garden of Eden, an act of sin that supposedly "extinguished the light of the world" (Bloch 1980, 20; Ganzfried 1961, 2: 72; Barack 1965, 98). In any case the problem stems from the fact that she is supposed to say a blessing before lighting the candles and that the blessing officially begins the Sabbath. "The blessing must be said before the lighting—but once the blessing has been pronounced, the woman is no longer permitted to light the candles. To get over this hurdle, the rule in this particular case is that the woman lights the candles *before* the blessing, then, with her eyes closed, she recites the blessing, and only afterwards looks at the candles burning, as if she had just lit them" (Himelstein 1990, 62; Lauterbach 1973, 470; Steingroot 1995, 100). Instead of closing her eyes, she may cover them with her hands (Donin 1972, 73; Ganzfried 1961, 2, 72; Bloch 1980, 130; Sperling 1968, 119; S. Cohen 1995, 25). Another solution, if it is after sunset, is to ask a Gentile, that is, a *Shabbes Goy*, to light the candles after which a Jew can recite the blessing (Broyde and Jachter 1993, 93). These are other representative instances of circumventing custom.

THE *ERUV* AS SYMBOLIC SPACE

An *erub* or *eruv* has been defined as "an enclosure of real or symbolic walls surrounding a community, which Halakhically permits Jews to carry on the Shabbat" (Weiss 1987, 40). Essentially, the device converts "a number of homes into a single house" (Rowland 1982, 49). Even a group of boats can form a fictive defined common space by being tied together (Neusner 1992–1993, IId, 32). Typically, an *eruv* is built by hanging rope, wire, or nylon cord (Kolatch 1985, 277) from poles surrounding a designated area or using preexisting telephone poles or fences.

As it is forbidden on the Sabbath to carry anything out of one's home, the construction of an *eruv* basically extends the spatial limits of the "home" such that women, for example, can wheel baby carriages through the streets to the synagogue (assuming the synagogue is located within the *eruv*). Otherwise women would be housebound, being forced to stay at home with their infants. Thanks to the *eruv* women find it easier to participate in services because they can bring their infants in baby carriages with them (Weiss 1987, 40; Vecsey 1979, 13). Physically disabled individuals confined to wheelchairs can also be wheeled to a synagogue (Metzger 1989, 85; Neuwirth 1989, 568; Trillin 1994, 50; Diamond 2000, 51). They could not attend services without an *eruv* if a non-Jew was not available to push their wheelchairs. Within the boundaries of an *eruv*, a Jew would be allowed to help such nonambulatory fellow Jews. Men and women can also carry objects to their neighbors' homes, for example, carrying a "casserole to a shut-in across the street" (Trillin 1994, 50), assuming again that these houses are contained within the confines of the *eruv*.

One woman gave testimony illustrating how the construction of an *eruv* immeasurably improved the quality of her life. Her eight-year-old son could carry a toy car with him and her fourteen-year-old daughter could carry a comb with her on the Sabbath. "It's so nice on a snowy day to be able to wear your warm boots and carry your indoor shoes with you. I can bring my glasses and my keys" (Vecsey 1979, 13). There are numerous technical discussions as to how to set up an *eruv* with special attention to such details concerning construction and location (Eider 1968; Schachter 1983; Bechhofer 1998; Graus 1999).

Although there does not seem to be any mention of the concept of *eruv* in the Dead Sea Scrolls, it has been suggested that by the end of the first century C.E., the *eruv* had become part of Sabbath tradition (Kimbrough 1966, 502). We find an entire tractate of the Mishnah devoted to the *erub* or *eruv*. In fact, titled "Erubin," it immediately follows the section concerned with Shabbat (Neusner 1988, 208–229). Many of the *eruv* rules concern details of measurement. For example, partitions are supposed to be "ten handbreadths high." So one cannot draw water from a cistern that is between two courtyards unless a partition ten handbreadths high is made for it (224). Or if a caravan is encamped in a valley, the travelers may surround the camp with a fence made out of cattle yokes, and if they do this, they may carry things within the enclosure "on condition that the fence be ten handbreadths high" (209). Another measurement was the figure of two thousand cubits as the absolute limit beyond a settlement's boundaries where an observant Jew might be permitted to walk (Gilat 1963, xxv; Neusner 1988, 218).

There is an interesting example of circumvention in connection with that limit. The Sabbath law dictates that one must not leave one's city or community beyond a distance of two thousand cubits, but there were several exceptions. These included a midwife called on in an emergency situation to help deliver a baby, or an individual summoned to assist in extinguishing a life-threatening fire. The problem was that after the midwife or acting fireman carried out their mission, they were, according to the same Sabbath law, required to remain where they were (within an area of a circumference of four cubits) until the end of the Sabbath. A rabbi realized that under such a restriction of having to remain "immobile till the end of the Shabbat at the spot where they rendered help," few individuals would ever leave their original homes to offer assistance. So the rabbi ruled that anyone leaving home on the Sabbath on a mission of mercy would be given the status of the inhabitants of the place where the help was needed. Accordingly, they would be able to move two thousand cubits in all directions once the assistance had been rendered (Berkovits 1983, 12). This did not solve the problem completely, but a two thousand cubits limit for the return trip was a much better option than remaining trapped in a four-cubit square.

Another ingenious technique for getting around the two-thousand-cubit constraint on the Sabbath is described by Solomon Schechter in a neglected brief 1892 essay entitled "Legal Evasions of the Law." After noting that the two-thousand-cubit limit was a rabbinical restriction rather than a question of biblical law, Schechter explains:

> Now the legal fiction often alluded to consisted in putting a meal at a certain point (at the end of the 2000 yards' limit). The person so acting was regarded as having removed his habitation from the town, and as having fixed it at the new point. He could thus walk 2000 yards further on, whilst he lost the right to walk 2000 yards in the opposite direction. . . . But this concession was only allowed for the furtherance of some religious object; for instance, to pay a visit of condolence, to attend a wedding banquet, to meet a master or friend, or perform similar acts. (1892, 562; cf. Ganzfried 1961, 2:142; Kolatch 1985, 279)

In another account of this device, it is indicated that enough foodstuffs for two meals (rather than one) can be placed up to two thousand cubits from one's home, but this must be done before the onset of the Sabbath. This "creates the legal fiction that one's domicile extends to the point at which the foodstuffs have been placed, and allows the person for whom they were placed to walk an additional 2000 cubits from that spot" (Roth 1986, 25n35).

One of the fears underlying the construction of an *eruv* is that one may inadvertently move from a private domain into a public one. One instruction mandates that "He who went beyond the Sabbath line, even by a single cubit, should not reenter" (Neusner 1988, 216). The taboo against crossing the line involves some unusual and quite fascinating hypothetical situations: "A man should not stand in private domain and urinate into public domain."

By the same token he should not stand in public domain and urinate into private domain. "And so too he should not spit [across the Sabbath line]" (227). All this has to do with the prohibition against carrying anything on the Sabbath, whether from private to public or public to private areas.

Strange as it may seem, these hypothetical matters have been carefully considered by various rabbinical authorities. In the Babylonian Talmud, there are more than three hundred instances of a device called *teyku*, which refers to an insoluble problem (cf. Breuer 1972, 526). Supposedly the term *teyku* is "an abbreviated form of *teykum*" meaning "let it stand," in other words, give up, for there is no answer to the dilemma (Jacobs 1981, 14; 1984b, 29). Here is one illustrative example of a *teyku*: "Rava set a problem: What is the law if a man stood in a private domain but with the end of his penis in the public domain? Do we consider it (lit. 'go after') from the point of view of the original movement (of the urine) or do we consider it from the point of view of the place from which it (the urine) comes out? TEKYU." Here is the discussion:

> The *Mishnah* (Eruvin 10:5) rules that it is forbidden for a man to stand in a private domain on the Sabbath and urinate into the public domain because by so doing he expels the urine and so is said to have carried or thrown it from the private to the public domain. Rava's problem is where the tip of the penis is in the public domain, i.e., does the *Mishnah* only refer to where the penis, too, is in the private domain? The formulation of the problem is given as: do we look at the matter from the point of view of the source of the urine in the body (which is in the private domain) or do we say that since the urine actually emerged from the body in the public domain and is deposited there, there has been no "carrying" from the private to the public domain. (Jacobs 1981, 44)

The reader should not be surprised to learn that this particular passage from the Mishnah inspired an eighteenth-century satirical work that described the "Kosher" Jew as "one who does not urinate in public places on the Sabbath" (Friedlander 1986, 142).

Raising hypothetical questions about objects spanning borders is not that uncommon in Jewish tradition, even when an *eruv* is not specifically involved. Telushkin retells a Talmudic tale, which begins: "If a fledgling bird is found within fifty cubits [about seventy-five feet] . . . [of a man's property], it belongs to the owner of the property. If it is found outside the limits of fifty cubits, it belongs to the person who finds it." The narrative continues, "Rabbi Jeremiah asked the question: 'If one foot of the fledgling bird is within the limit of fifty cubits, and one foot is outside it, what is the law?' It was for this reason that Rabbi Jeremiah was thrown out of the house of study" (Telushkin 1992, 49–50).

The construction of an *eruv* is clearly a way around the restriction concerning the movement from private to public space. Essentially, it converts public space into an extension of private space. By means of this artifice, observant Jews are released from the confinement of their own homes on the Sabbath.

A contemporary Jewish joke demonstrates the utility of an *eruv* even though there is no actual mention of an "*eruv*" in the text. The joke does, however, celebrate the basic underlying concept of the value of the extension of space and, in this case, time as well. The joke goes like this:

> A Jew, a Christian, and a Muslim were having a discussion about who was the most religious. "I was riding my camel in the middle of the Sahara," exclaimed the Muslim. "Suddenly a fierce sandstorm appeared from nowhere. I truly thought my end had come as I lay next to my camel while we were being buried deeper and deeper under the sand. But I did not lose my faith in the Almighty Allah. I prayed and prayed and suddenly for a hundred meters all around me, the storm had stopped. Since that day I am a devout Muslim and am now learning to recite the Quran by memory." "One day while fishing," started the Christian, "I was in my little dinghy in the middle of the ocean. Suddenly a fierce storm appeared from nowhere. I truly thought my end had come as my little dinghy was tossed up and down in the rough ocean. But I did not lose my faith in Jesus Christ. I prayed and prayed and suddenly, for three hundred meters all around me, the storm had stopped. Since that day I am a devout Christian and am now teaching young children about Him." "One day I was walking down the road," explained the Jew, "I was in my most expensive designer outfit in the middle of New York City. Suddenly I saw a black bag on the ground in front of me appear from nowhere. I put my hand inside and found that it was full of cash. I truly thought my end had come as it was a Saturday and we are not allowed to handle money on the Sabbath. But I did not lose my faith in Jehovah. I prayed and prayed and suddenly, for five hundred meters all around me, it was Tuesday."

The construction of an *eruv* in modern times is typically accomplished simply by stringing wires around the space to be enclosed with the wires attached to poles (e.g., telephone poles or streetlights already in place). An *eruv* can consist of a single courtyard or can encompass as much as a six-square-mile area as was proposed for a locale in London (Trillin 1994). The concept of *eruv* seems analogous, at least in terms of structure, to a well-known metaphorical concept in Halachic practice, usually referred to as "building a fence around the Torah." This strategy justifies the interdiction of an action that, while not actually constituting a violation of the Sabbath and the like, might, if carried out, lead to another action that would be a violation. For example, one should not handle a saw on the Sabbath lest it be used to saw wood, which would be a violation (Jacobs 1984b). Similarly, one should not handle a match or a pencil on the Sabbath because it could lead to a transgression such as lighting a fire or writing (Dresner 1970, 23). The prohibition against driving on the Sabbath has been interpreted as building a fence around the law thereby fencing in "sanctity of Shabbat" (Weinberger 1991, 17). This technique of building fences around the Torah has resulted in the accretion over time of Sabbath restrictions to the point that probably very few individuals are fully aware of the totality of all Sabbath rules and regulations.

The existence of jokes about Sabbath restrictions constitutes proof positive of the importance of such restrictions in Jewish daily life. What is a matter of life and death to the Muslim and Christian—being buried alive in sand or being drowned at sea—is equated in the joke to the stereotypic Jewish interest in money and how Jews chafe under the Sabbath constraints forbidding commerce and financial matters on that day.

The end result of the dozens of rabbinical additions to the relatively few specific actions enjoined by the Old Testament is a huge mass of negative injunctions. As Jastrow phrased it in 1898: "It is well known how the further elaboration of those instructions led to nigh endless restrictions. The people were not to journey on the Sabbath, not to ride, nor even to walk beyond a certain distance; no burdens were to be carried, fire was not to be touched, no meals were to be cooked, no business of any kind to be carried on" (322). A well-known Talmudic aphorism from the Hagigah says it more succinctly: "The laws of the Sabbath . . . lo, they are like mountains hanging by a string, for they have little Scripture for many laws" (Neusner 1988, 330). In some translations of this epitomizing classic articulation, the metaphor is expressed somewhat differently: "The rules about the Sabbath . . . are as mountains hanging by a hair, for Scripture is scanty and the rules many" (Beare 1960, 131n4). "Mountains hanging by a hair" is surely a striking and a seemingly apt summation of the Orthodox Jewish Sabbath regulations. At the same time, as novelist Herman Wouk, himself an observant Orthodox Jew, commented, "The restrictions of the Sabbath, which seem to tug at every turn of American life, were second nature to our fathers" (1959, 61). As we noted earlier, custom has been defined as second nature, implying that it is more or less taken for granted, taken as given, by those in its sway.

OTHER SABBATH CUSTOMS

The prohibition against carrying anything on the Sabbath can cause considerable personal inconvenience. For example, one cannot lock the front door of one's apartment or home because that would entail carrying a key. The way out of this problem is to "wear" the key as an article of jewelry (Neuwirth 1989, 231). A woman can wear a "key" pin and a man can wear a "key" tie clasp. Such an article of clothing, when worn, does not constitute "carrying" an object. So it is that an individual can lock his or her front door with a tie clasp or a piece of jewelry. These so-called *Shabbos Keys* must be functional such that a tie clip made out of a key "may be worn only if it actually serves to hold a tie in place" (Cohen 1995, 130, 138). In the same way, while a key cannot be attached to a belt, it can be worn as the replacement for the movable tongue of a belt buckle as long it is installed prior to the onset of the Sabbath (130). If there is an *eruv*, one could leave the house prior to the onset of the Sabbath carrying a key so that one could reenter one's house after Sabbath (Neuwirth 1989, 422). Incidentally, a Jew's animals are also subject to the same Sabbath restrictions with respect to carrying burdens. A pet dog, for example, if there is no *eruv*, should not be allowed out "carrying" an identification tag suspended from its neck (377). Presumably this rule is in effect whether or not the dog is actually Jewish. That is meant as a facetious comment but there is actually a joke about this issue. A Jew goes to a rabbi and asks if he will perform a Bar Mitzvah for his dog. The rabbi is outraged. "I can't perform a Bar Mitzvah for a dog. That's ridiculous. I refuse to do so." "That's all right," replied the Jew, "I'll just take him back to the rabbi who circumcised him."

An analogous example would be to pin a handkerchief to one's coat (Rosten 1970, 324) or inside one's sleeve or to tie it around one's waist—pockets cannot be used (Kaye 1987, 17)—so that technically, one would not be carrying a handkerchief, which is forbidden (Peli 1991, 62). In Eastern Europe, it can be "tied around the wrist or tucked into the belt rather than carried in the pocket" (Zborowski and Herzog 1962, 50). Other permissible techniques include wrapping it around the neck like a scarf (S. Cohen 1995, 128), using it as a belt, or firmly sewing it into a pocket so long as this is done before the Sabbath (Neuwirth 1989, 229–230). (Sewing is one of the forbidden forms of work.) For the same reason, a woman must be sure to wear her gloves all the time so that she does not risk "carrying" them by accident (Kaye 1987, 17). Similarly, one is not permitted to carry a pair of glasses from one's house to the street, but it is permitted to go out while wearing the glasses (Schlossberg 1996, 18). There is even a joke that depends upon this technique of "wearing" a forbidden object as an article of clothing in order to circumvent the Sabbath restriction. It is normally forbidden to fly on the Sabbath, just as it is forbidden to drive. So the joking question goes: When is it permissible to fly on the Sabbath? Answer: When one buckles one's seat belt and by so doing wears the airplane.

The issue of intent seems to be held in abeyance. As one author phrases the issue: "It is forbidden for a woman to carry a nut on the Sabbath for her infant but is she allowed to 'wear' the nut as an adjunct to her cloak? May she fix the nut to her cloak even though her true intention is only to carry out the nut for her infant?" The author continues by remarking that this "whole question of subterfuge on the Sabbath" was debated as early as the second century (Jacobs 1981, 28)

Young girls with their typical teenage concern for their appearance are frustrated by the "carrying" prohibition as it prevents them from taking even minimal cosmetics with them to the synagogue. Their solution is to take the needed items ahead of time, that is, before the Sabbath, to the synagogue where they are secreted somewhere in the bathroom and readily available to be used after arrival for the Sabbath services. Here is an account of this practice:

> When I was a teenager, I would periodically apply my talents towards finding a good safe hiding spot for my comb and lipstick in the small ladies' room of my shul. I couldn't carry these items with me, and yet there was no way on earth I would walk into shul without recombing after the ten-minute walk there. So I had to provide for these things properly. Best friends were those girls to whom you would tell where your "Shabbos comb and lipstick" were hidden. When I was married, and moved away, I left my comb and lipstick in place. It was like leaving a small part of me behind in the shul of my youth. I wonder if it's still in place. I know no one is looking anymore, because an eruv has since been put up in that neighborhood. (Greenberg 1983, 47–48)

There are several techniques that can be adopted to avoid violating the carrying prohibition. For example, if two people combine forces to engage in a "forbidden" activity, such as carrying a child on the Sabbath, an activity one of them in theory could have done by him- or herself, then both are exempt because "neither is doing a complete *melacha*" (Spirn 1992, 114). This is a technique of some antiquity as it is attested in the Babylonian

Talmud. "He who takes out a loaf of bread into the public domain is liable. If two people took it out, they are exempt" (Neusner 1992–1993, IIc, 103). There is no mistaking the principle here: "A single individual who performs a forbidden action is liable; two people who carry it out are exempt" (104). The stratagem of having "two people performing a single act . . . converts every prohibited act on the Sabbath into a rabbinic prohibition" (Tendler and Rosner 1987, 57) as opposed to the more serious biblical or Torah violation. The underlying logic of this subterfuge is astonishing. It is as if one were contending that the commission of a crime jointly by two individuals in concert would excuse both of them inasmuch as each had committed only half a crime! But this explains in part why doctors who need to carry instruments across a public domain, that is, in an area not included in an *eruv*, may ask another Jew to help him carry them. If two Jews carry them, it is a lesser offense. Another technique is a form of *shinui* such that the doctor carries the instruments on top of his head (Sokol 1986, 169). Other *shinui* techniques recommended for carrying medicines in an area where there is no *eruv* include placing them "on one's head, under one's hat, inside one's shoes or between the clothes one is wearing" (Neuwirth 1989, 526).

Another contrivance is based upon the rule that the Torah forbids one to transfer objects more than a distance of four *amot* (Neuwirth 1989, 202). Four *amot* or cubits is the limit (approximately seven feet) that one is permitted to carry an object in a public domain (Neusner 1992–1993, IId, 19). However, a person can carry something (e.g., a crying child or a child who refuses to walk) just three *amot* and then stop, wait, and go another three *amot*, stop, wait, and continue in like fashion. This artifice is apparently forbidden by the rabbis, but it would not violate the Torah four-*amot* limit. In other words, one would be violating "only a rabbinic, rather than a biblical, prohibition" (Spirn 1992, 115). Another technique in such circumstances that can be used if there are several Jews in the area is to have each Jew carry the child a distance of less than four cubits, stop before exceeding the limit, and hand the child to another Jew who does likewise. If there are only two Jews, they can alternate carrying the child in such a fashion (Cohen 1995, 154, 155).

Sometimes crises arrive, however, that are not so easily resolved. For example, one account describes the sense of guilt produced in the children of Orthodox parents if they "find a coin in the pocket of the coat they are wearing on the Sabbath, and agonize over whether it is worse to take the coin out and thus touch money on the Sabbath, or leave it there and have to carry it around all day" (Kaye 1987, 57). This is why it is advisable for every observant Jew to check his or her pockets carefully to see if they contain anything, and this should be done any time the Jew prepares to leave the house on the Sabbath (Cohen 1995, 152). As for the dilemma caused by suddenly finding a coin or other object while walking in a public domain on the Sabbath, there are several solutions. One could turn the pocket inside out thereby causing the object to fall out or one could set the item down in an unusual manner, for example, by holding it on the back of one's hand or by roughly (as opposed to gently) dropping it (153).

As might well be imagined, there have been respected modern students of Jewish law who have criticized what they consider to be the lack of common sense in the *reductio ad absurdum* aspects of the carrying prohibition. Boaz Cohen, for example, comments, "We will not consider one who carries a watch, a handkerchief, a key, or a cane as a Sabbath breaker." He then refers to a like-minded colleague who favors "permitting the carrying of an umbrella on the Sabbath" (1977, 93). If a person has a physical disability, he may use a walking stick to assist him in walking to the synagogue on the Sabbath on the grounds that the stick is "indispensable" and thus "not treated as an object that is carried, but like a shoe that is worn on the foot" (Jacobs 1999, 107). This is similar to the common sense that eventually prevailed permitting Jews to carry a pocket watch on the Sabbath (Pollack 1971, 167), though it had earlier been forbidden (Ganzfried 1961, 2, 110).

The prohibition against carrying an object has caused problems for the ultra-Orthodox who would like to protest the desecration of the Sabbath by secular Jews, among others. In theory, they would like to picket entertainment venues such as movie theaters or interrupt traffic, that is cars driven by Jews on the Sabbath. But as they are not permitted to carry anything, they cannot march hoisting the standard signs usually displayed in such public demonstrations. In actuality, the ultra-Orthodox do violate their own rules by carrying stones on the Sabbath and hurling them at passing cars in their neighborhoods (Zemer 1999, 284). According to one "apocryphal story," when a taxi drove into a strict Orthodox district of Jerusalem (presumably Meah Shearim) after the onset of the Sabbath, the taxi was soon surrounded by an angry mob who "pulled the taxi driver from his vehicle and stoned him to death." This may, however, just be a cautionary tale intended to warn tourists against desecrating the Sabbath in this particular section of Jerusalem (White 1993, 184).

Another Sabbath restriction refers to "tearing." Nothing can be torn on the Sabbath. Even opening the spout of a milk or orange juice carton would be construed as forbidden act of tearing. For this reason, it is considered best to open all such containers before the Sabbath. If one forgets, there is a way around the restriction. One can puncture the bottom of the carton, which makes it unfit for further use, and then open the spout and pour the contents into another container (Cohen 1991, 184). The rationale of this circumvention depends upon a distinction between "destructive" and "constructive" tearing. Since all of the thirty-nine prohibited forms of work are supposed to relate to the *construction* of the Tabernacle, it is only "constructive" acts that are forbidden. In contrast, destructive acts are permitted. So in the example of opening a milk or orange juice carton, if one gently tore open the normal spout flap, this would be construed as "constructive" tearing as it would allow the spout to be reclosed and reopened. Cutting open a carton in a manner that permanently destroys its utility is considered "destructive" tearing and that is permitted (S. Cohen 1995, 84–85).

As for closing a container, there are other circumventions. It is forbidden to tie or untie knots on the Sabbath. So if one wanted to store food in a plastic bag, one should not gather the top of the bag and "tie it onto itself in a single knot." However, "It is permissible to use a plastic twist-tie on Shabbos to securely close a bag" (Cohen 1991, 189–190; S. Cohen, 1995, 222). Some of the circumventions are quite ingenious. For example, it is forbidden to wash or even rinse dishes on the Sabbath, but to prevent food residue from hardening on dirty dishes piled in a sink, there are several possible alternatives. "One may leave a pan of soapy water in the sink before Shabbos, and stack the dishes in the pan" or "One may stack dirty dishes in a sink and wash his hands over the sink, allowing the water to flow over the dishes" (Cohen 1991, 204). This kind of logic does not prevail in all instances. For example, it is forbidden to water plants on the Sabbath and it is consequently forbidden to wash one's hands over growing plants because even though the primary intent may be to wash one's hands, the act will inevitably result in the plants being watered (Cohen 1988, 46).

Another very practical problem created by this rule prohibiting tearing concerns the use of toilet paper. Most toilet paper comes in rolls of tissue, a section of which is normally torn off to clean one's posterior after an act of elimination. As tearing anything is proscribed, the way around this regulation is to pretear toilet paper prior to the Sabbath. In hotels frequented by Orthodox Jews, one finds in the bathroom either pretorn toilet paper or a set of facial tissues (the use of which does not require any act of tearing). On one occasion in the early 1970s, an American Jew, not fully cognizant of this practice, was visiting an observant household in Israel. Seeing the small pile of pretorn toilet paper in the bathroom, the American wrongly assumed that it had no particular purpose and blithely flushed it down the toilet. The American's Israeli host later scolded the visitor for this thoughtless act inasmuch as it left the household toilet-paperless over the Sabbath.

There are other sanctioned ways of circumventing the taboo against tearing toilet paper. "If a gentile is available, one should hint to him to tear the paper. However, one should not tell the gentile explicitly to tear it. One may say, for example, 'My toilet paper is not torn apart and I cannot use it in that manner.' This is permitted even though the gentile will deduce from this statement that the Jew wants him to tear the paper" (S. Cohen 1995, 97). Similarly, one can say to a non-Jew on the Sabbath "I have no toilet paper" so that the latter will gather that he or she should tear sheets off the roll (Neuwirth 1989, 455). But if there is no *Shabbes Goy* at hand to whom to hint, there are yet other resourceful alternative techniques.

As mentioned earlier, there is another form of circumvention acceptable in some circles and that is to perform a standard act in a nonstandard manner. Here is one account of this option:

> Sheets of paper towels or toilet paper should be torn from the roll prior to Sabbath. One should be aware that even certain kinds of interleaved tissues might be joined to each other, and these should be separated before Sabbath. If tissues have not been prepared and no other paper is available on Sabbath, there is a view that toilet paper may be torn, but not on the perforations and in an unusual way, e.g., with the feet. (Pick 1998, 73)

Another authority suggests if all else fails, "it is permitted to tear the paper from the roll in an unusual fashion, e.g., by tearing with one's teeth, elbows or feet" (S. Cohen 1995, 98). Another form of *shinui* in the case of toilet paper consists of the following technique: "One could hold the roll down with one elbow, while tearing the paper off with the wrist of the other arm" (Neuwirth 1989, 333) or "One may use the paper without tearing it from the roll and, when finished, insert the used portion of the roll in the toilet and flush. The paper in the bowl will thus be torn automatically from the rest of the roll" (S. Cohen 1995, 97). In this way, the individual him- or herself is technically not tearing the toilet paper. Instead, the paper is torn by the flushing action of the toilet. Still another alternative is to use facial tissues in the bathroom inasmuch as the use of this type product does not require any act of tearing, and it is not usually used as toilet paper. However, the more common custom is to simply pretear the toilet paper prior to the advent of Sabbath.

The pretearing strategy can also be employed in connection with infant hygiene. Since a sponge, wash cloth, or soap bars cannot be used on the Sabbath—it is not permitted to "wring out" objects such as a wash cloth or a sponge—one can circumvent this difficulty by utilizing "absorbent cotton balls, or soft paper tissues prepared to proper size in advance" to cleanse the diapered area. If soap and water are required, liquid rather than bar soap is permissible. Bar soap is forbidden on the Sabbath because it violates several rules, one of which is scraping (Cohen 1991, 178). For this reason, liquid soap is commonly used on the Sabbath (e.g., in hospitals) (Sokol 1986, 191; Neuwirth 1989, 635). In any case, the excess moisture on the infant may be wiped up using "facial tissue, previously cut toilet tissue, or a large absorbent cotton ball" (Tendler 1988, 52).

There are some quaint forms of *shinui* that serve to circumvent the prohibition against "kneading," which is defined as "binding together small particles by means of a bonding agent to form one mass" (Cohen 1991, 142). These include reversing the usual order of combining the ingredients in food preparation—for example, instead of pouring milk on cereal in a bowl, one would put the milk in the bowl first and then add the cereal, stirring a mixture with crisscross strokes instead of the usual typical continuous circular motion, stirring a mixture with one's bare hand or finger, or using the handle of a spoon or fork, or a knife-blade (Cohen 1991, 149–152; 1993, 97–99). This technique is apparently traditional. In the Babylonian Talmud, for example, we are told that one may crush peppercorns on the Sabbath by using a knife handle, as this constitutes an unusual way of doing this. The usual way would utilize a peppermill (Neusner 1992–1993, IIe, 74). Similarly, if one forgets to grate horseradish, one of the usual components of a Passover seder, before the seder has begun, as one should, it is permissible to do so as long as one turns the grater "upside down" (Steingroot 1995, 37). Neusner calls this general principle that "one may do something in an unusual way but not in the usual way" a Mishnah rule (1992–1993, IIe, 76). All of these examples of *shinui* constitute instances of sanctioned circumventions. *Shinui* techniques are recommended in a very broad spectrum of activities. For instance, it is forbidden to remove fragments of a broken windowpane on the Sabbath, as it would violate the "Building" *melacha*. But if there is a danger that someone might cut him- or herself and if there is no non-Jew available to remove the remaining glass, "one may remove it oneself, using a method which one would not normally employ, for example, by kicking it out" (Neuwirth 1989, 339).

Another instance of *shinui* concerns what to do on the Sabbath if there is a drainpipe clogged by twigs that is causing water damage to one's roof. One may tread on the blockage with one's foot (as opposed to using a shovel or one's hands) in order "to push the impediments through the pipe" thereby restoring the proper drainage (Roth 1986, 26).

It is worth remarking that the technique of *shinui* adopted on the Sabbath to avoid desecrating the day has a close analog in recommended practices during the sabbatical year. Examples would include the particular custom connected with pruning olive trees. This might be done to obtain wood for building, according to a passage in the Mishnah. It is forbidden to do anything that might stimulate the growth of new branches during the sabbatical year. So instead of covering a truncated olive tree with dirt, which is said to be the usual way of sealing the surface of a stump when one cuts back a tree to cultivate new branches, one must instead cover the stump with stones or stubble, which indicates that the farmer in question is not attempting to cultivate the growth of new branches (Neusner 1988, 77). Another instance of what appears to be a form of *shinui* would be the rule that requires that figs coming to fruition in a sabbatical year may not be harvested with the normal fig knife but must be harvested with an ordinary knife, or that grapes must not be trampled in a vat but may be trampled in a trough (86–87). Still another example concerns the trimming of hedges. Since this activity is done for aesthetic reasons and not to stimulate the growth of the hedges, it is permitted during *Shmittoh*, the seventh year. But just to be on the safe side, "one should change the way he usually cuts it (e.g., a straight cut at a higher point as opposed to the usual diagonal cut, or vice versa) and also use a different instrument than usual" (Marchant 1986, 170).

Another interesting example of *shinui* is also afforded in the case of writing, which is not permitted on the Sabbath. Even writing letters in the condensation that forms on windowpanes is proscribed (Neuwirth 1989, 339). In Israel, Orthodox women employed as hospital nurses, assuming they did work on the Sabbath, had a problem with respect to keeping patients' records on that day. Patients, too, if they needed to be admitted to a hospital on the Sabbath, were not permitted to sign admission forms or once admitted could not sign a consent form allowing a doctor to perform surgery (Cohen 1995, 14).

The same difficulty occurred with Orthodox men serving on the police force. Again, assuming such men worked on the Sabbath, they were often required to write up reports of murders or robberies if they occurred on that day. The circumventive solution was to write in an unusual or exceptional way. A nurse or patient or policeman could thus write with the left hand if they were right-handed or with the right hand if they were left-handed (S. Cohen 1995, 14; Halperin 1986, 134). Other alternatives included writing in non-Hebraic script or by writing with invisible ink, which could be developed to appear later (Abramov 1976, 205). The charter so-to-speak for such circumventions is set forth in the Shabbat section of the Mishnah. If one writes with ink or with anything that leaves a mark, one is liable to a sin offering; but if one wrote with fluids such as water or fruit juice, or with dirt from the street, or with sand, or with anything that does not leave a lasting mark, one would be exempt. Another apparently acceptable circumvention consists of writing with the back of one's hand or with one's foot, mouth, or elbow (Neusner 1988, 195). A manual for physicians, for example, suggests that a doctor using a standard, nonelectric typewriter might employ a *shinui* (e.g., "pressing keys with the dorsum of fingerjoints") (Sokol 1986, 188), but not merely typing with the left hand (273n39). Performing an act on the Sabbath in an unusual manner, such as using a form of *shinui* involving a change of hands, is not always a viable option. For instance, one would not want a right-handed dentist to perform a root canal operation with his left hand (Tendler and Rosner 1987, 52).

A more idiosyncratic circumvention was devised by Martha Bernays, Freud's bride-to-be, who was the daughter of Orthodox Jewish parents. Out of respect for her mother, Martha, who wrote Freud almost daily, would not do so on the Sabbath (Grollman 1965, 70). However, later during their long engagement Martha did dare to write Freud on the Sabbath, but she would do so in the garden using a pencil rather than writing with pen and ink inside the house in her mother's presence. Freud, who described himself as a "godless Jew," was quite annoyed by this and chastised Martha for being too "weak" to stand up to her mother (Jones 1953, 116).

Another, more conventional form of circumvention with respect to writing occurs during Sabbath services where pledges for cash offerings are made by marking cards or using string. Sometimes congregants are handed cards bearing their names along with various dollar amounts. A congregant can indicate his or her choice of an amount to be donated by attaching a paperclip (Neuwirth 1989, 446). This avoids the proscribed act of writing. Merely marking a donation card evidently does not count as writing.

> To write down the amounts donated is, of course forbidden, which is why the cards and string are used. This is not a circumvention of the law against writing on the Sabbath, nor is it against its intent. Card marking in this way is simply not subsumed by the law under the heading of writing and it patently is not "writing." It follows from this that no intent of any law is being flouted. (Jacobs 1999, 100)

In some synagogues, one simply bends or folds down the appropriate portion of the pledge card rather than marking it (Neuwirth 1989, 446). In this way, there isn't even a question of whether "marking" the card in any way constitutes a form of writing.

Erasing writing is also forbidden. If, for example, a cake decoration includes words written in the icing, it is not permitted to cut the cake in a way that destroys any letters. One can, however, cut the cake between the words or letters. The same rule holds with respect to writing or a sticker on fruit such as an orange or banana (Cohen 1991, 140).

Because it is forbidden to light a fire on the Sabbath, it is somewhat difficult to serve hot food on that day. But whereas cooking of any kind is not permitted, cooking being defined as "using heat to alter the quality of an item" (Cohen 1991, 1), it is permissible to maintain the warmth of a dish cooked before the onset of Sabbath. However, according to one authoritative source (Neuwirth 1989, vol. 1, 4), no food can be warmed to a temperature above 45 degrees Centigrade (113 degrees Fahrenheit). Another authority indicates 43 degrees Centigrade (110 degrees Fahrenheit) (Cohen 1991, 4). The prohibition against altering the temperature on the Sabbath results in a number of restrictions. For example, one cannot remove the amount of water in a pot because reducing the amount might cause the remaining water to boil more quickly. For the same reason, one should not stir or cover a pot of partially cooked food or liquid. By the same reasoning, one may not close an oven door, as that would cause the interior temperature to rise. Accordingly, one should take care not to open an oven door if there is a chance that the food inside is not fully cooked, as it would not be permitted to close the oven door once having opened it (8–9).

The way around this rule is to prepare a special dish on Friday afternoon consisting usually of meat, beans, barley, potatoes, chickpeas, or some similar combination of ingredients. "Hungarian Jews may use beans, Polish Jews potatoes, Sephardic Jews rice" (Danzger 1989, 214). This dish, called *cholent*, is placed in the oven before the Sabbath begins and left to cook all night at a low heat (below the 45 degrees Centigrade limit). The word *cholent* may be of French origin (Trepp 1980, 71; Lowenstein 2000, 124), perhaps from *chaud* (heat) and *lent* (slow) referring to "slow heat." Typically, this stew "is cooked for several hours on Friday afternoon and then allowed to simmer for 18 hours or more until Saturday lunch" (Naron 1984, 12). At noon on the Sabbath it is taken out of the oven to be eaten. One source says, "It is the only dish that Jews the world over have in common because it was created to permit them to eat hot food on the Sabbath without breaking the Sabbath laws, which are the same for Jews everywhere" (Asheri 1978, 100). Another says, "Cholent is one of the most authentic of all Jewish dishes. It fills the need for a hot food that can be eaten during the day without transgressing the prohibition of putting food on the stove on the Sabbath itself" (Schlossberg 1996, 49). The *cholent* can be placed on an electric hot plate so long as the plate has only one temperature setting and that it is turned on before the onset of the Sabbath (Cohen 1991, 43). One way of simulating a nonadjustable hot plate on a stove is to remove the relevant control knob (Halperin 1986, 39).

There is another technique of circumvention, which may be utilized in connection with "keeping food warm." A pot containing food may not be placed on a stove burner because that would be tantamount to placing it on a form of fire. But one is permitted to place a small sheet of tin or aluminum or a "metal dish upside down" on the burner and then place the pot on that so long as the intervening metal sheet or dish is not made red-hot by the burner (Neuwirth 1989, 14–15). This piece of sheet metal is sometimes called a *blech* (Naron 1984, 13; Palatnik 1994, 147; Kolatch 1995, 166; Rabinowitz 1997, 103). It is placed over the stove-top burners, which are kept at a low heat. This must be done before the Sabbath. The "hot" food, also prepared in advance, is placed "on the *blech* to remain at a warm-to-low simmer until it is ready to be eaten" (Palatnik 1994, 147). (For the regulations governing the use of the *blech,* see Cohen [1991, 43–45].) There are still restrictions, however. For example, one is not supposed to add seasoning to a pot of hot soup even after the pot is removed from the *blech* because the heat of the soup will cook the seasoning (18).

There is also an additional food item served on the Sabbath that was specifically devised to avoid violating one of the prohibitions. The law in question is referred to as "Selection," and the rule is, "It is, in general, forbidden to separate or sort out two kinds of articles which are mixed together" (Neuwirth 1989, 35). The law is also known as "Sorting" (Cohen 1991, 83). A consequence of this rule is that "One must be careful, when preparing food on Shabbath, not to remove the bones from fish or meat" (Neuwirth 1989, 38). An Orthodox Jew, for example "will not remove bones from the chicken but can remove the meat of the chicken from the bone" (Naron 1984, 9–10). It is harder to do this with fish. Bones, therefore, must be removed prior to the Sabbath. One way of avoiding the difficulty with respect to fish is to prepare gefilte (filled or stuffed) fish, which has become a standard item in Jewish traditional cuisine (Neuwirth 1989, 39; Danzger 1989, 213; Lowenstein 2000, 125). As one authority phrased it: "*gefilte fish* was adopted for Sabbath use, for this way all the bones are removed before the Sabbath" (Himelstein 1990, 67). Another reason why it is customary for Jews to eat fish on the Sabbath, according to one source, is to remind them of the mercies of God. "Even as fish have no eyelids, so that their eyes are never closed, so the eyes of the Lord are open at all times to watch over those who fear him" (Sperling 1968, 129–130).

The rule against separating the bones of the fish from the fish flesh is part of a larger set of regulations forbidding the removal of food from a mixture that includes unwanted items labeled "waste." For example, according to one authority, it is not permitted to remove spoiled grapes from a cluster, but one must instead take the fresh grapes, leaving the unwanted ones behind (Cohen 1991, 97). There are ways around this rule, however. If, for example, a particle of dirt or an insect falls into a drink or food, one cannot remove the particle or insect by itself, but may scoop it out with some of the drink or food (106). Following the same logic, one should not remove watermelon seeds unless one takes some melon along with each seed, or remove fish bones unless one takes a bit of fish with each bone (105–106). In other words, no act of separation takes place. The impurity or "waste" remains as part of a mixture. One permissible circumventory technique is possible if the food in question is already in the mouth. Thus one can spit out the watermelon seeds, or pull out fish bones from a piece of fish in one's mouth (104).

The mouth is also involved in another food practice. One of the thirty-nine forms of *melakah* is "Threshing," which has been extended to include extracting liquid (Cohen 1991, 118). This means that it is forbidden to squeeze a lemon. However, it is permissible to put a wedge of lemon (or orange) in one's mouth and suck the juice from it. In another rule, in order to get around the prohibition against squeezing a lemon to put its juice into one's cup of tea, one can cut a slice of lemon and put it in the tea so long as one does not press the lemon slice against the side of the cup (127).

THE *SHABBES GOY*

Almost all of the Sabbath rules can be circumvented simply by having a non-Jew or Gentile, otherwise known as a *Shabbes Goy*, carry out the proscribed activity. For example, "One may, on Shabbath, request a non-Jew to take something out of, or put something into, an electric refrigerator, even if the act of opening the door will (a) immediately activate the motor of the refrigerator and (b) switch on the internal light. . . . Similarly, one may ask a non-Jew to close an open refrigerator, even if this will extinguish an internal light" (Neuwirth 1989, 486).

The use of a *Shabbes Goy* is, however, subject to a strict rule. That rule is that one may not directly ask a Gentile to do work on one's behalf on the

Sabbath (Broyde and Jachter 1995, 84). Some authorities allow asking a Gentile to do work on the Sabbath provided that the request is made before the onset of the Sabbath. Normally, a Jew is not allowed to enjoy the benefit of any prohibited act performed by a Gentile. The reason for this is to remove any incentive for a Jew to have a Gentile do work for him or her on the Sabbath (Cohen 1988, 14). If a Gentile performs an act for his or her own purposes, then the Jew is allowed to benefit from that act. For example, "If a Gentile turned on a light in a dark room in order to read a newspaper, a Jew is also permitted to read in that room" (15). In other words, the turning on of the light was in theory not done at the request or behest of the Jew. A passage in the Shabbat tractate of the Babylonian Talmud confirms the traditionality of this reasoning: "Samuel visited the household of Abin of Toran. A gentile came and lit a lamp. Samuel turned away. When he saw that the gentile had brought a document and was reading it, he noted, 'He lit it for himself,' so he, too, turned toward the lamp" (Neusner 1992–1993, IId, 125).

A distinction is made between violations that are proscribed by the Torah and those that are forbidden by rabbinical pronouncement. A Jew can ask a Gentile to perform an act forbidden by rabbinical decree if, for example, there is a serious risk of substantial financial loss. If for instance, a freezer full of meat became disconnected on the Sabbath, thereby risking the loss of the entire meat contents, a Jew could tell a Gentile to plug in the freezer so long as he or she did so indirectly by saying, "If the plug remains disconnected, the food will spoil" (Cohen 1988, 31). If the substantial loss requires the breaking of a Torah Sabbath rule as opposed to a rabbinical one, then a special form of circumvention is permitted. A Jew can tell a Gentile to tell another Gentile to carry out the forbidden act. This device known as *amira l'amira* (tell to tell) is permissible only if the second Gentile is acting as an agent of the first Gentile and not of the Jew. The Jew may not engage the first Gentile to act as a broker and for that matter, if the second Gentile carries out the forbidden act knowing that it is being done for a Jew, the Jew is not supposed to derive any benefit from that act (54–55). This device of asking one Gentile to tell another Gentile to carry out an action that is forbidden on the Sabbath is a quite remarkable example of circumvention.

Ideally, a Gentile or in some cases a nonobservant Jew will simply act on his or her own without being asked to turn on lights or turn off a radio or television. Of course, one means of circumvention available to the Jew is to turn on the radio or television prior to the onset of the Sabbath. The taboo essentially concerns the act of turning on or off the entertainment device, not necessarily listening to or watching it. Still, there was a nationwide debate in Israel over whether telecasts on the Sabbath should be permitted (Gurevitch and Schwartz 1971).

Playwright Anna Deavere Smith presents a pointed and poignant portrait illustrating the radio dilemma in her *Fires in the Mirror*. Inasmuch as her dramatic vignettes were purportedly based upon a kind of fieldwork, namely, interviews with inhabitants of a well-known Jewish section of Brooklyn, Crown Heights, we may reasonably assume that her rendering of the results of a telephone interview with a Lubavitcher woman is based on an actual incident.

Near the end of the Sabbath, a baby was playing with the knobs on a stereo system. "Then all of a sudden, he pushed the button—the *on* button—and all of a sudden came blaring out, at full volume, sort of like a half station of polka music . . . and we can't turn off, we can't turn off electrical, you know electricity, on Shabbas." The volume was so great that a young visitor in the house began to complain of getting a headache and asked the woman of the house if anything could be done about turning off the radio. The woman mused, "Couldn't we get a baby to turn it off: we can't make the baby turn it off, but if the baby, but if a child under three turns something on or turns something off it's not considered against the Torah. So we put the baby by it and tried to get the baby to turn it off; he just probably made it worse. . . . I said I would go outside and see if I can find someone who's not Jewish and see if they would like to—see if they could turn it off. So you can have somebody who's not Jewish do a simple act like turning on the light or turning off the light, and I hope I have the law correct, but you can't ask them to do it directly, if they wanna do it of their own free will." The woman then proceeded to go outside for help. "And I saw a little boy in the neighborhood who I didn't know and didn't know me—not Jewish, he was black and he wasn't wearing a yarmulke because you can't—so I went up to him and I said to him that my radio is on really loud and I can't turn it off, could he help me." The little boy follows the woman into the house "and so he goes over to the stereo and he says, 'You see this little button here that says on and off? Push that in and that turns it off.' And I just sort of stood there looking kind of dumb and then he went and pushed it, and we laughed that he probably thought: And people say Jewish people are really smart and they don't know how to turn off their radios" (Smith 1993, 6–7, 8).

Although one is not supposed to directly request help from the *Shabbes Goy*, it is evidently permissible to hint so long as the hint is subtle enough. For example, in one discussion, it is stated that it is not permitted to ask a Gentile maid to turn on lights on the Sabbath, because that would entail turning on the electricity. However, it would be all right to ask the maid to turn off the lights, because the ensuing darkness in the room would only be an indirect result of the lights having been turned off. The action could not be said to *create* the darkness, supposedly it only *resulted* in the darkness (Katz 1991, 26). The hinting issue concerns the manner in which the maid is asked to extinguish the lights. For example, according to one authority, "it is proper to say: 'I can't sleep because the light is on.' Do *not* say: 'Do you think you could do something about the lights?' or 'I wish the lights were turned off' " (27n26). One Sabbath primer proposed that one should use a "noninstructive" hint such as, "It's rather dark in here," but not an "instructive" hint such as, "Please do me a favor; there is not enough light in this room." In the same fashion, to get a light turned off, one could say, "What a waste of electricity!" as a "noninstructive" hint but not an "instructive" hint such as, "Why didn't you turn out the light last week when I was trying to sleep?" (Pick 1998, 112). As one might expect, there is not total agreement as to how broad the hint can be. Another authority, for example, specifically notes, "One may not say to a Gentile 'Please help me out. The lights are on in the bedroom and I cannot sleep' " (Cohen 1988, 22). The reason for this is that the Jew has asked the Gentile to perform an action when he says, "Please help me out." Nor can the Jew say, "I can't turn off the lights because it is Shabbos" (22). What is permitted is a suggestive statement rather than a request or command. But even a suggestive statement may lead to difficulties. Once again, the question of appearances is involved. Passersby might wrongly assume that the Jew had instructed the Gentile to turn off the lights rather than merely hinting that he or she should do so.

The Gentile's response to a hint can also cause problems. If the Gentile asks point-blank, "Would you like me to turn off the lights?" the Jew may not respond "yes" as this would be equivalent to the Jew's making a direct request. All the observant Jew can do in such a situation is to repeat, "I will not be able to sleep with the lights on" or "I can't tell you what to do" and hope for the best (Cohen 1988, 26).

Upon reflection, it becomes obvious that the very insistence upon hinting is itself a perfect example of circumvention. In this sense, verbal circumlocution counts as circumvention. That is why it is not surprising that there is an entire book devoted to precisely how a Jew should or should not ask a Gentile to do something on the Sabbath (Cohen 1988). The basic principle seems to be that one can never make a direct request to a *Shabbes Goy*. Making a direct request would be tantamount to the Jew carrying out the forbidden activity him- or herself.

Sometimes the *Shabbes Goy* receives remuneration for services rendered.

In Eastern Europe, for example, the Sabbath candles cannot be blown out by members of the family "because on the Sabbath a Jew must avoid all contact with fire or with anything related to it. Therefore at bedtime all lights will be extinguished and all fires taken care of by someone who is not subject to the severe Sabbath regulations. Often some non-Jew, a *shabbes goy* is paid by the community for this service" (Zborowski and Herzog 1962, 47). Incidentally, the prohibition against putting out a fire on the Sabbath is so strict that in the case of a house fire, one is theoretically not allowed to tell a Gentile "Put it out." According to the Babylonian Talmud, there is even a difference of opinion as to whether one can or cannot say "Whoever puts it out won't lose," which is presumably a not so subtle hint that the *Shabbes Goy* who extinguishes the fire might receive a reward for so doing (Neusner 1992–1993, IId, 121).

Incidentally, if a fire breaks out on the Sabbath, not only is it forbidden to put it out, but also it is not permitted to save anything from the flames except for sacred books and a token amount of food and clothing (Jacobs 1984b, 152). On the other hand, although it is true that any fire that does not endanger human life may not be extinguished on the Sabbath, it is permitted to place "new, water-filled clay jugs around the periphery of a fire, despite the fact that the spreading fire will burst the jugs, thereby enabling the water to extinguish the fire" (Halperin 1986, 62). This is yet another ingenious example of circumvention.

There are some requests made of the *Shabbes Goy* that are so onerous or unpleasant that probably no amount of possible payment would induce him or her to perform the requested activity. The prohibition against shearing includes cutting hair or nails on the Sabbath. According to one source, "cutting nails with scissors or a nail clipper falls under the Biblical prohibition of shearing, whereas biting or tearing off nails is prohibited Rabbinically" (S. Cohen 1995, 160). The same source also describes a hypothetical situation in which a woman scheduled to visit the *mikveh* (ritual immersion pool) Friday night forgets to cut her fingernails before the Sabbath. In such a case, "she should have a gentile tear or bite off the fingernails. If this is impossible, or if the gentile is unwilling to do this, she may have the gentile cut off the nails with an instrument" (166). One wonders just how many *Shabbes Goys* would be willing to bite off a Jewish woman's fingernails to help her avoid violating a Sabbath prohibition!

The topic of cutting hair calls to mind one of the most startling examples of circumvention in Orthodox Judaism. Rabbis decided that women's hair was distracting to men and that it might keep the men from attending to their mandatory study of Torah or from praying properly. Consequently, Orthodox Jewish women were obliged to cut off their hair before marriage (Gaster 1955, 105).

There is no biblical rule requiring them to do so (Bronner 1993, 466), although feminist readers might note that in the laws governing the treatment of women captured as prisoners of war being considered as possible mates, such women had to shave their heads (Deut. 21:12). Then the male captors had to wait a month when presumably they might change their minds and release the women (Bronner 1993, 466). The equation of Orthodox women brides with such prisoners of war speaks volumes about the male chauvinist attitudes that continue to permeate Orthodox Jewish culture. It was also feared that good-looking, well-groomed Jewish women might attract the attention of lecherous anti-Semites (Rosten 1970, 338). This was yet another reason given for the rule that Orthodox women should cut off their hair and keep their heads covered. There is an echo of this custom in the New Testament. We are told: "But every woman that prayeth or prophesieth with her head uncovered dishonoreth her head: for that is even all one as if she were shaven. For if the women be not covered, let her also be shorn: but if it be a shame for a woman to be shorn or shaven, let her be covered" (1 Cor. 11:5–6). What is of interest in the present context is that Orthodox women traditionally wore a *shaytel* (*sheitel*) after marriage. A *shaytel* is a wig and was made "either of the user's own hair, of someone else's hair, or of artificial hair" (Rosten 1970, 337). So the rule that women were not allowed to wear their hair after marriage remained intact. Nevertheless, with the help of a sanctioned circumvention, they could continue to wear their own hair just so long as it was in the form of a wig!

With respect to what a Jew can or cannot say to a *Shabbes Goy* under difficult conditions, an interesting test case has to do with a burglar alarm system. The problem arises in the event such an alarm goes off on the Sabbath. Normally, security guards are immediately dispatched to the scene of the potential crime and they drive there as quickly as possible in order to interrupt the robbery and apprehend the intruder. If the guards are not Jewish, the issue rests on the prohibition against telling a Gentile to do work that is forbidden to Jews on the Sabbath. "Accordingly, it should be prohibited to obligate him to drive to the site of the break-in on Shabbat. Yet, the prohibition only applies to telling a Gentile to do Torah prohibitions and it does not apply to telling him or her to transgress Rabbinic prohibitions in circumstances of great need. To avoid this problem, the Gentile can be told to avoid driving to the break-in (the only certain Torah prohibition). If he then drives to the site, it is not at the behest of the Jew, and there is no prohibition" (Oratz 1993, 86). So this particular example of circumvention consists of a Jew asking a Gentile security guard not to drive to a possible break-in on the Sabbath but assuming or hoping that the guard will ignore this absurd request.

Sometimes the need for the services of a *Shabbes Goy* is really pressing. For example, cows need to be milked and it is painful for the animals if they are not milked. The rule is "It is forbidden to milk an animal on Shabbath" but "One may have an animal milked by a non-Jew, in order to save it suffering" (Neuwirth 1989, 391). Even the rule prohibiting asking a *Shabbes Goy* on the Sabbath itself to perform a prohibited task may be put aside. "One may tell a non-Jew on Shabbath to milk one's cows, to save them the suffering they would be caused if they were not milked for a whole day" (465; Katz 1989, 70). "A Jew may be present while the non-Jew is milking, to ensure that he does not take any of the milk for himself, but the Jew may not speak to the non-Jew about such matters as remuneration" (Neuwirth 1989, 465). After the Sabbath, the Jew is permitted to pay the *Shabbes Goy* for services rendered, but not on the Sabbath itself. The Jew cannot even indicate to the *Shabbes Goy* where the money has been placed so that the *Shabbes Goy* could pick it up by him- or herself (466). The Jew can, however, remind the *Shabbes Goy* in this instance of the necessity of cleaning the cows' teats with a wet cloth so long as he does not do so directly. The Jew must merely "hint to the non-Jew of the need to clean the teats" saying, for example, "This milk won't be any good if the teats of the animal aren't cleaned before milking" (465). However, milk "which has been extracted on Shabbath, even in a permitted matter, whether by a non-Jew or by means of a milking machine . . . may not be drunk on that Shabbath" (391). So even though the *Shabbes Goy* can milk a Jew's cow, the milk produced thereby cannot be drunk by the Jew on the Sabbath. If no *Shabbes Goy* is available and the cows are suffering, there is one other recourse. "In the absence of a non-Jew, one should milk to waste," which includes letting the milk go down the drain (392; Pick 1998, 49).

More controversial is the circumvention employed to get around the prohibition against transacting business on the Sabbath. A Jew could enter into a partnership with a non-Jew so that the non-Jew could plough a field with the Jew's animal on the Sabbath or the non-Jew could keep a shop open on the Sabbath. We know the practice existed because a famous rabbi had this to say: "It is also forbidden for a Jew to use evasive tactics with his Gentile partner with whom he ploughs and sell him the animal he ploughs with or the goods in his shop and then buy the animal back after the Sabbath—for it is deceitful and is forbidden unless he parts with the animal or goods completely" (Katz 1989, 34). On the other hand, the transfer of ownership by a Jew to a non-Jew seems to be a standard form of acceptable legal circumvention (Shilo 1982). The transfer, however, must be fully legal and known by others to be legal to avoid giving the "appearance" to onlookers that a Jew had hired a non-Jew to run his business on the Sabbath, which would constitute a violation as it is prohibited for a Jew to allow a Gentile to operate a Jewish business on the Sabbath (Cohen 1988, 77, 104).

This form of circumvention is also practiced on other occasions than the Sabbath. For example, during Passover, Jews are not permitted to eat leavened bread. "Seven days shall ye eat unleavened bread; even the first day ye shall put away leaven out of your houses" (Exod. 12:15); "Seven days shall there be no leaven found in your houses" (Exod. 12:19). The rule is repeated: "Seven days thou shalt eat unleavened bread, and in the seventh day shall be a feast to the Lord. Unleavened bread shall be eaten seven days; and there shall no leavened bread be seen with thee, neither shall there be leaven seen with thee in all thy quarters" (Exod. 13:6–7). However, rabbinical practice permitted Jews to store leavened bread in their quarters or homes if, and only if, such bread belonged to Gentiles. To this end, rabbis recommended "selling all leavened products and utensils to a gentile for a sum of money, and then repurchasing the food and dishes eight days later, after Passover" (Brooks 1990, 26).

This legal fiction is definitely traditional, as chapter 114, "The Selling of Hametz," in the *Code of Jewish Law* attests (Ganzfried 1961, 3: 34–39). As noted above, observant Jews are required to remove all traces of leaven from their homes. "Any product made of any of five specific grains which has been allowed to ferment or any leavening agent is generally referred to as *hametz*" (Himelstein 1990, 104) and this includes even crumbs. It is forbidden to have *hametz* in the home during Passover. However, this can cause problems. For example, whiskey is considered *hametz* as it is fermented from wheat and in theory must be gotten rid of. As one authority noted, Jewish owners of inns in Poland would face ruin "if they had to get rid of all their stocks of alcohol containing *chametez*" (Jacobs 1999, 127).

Here is another version of the recommended circumvention: "What one may do is to sell all his *hametz* to a non-Jew for the duration of Passover. This way, the person does not, indeed, own any *hametz* during the festival" (Himelstein 1990, 105). The authority in this case insists that "It is important to stress that this is not a legal fiction . . . the *hametz* must be locked away in a specific place within the home, and that place must be rented to the non-Jew for the duration of Passover" and "the non-Jew must give a nominal deposit to buy the *hametz*, with the understanding that he has the right to obtain it all if he later pays the full market price for it. Every person who sells *hametz* must then be willing to part with his *hametz* should the non-Jew be willing to exercise his option. . . . Of course, the non-Jew generally does not exercise his option" and the sale is terminated after Passover ends (105). Jacobs agrees, "the sale is a real sale, drawn up according to the requirements of Jewish law. It is not as if one is trying to circumvent the Torah law since, as the rabbis explain it, the Torah only forbids the ownership of *chametz* by a Jew during Pesach" (Jacobs 1999, 127; 1984b, 141).

There is another striking example of the legal fiction involving the sale of goods or property to a non-Jew. Remember the rules governing a sabbatical year set forth in Leviticus (25:1–6), according to which, every seventh year, there was to be a "Sabbath of rest unto the land, a Sabbath for the Lord: thou shalt neither sow thy field, nor prune thy vineyard" (Lev. 25:3). No matter how inconvenient it might be to desist from most normal activities on a Sabbath day, the idea of a farmer not being permitted to utilize his land in any way for a whole year is obviously much more serious. (Many of the rules governing what agricultural workers could or could not do in a sabbatical year are contained in the Shebiit tract in the Mishnah. See also Marchant [1986].)

The issue arose in Palestine in the 1880s. A farmer there sent an inquiry in 1887 to three Russian rabbis asking if he were allowed to cultivate his land in 1889. As usual, there was disagreement as to how to proceed. One solution proposed was to temporarily sell the land to a Gentile (Abramov 1976, 48; Kolatch 1985, 321). The leading Sephardic rabbi in Palestine at that time agreed to this device of a "quasi-conveyance of the land to a non-Jew," but the Ashkenazic rabbis did not. In the fall of 1888, they issued a proclamation stating:

> We inform our brethren the settlers that, in accordance with our religion, they are not permitted to plough, to sow or to reap, or to allow gentiles to perform these agricultural operations in their fields (apart from such work as may be necessary to keep the trees in a healthy condition, which is legally permitted). Inasmuch as the settlers have hitherto endeavoured to obey God's law, they will, we trust, not violate this biblical command. (Abramov 1976, 48–49)

As it happened, the Ashkenazic rabbis lacked power to enforce their dictum and so the settlers did cultivate their lands in 1889. However, the issue in question is not completely dead. Realists still have to insist "to leave all the land in a Jewish state in the twentieth century untilled very seventh year would be its destruction" and that "to 'sell' the land of Israel every seventh year is a farce" and "is it not a self-demeaning procedure to sell the entire agricultural area of the Jewish people in the State of Israel to non-Jews every seventh year—for this is what we would have to do if all Israel were Torah-observant!" (Berkovits 1983, 96–97). Critics of this crafty ploy of selling one's land to a Gentile for the duration of the seventh year contend, with some justification, "The resort to legal fiction is here so blatant that it borders on sheer evasion" (Jacobs 1984b, 143).

Lest anyone think that the problem of tilling the soil in the seventh year has disappeared in modern times, it should be noted that according to a radio report in 2000, some Israeli farmers apparently went to considerable lengths to ensure that their lands lay fallow for the required period. In order not to violate the interdiction, they covered their fields with plastic sheeting and then strewed these sheets with earth imported from outside the Holy Land. In this way, technically speaking, they did not transgress the seventh year prohibition against planting crops in Israeli soil.

In a discussion of the issue of whether it is proper to "hire an Arab to do the work in the garden," the following answer is given. Whereas some authorities "are of the opinion that if a non-Jew does work on the land of a Jew during the *Shmittoh* year then the Jew is transgressing, however, they are of the view that if the non-Jew is paid in a way that it not recognizable that his payment is for work done during the *Shmittoh* year, e.g., he is given a lump sum before *Shmittoh* for several years work, then it is permissible" (Marchant 1986, 167). This is a fine example of circumvention and there is an analog in Sabbath practice. For instance, babysitting on the Sabbath is not permitted unless babysitting is also regularly provided outside Sabbath hours, that is, on other days, and payment for such service is made on a weekday. This gets around the prohibition against earning money on the Sabbath (Pick 1998, 21; Neuwirth 1989, 412–413).

It is worth noting that the idea of selling land to a non-Jew to resolve this question in the 1880s in Palestine was inspired by a similar technique employed by Hillel the Elder in the first century C.E. According to regulations set forth in Deuteronomy 15, the seventh year was a time to cancel all debts. "At the end of every seven years thou shalt make a release. And this is the manner of the release: Every creditor that lendeth aught unto his neighbor shall release it; he shall not exact it of his neighbor, or of his brother; because it is called the Lord's release" (Deut. 15:1–2). The custom of periodically remitting debts along with liberating slaves was also an institution found in Assyria and Babylon (Hallo 1977, 13). In any case, the problem was that since all loans were canceled in the seventh year, it became almost impossible for anyone to obtain a loan as that seventh year approached because the lender knew that any money loaned at that time would become essentially a free gift to the individual requesting the loan. Consequently, commercial activities were severely negatively impacted by this sabbatical rule. Hillel devised a clever legal fiction known as the *Prosbul* to circumvent the rule. This fiction allowed the parties involved in the proposed loan agreement to declare that the loan was given to a court for collection. Since the cancellation of debts in the sabbatical year was construed to apply only to individuals and not to public institutions, Hillel's proposal to make loans a public rather than a private personal matter succeeded in circumventing the debt cancellation requirement (Abramov 1976, 47). The net result of this device "served both the rich and the poor. The rich did not lose their money; the poor in need of a loan, were able to find people who were willing to lend it to them" (Berkovits 1983, 14). (For further details of *Prosbul*, see the relevant section of the Shebiit tract in the Mishnah [Neusner 1988, 91–92 and chapter 180, "Cancellation of Debts in the Sabbatical Year," in the *Code of Jewish Law* (Ganzfried 1961, 4: 65–67)].) This also demonstrates that the effort to find a legally permissible means of circumventing a Halachic law is part of a very longstanding traditional part of Jewish culture. Indeed, one rabbi not entirely unsympathetic to Halacha admitted, "A superficial study may give the impression that often, instead of outrightly rejecting a biblical command, the Halakha attempts to get around it" (Berkovits 1983, 75).

Another example involving finance is the *heter iska*, "a contract which permits a creditor to enter a partnership by circumventing the prohibition of taking interest. He would not be allowed to lend the merchant money at interest, but by becoming a partner in the transaction, the same end is accomplished" (Sigal 1966, 25).

With respect to the seventh year custom, one could, perhaps, suggest that the custom of canceling debts in and of itself represents a form of circumvention. In that sense, it would constitute a perfectly legal way of avoiding the repayment of a debt incurred. In that context, it is interesting to consider a strange ritual associated with the celebration of Yom Kippur, the Day of Atonement. On the eve of Yom Kippur, a traditional ritual consists of singing or saying a seemingly bizarre linguistic formula called *Kol Nidre*. This legalistic declaration cancels much more than mere debts. The renunciatory text consists in part of the following:

> All vows, obligations, oaths, anathemas . . . or any other expressions by which we shall have vowed, sworn, devoted, or bound ourselves to . . . we repent of them all; they shall all be deemed absolved, forgiven, annulled, void, and made of no effect; they shall not be binding, nor shall they have any power, the vows shall not be reckoned vows, the obligations shall not be obligatory, nor the oaths considered as oaths. (Deshen 1979, 121–122)

This formula has perplexed rabbis over the centuries, but the formula has persisted showing the "hold of popular custom" (Deshen 1979, 123). One clue is provided by the fact that Yom Kippur is supposed to "be a Sabbath of rest unto you" (Lev. 16:30) and is commonly called Shabbat Shabbaton, the "Sabbath of Sabbaths" (Greenberg 1983, 338; Deshen 1979, 126). In other words, all the restrictions that apply to the Sabbath also apply to Yom Kippur. Since Sabbath observance includes numerous examples of circumvention, it is really not so surprising that Yom Kippur should begin with a legalistic formula negating ordinary everyday oaths and obligations. As a matter of fact, the final section of the Shabbat tract of the Mishnah begins, "They abrogate vows on the Sabbath" (Neusner 1988, 208). This is amplified in the Babylonian Talmud specifying that the vows in question have to do with Sabbath observance (Neusner 1992–1993, IIe, 144). The *Kol Nidre* as a feature of Yom Kippur, the "ultimate Sabbath," would seem to provide a similar prescribed way around living up to previous agreements.

The Hillel device of the *Prosbul* might then be an example of a circumvention of a circumvention. The initial custom of requiring individuals to cancel debts in the sabbatical year was a means of circumventing the repayment of financial obligations. But inasmuch as this proved to be a serious obstacle to conducting business, it was necessary to find a way around that custom by essentially transferring the debt to a court that is structurally analogous to selling land or a business to a Gentile.

The traditionality of the legal fiction of selling a proscribed item to a non-Jew is also attested in joke form. The joke assumes knowledge of the fact that most Jewish congregations prohibit smoking on synagogue premises (Zemer 1999, 345). Members of an Orthodox congregation were startled on the Sabbath to see their rabbi smoking a cigarette out in front of the synagogue. "Rabbi," they asked, "How can this be that you are smoking on the Sabbath?" (Smoking involves lighting a fire and as such is strictly forbidden on the Sabbath.) "No problem," replied the Orthodox rabbi, "I sold my lungs to a gentile."

The whole notion of *Shabbes Goy* demonstrates the fact that observant Jews are obliged to depend upon non-Jews or nonobservant Jews to carry out essential services. To put this into historical perspective, it should be realized that almost all of Halachic law was developed in the Jewish Diaspora. It was during the long period of exile (*Galut*) that Jews codified and amended what has evolved into Halachic law. This means that the Jews who lived according to this law were always a minority population (Halkin 1980–1981, 24). In such a situation, essential services (hospitals, police forces) were managed by the majority populations. In other words, Jews could afford to cease all meaningful activity on the Sabbath because others could be depended upon to carry on with manning emergency rooms in hospitals and the like. It is only with the establishment of the State of Israel in 1948 that the use of a *Shabbes Goy* became more problematic. Although the Orthodox community in Israel resents what they perceive to be the pernicious influence of the secular Jews (as well as Conservative, Reform, and other non-Orthodox religious Jews), it is necessarily dependent upon these individuals to carry out essential tasks on the Sabbath. As one author phrases it, "Whereas in the Diaspora, essential services were performed on the Sabbath by the Shabbes Goy, in Israel they were being performed by the Shabbes Jew" (Abramov 1976, 211). These services include "lighting the streets at night, telegraph and telephone, water-supply" (Halkin 1980–1981, 25). Another author aptly summarizes the problem:

> How is the Sabbath to be observed in a highly industrialized society that depends on continuous-process industries that cannot be turned off every Friday at sunset? Are they to be serviced only by non-religious Jews, just as the police force, for instance, is to be recruited only from among non-Sabbath-observant citizens? Is this what the Torah intended by a Jewish people living in its own land, a land dependent on the Jewish "shabbes-goy"? (Berkovits 1983, 91)

As another author puts it, "With the establishment of the state of Israel, an entirely new situation arose—the observance of the Sabbath *without* the 'Shabbes goy.' It was completely unthinkable, both ideologically and practically, for the state to function on the principle that certain areas of the national economy and public services were to be manned only by, and indeed reserved for, non-Jews" (Rabinowitz 1971, 29–30). In Israel, this has led to the "Shabbes Jew" replacing the *Shabbes Goy*. The Orthodox Jew in this context is cast in the role of being "a parasitic sect, living off the services of non-Orthodox Jews" (Abramov 1972, 8).

Some Jews have become defensive about using the services of a *Shabbes Goy*, especially because in theory "it is forbidden to circumvent the laws of the Sabbath deliberately" (Barack 1965, 38). They firmly insist that it is not a case of circumvention at all. "The institution of the 'shabbos goy' is not an evasion of the law, it is not a trick resorted to by the rabbis in order to get round the law" (Jacobs 1999, 100). This and other similar disclaimers call to mind the classic line from *Hamlet*: "The lady doth protest too much, methinks" (III, ii, 242).

CIRCUMVENTION AND JEWISH MENTALITY

It is not possible to overestimate the importance of the Sabbath for Jews and not just for Orthodox Jews. There are dozens of attestations of this. "Shabbat is more than just one institution among many, for Jews. It is the very heart of the Jewish religion" (Kertzer 1993, 209). A proverb also confirms the centrality of Sabbath for Judaism. Like all true folklore, this proverb manifests multiple existence and variation. Some of the variants include: "As Israel has preserved the Sabbath, the Sabbath has preserved Israel" (Trepp 1980, 67); "More than Israel has kept Shabbat, Shabbat has kept Israel" (Kertzer 1993, 209); "More than the Jews kept the Sabbath did the Sabbath keep the Jews" (Rosten 1972, 394).

But while the Sabbath remains a staunch bulwark of Judaism, the "mountains hanging by a hair" have proven in some instances to be an insufferable burden. Hence the elaborate mechanisms for getting around the innumerable restrictions. It is worth noting that the propensity for circumvention is by no means confined to the Sabbath rules. The other principal mark of Orthodox Judaism consists of dietary restrictions. The concept of kosher is sufficiently complex as to require an entirely separate treatise. It is enough to say that keeping kosher involves eating meat from animals properly ritually slaughtered, avoiding certain foods, and not mixing meat and milk products. The latter law, *kashrut,* means, for example, that an Orthodox Jew could not possibly eat a cheeseburger (which consists of a forbidden combination of meat and milk products). It turns out that among some rabbis, "There is no objection to eating meat dishes after milk, only to eating milk after meat" (Jacobs 1999, 90). The reason given for this is that meat particles are more likely to remain in the mouth than is the residue of dairy products (excepting hard cheese). But even with respect to eating meat after milk, there are rules governing how long after eating meat one must wait before ingesting a milk product, lest one risk mixing meat and milk inside one's body (Kaye 1987, 127; Greenberg 1983, 105). According to one authority, "Milk and foods derived from it may not be consumed sooner than six hours after the consumption of meat, though meat may be eaten two hours after milk" (Woolf 1945, 169). A different opinion is that in the case of someone wishing to consume a "cream soup" (containing a dairy product) in a restaurant before eating a meat entrée, one would let a half-hour elapse after ingesting the soup plus rinsing one's mouth thoroughly before being permitted to eat the meat course (Jacobs 1999, 94). Yet another authority indicates that a six-hour waiting period applies no matter whether meat or milk product is eaten first:

> Among observant Jews, a six-hour interval is required between the consumption of one and of the other, and separate cooking utensils, china and crockery must be used for each. If a "milk" plate accidentally comes into contact with a "meat" plate, or vice versa, it must be broken, and if this happens in the case of a steel object (e.g., a knife, fork or spoon), the latter must be scalded, passed through fire or plunged into the earth for a specified time. (Gaster 1955, 211–212)

A knife, for example, which might have particles of "forbidden food" adhering to it is put into the earth to remove these particles (Jacobs 1999, 83). One version of the pertinent rule insists that "a knife that cut meat must be thrust into ten different spots of hard earth before it may be used to cut cheese" (Halperin and Oratz 1994, 75).

A highly reliable source in Baltimore informs me that instead of waiting for so many hours between eating meat and then milk or vice versa, one can dispense with the waiting period if one brushes one's teeth in between. This appears to be an update of an older lenient rule with respect to the required waiting period. According to this rule, if one removed particles of meat in the mouth by chewing bread or something abrasive, one needed to wait only one hour before eating cheese after meat (Pollack 1980). This is a fine example of circumventing custom. The variations in the waiting period involved in this customary behavior are really quite extraordinary ranging from one hour, three hours, six hours, and in the case of one pious individual, twenty-four hours. The latter Jew "would refrain from eating milk dishes until 24 hours had elapsed since he had eaten meat" (Jacobs 1999, 97).

There are even special rules for children in this regard. A child under three years of age may eat dairy products immediately after eating meat though "the child's mouth should be externally cleaned of any meat residue." A child between the ages of three and six should wait one hour after eating meat before ingesting a dairy product. A child six or older should obey adult rules with respect to the time interval (Cohen 1993, 35).

Once again, we find an "appearance" issue. It is not just that one cannot commingle meat and dairy, but that one cannot even appear to have done so. In chapter 46 of the *Code of Jewish Law* that discusses "Forbidden Foods," we find the following: "If we prepare a dish of meat with an extract of almonds, we must put whole almonds in it on account of its deceptive appearance (because it [the almond extract] looks like milk, thus averting the suspicion of having transgressed the law, by having boiled meat and milk together)" (Ganzfried 1961, 1: 147). Similarly, one may have a problem serving kosher margarine, a purely vegetable product, at a meal where meat is on the menu, the reason being that margarine looks very much like butter, a dairy product. A guest might wrongly jump to the conclusion that the presence of what appeared to be "butter" on the table constituted a violation of the meat/dairy commingling rule. The same difficulty might arise in the use of a nondairy creamer for coffee served at a meal that included meat (Kolatch 1985, 262–263).

Washing dishes also presents a problem for the observant Jew. In theory, dishes that contained meat and dishes that contained dairy should not be washed in the same sink. This is why "many orthodox families insist upon separate sinks for washing dairy and meat utensils" (Halperin and Oratz 1994, 96). The introduction of the modern household dishwasher has led to new legislation. The same dishwasher can be used to clean both dairy and meat dishes so long as separate racks are used for dairy and meat dishes, dairy and meat dishes are washed at different times, and the rinse water for one set of dishes is not used for the other set. Also there should be an additional rinse in between the washing of the dairy and the meat dishes (100). Part of the rationale for the additional rinse is that it may help in the elimination of "scraps or bits of food that may still adhere to the inside of the machine" (Schwartz 1990, 430).

The required separation of meat and dairy has led to a truly ingenious though simple invention by the Institute for Science and Halacha. The invention is referred to as "kosher steam" (Precker 1981, 74). In hotels, hospitals, and other large institutions, "water from a single source was heated and circulated through steam tables that held both dairy and meat dishes, which cannot be mixed." The rabbis ruled that even the thickest of pots was porous enough that elements from both sets of dishes would enter the steam, thereby "rendering everything unkosher" (cf. Schwartz 1990, 430). The way out of this dilemma hinged on a principle based on Jewish law that if the steam were inedible, the entire procedure was acceptable. The question then was: How does one make steam "inedible"? "According to Halacha, one of the tests to determine if food is fit for consumption is whether or not a dog will eat it" (Halperin and Oratz 1994, 152). "A clever Institute troubleshooter added a few drops of harmless pine oil to water, and the laboratory dog wouldn't touch it" (Precker 1981, 74; Halperin and Oratz 1994, 154). As a result, hotels catering to Orthodox Jews were able to serve hot lunches that included both meat and dairy dishes.

Other dietary restrictions include forbidden foods such as pork and shellfish. What is fascinating in the present context is the way in which some

Jews find ways around the dietary restrictions. For example, at some upscale delicatessens, one can purchase turkey that tastes like ham, or one can eat fish that has been molded into the form of shrimp. Similarly one can purchase "Turkey bacon" (imitation bacon made from light and dark turkey meat) or "Baco-Bits," which simulate the flavor of bacon. Modern food technology produces soybean-based "meats" that are intended to taste like ham and bacon (Diamond 2000, 119). Some Jews who refuse to eat pork at home will eat it in a Chinese restaurant (Tuchman and Levine 1993, 1996). Philip Roth in *Portnoy's Complaint* comments on this phenomenon, remarking that lobster remains off limits. "Even in the Chinese restaurant, where the Lord has lifted the ban on pork dishes for the obedient children of Israel, the eating of lobster Cantonese is considered by God . . . to be totally out of the question. Why we can eat pig on Pell Street and not at home is because . . . frankly I still haven't got the whole thing figured out" (1967, 90). But Roth does offer an explanation: "Suddenly even the pig is no threat—though, to be sure, it comes to us so chopped and shredded, and is then set afloat on our plate in such oceans of soy sauce, as to bear no resemblance at all to a pork chop, or a hambone, or, most disgusting of all, a *sausage* (ucchh!). . . . But why then can't we eat a lobster, too, disguised as something else?" (90). One sociological survey reported that Jews who were interviewed claimed that they "loved to eat egg rolls in Chinese restaurants because the pork and seafood tasted delicious but were so minced that they could pretend these ingredients were not there" (Tuchman and Levine 1993, 390; 1996, 27). Accordingly, Chinese food was considered by many Jews to be "safe *treyf*" (Tuchman and Levine 1996). The critical factor here seems to be "disguise," which we may consider as a clever form of circumvention.

Speaking of pork, there is quite a remarkable instance of circumvention concerning this taboo diet item. At one point, the Orthodox rabbinical community in Israel asked the government to forbid *kibbutzim* to raise pigs. Raising pigs, they contended, would be a violation of the sacredness of the land of Israel. The idea of an anti-pig-raising ordinance was not a new one. In one of the more legalistic tractates of the Mishnah, the Baba Qamma, we find, "They do not rear pigs anywhere" (Neusner 1988, 519). In 1957, the Knesset enacted the Local Authorities (Special Enablement) Law, which gave local authorities the power to initiate legislation "limiting or prohibiting the raising or keeping of pigs and the sale of pork products destined for food" (Rubinstein 1971, 221). In 1962, the more comprehensive so-called Pig Law was enacted. According to the provisions of this Pig-Raising Prohibition Law:

> A person shall not raise pigs, own them, or kill them for eating purposes. . . . Anyone not abiding by this law is subject to a fine. An owner of a place permitting others to use it for these purposes is subject to half this fine. The police or others who were appointed by the Minister of police can enter any place where they have reasonable suspicion to believe that it is being used for these purposes in order to search it. They can also seize pigs raised in violation of this law and confiscate them. These pigs will be destroyed. Owners can appeal this action in court.

Specifically exempted from the provisions of this law were five Arab villages, one Arab city (Nazareth), and two mixed Arab/Druze villages. Also exempted were zoos as well as scientific and research institutions using pigs for experimental, teaching, and research purposes (Rubinstein 1971, 221n95). Jewish settlements, however, were obliged to obey the law. Nevertheless, the residents of Kibbutz Sarid, among others, found an ingenious way around the prohibition. They raised pigs on wooden platforms so that technically, the pigs' feet never touched Israeli soil. There seems to be no limit to the ability of Jews to circumvent religious restrictions or secular laws inspired by religious convictions.

Occasionally, these food subterfuges can backfire. There is one instance of where observant Jews, thinking they were eating kosher, discovered to their horror that they had eaten *treif* (or *treyf*), nonkosher food, from the Hebrew *terefah* (Bloch 1980, 90), meaning "torn to pieces" (Rosten 1970, 410). "Neither shall ye eat any flesh that is torn of beasts in the field; ye shall cast it to the dogs" (Exod. 22:31). This took place when one hundred Orthodox Jews from Baltimore were on a fund-raising cruise in Chesapeake Bay. One of the "kosher" delicacies served was in the shape of imitation crab cakes. Later, upon inquiry, it turned out that "the imitation crab cakes were the real McCoy" (Schlossberg 1996, 75).

This event is somewhat similar to one that allegedly helped precipitate the formation of the movement known as Conservative Judaism. As the story goes, at a banquet in 1883 held on the occasion of the graduation of the first class from Hebrew Union College, a basically Reform group, shrimp was served. Shrimp as shellfish was definitely not kosher and this *treyf* banquet scandalized many Jews who as a result mobilized what eventually became the Conservative Jewish movement (Danzger 1989, 23).

Avoiding taboo food is also a theme found in jokes. In February 1998, I received the following text via e-mail from a valued informant in Haifa: A Jewish man moves into a Catholic neighborhood. Every Friday, the Catholics go crazy because, while they're morosely eating fish, the Jew is outside barbecuing steaks. So the Catholics work on the Jew to convert him. Finally, by cajoling and pleading, the Catholics succeed. They take the Jew to a priest who sprinkles holy water on the Jew and intones: "Born a Jew; Raised a Jew, Now a Catholic." The Catholics are ecstatic. No more delicious, but maddening smells every Friday evening. But the next Friday evening, the scent of barbecue wafts through the neighborhood. The Catholics all rush to the Jew's house to remind him of his new diet. They see him standing over a sizzling steak. He is sprinkling water on the meat and saying, "Born a cow, raised a cow, now a fish."

In a version of the same joke published in 1971, a friendless Jew cooks chicken on Friday nights and decides to convert to Catholicism in order to have friends. A priest tells him, "All you have to do is cross yourself every time you see someone and say, 'Once a Jew, now a Catholic,' and be sure to follow all the laws, and come to church and eventually you'll become a Catholic." The Jew does so, but he continues to cook chicken on Friday nights, causing complaints by the Catholics in the neighborhood. The priest asks the Jew about the rumor, but the Jew firmly denies it. Finally, the priest goes to the Jew's house on Friday to see if he is cooking chicken. "And he looks in the window. Here's the ex-Jew standing over a pot, cooking a chicken. And he's crossing the chicken saying, "Once a chicken, now a fish" (Dundes 1971, 196–197).

The point of the joke is that once a Jew, always a Jew. Despite the trappings of Catholicism, a Jew can no sooner become a Catholic than a chicken can become a fish. The joke declares that a Jew cannot possibly deny his or her ethnic heritage. Even if a Jew does convert, he can always return to Judaism without undergoing a Jewish conversion ceremony (Kolatch 1985, 36). At the same time, the joke illustrates how a Jew can circumvent a custom, namely, a once-traditional Catholic rule forbidding the eating of meat on a Friday. The fact that it is a Catholic custom that the Jew is circumventing does not alter the fact that a Jew is attempting to get around a dietary taboo. For that matter, it is a historical fact that some Jews did go through the motions of conversion to Catholicism in order to escape persecution, a real life-and-death example of circumvention.

It is worth noting that this particular joke was probably not originally a Jewish joke at all. An earlier text is contained in Poggio's classic fifteenth-century collection of facetiae. Poggio (1380–1459) included the following text in his 1450 compilation:

> A Spanish bishop who was traveling on a Friday stopped at an inn and sent his servant out to purchase some fish. The servant returned explaining that he hadn't been able to find any fish for sale, but told his master that he had seen two par-

> tridges. He was then ordered to go out, buy them, have them cooked, and brought to the table. The servant was amazed at this for he had assumed that the purchase was intended for Sunday, and he asked the bishop if he really meant to eat them on a day when meat was forbidden. To which the bishop replied, "I shall use them as fish." The fellow was even more startled at this answer, when the bishop explained, "You are aware that I am a priest, no? Well then, which is more difficult, making bread into the body of Christ, or partridges into fish?" Whereupon he made the sign of the cross, told them to change into fish, and he ate them as fish. (Bracciolini 1968, 176)

Here the point of this sacrilegious text is to make fun of the Eucharist, quite a different point from that found in the contemporary Jewish versions of the joke. Nevertheless, the theme of circumvention is surely present in this anti-Catholic joke. What this suggests is that the Jews are not the only people to practice the art of circumvention. It is likely that all peoples on the face of the earth devise ways of finding socially sanctioned loopholes around interdicted acts. The Jews are by no means unique in their penchant for circumvention. On the other hand, very few people seem to have perfected the art to the high level attained by the Jews. One might even go so far as to argue that one of the reasons why the Jews might have chosen to borrow this joke was precisely because it provided an excuse for a fantastic fictional example of circumvention. (For a valuable discussion of how non-Jewish jokes can evolve into Jewish jokes, see Raskin [1992, 167–180].)

Circumvention of custom occurs in yet other aspects of traditional Orthodox Jewish life. For example, traditional mourning ritual requires mourners to rend their garments as an expression of grief (Gen. 37:29, 34; 1 Sam. 4:12; 2 Sam. 13:31, for the rules of rending garments, see Ganzfried 1961, 4: 91–94). If observed properly, this would result in the ruination if not complete destruction of one's clothing. A standard dodge is to pin a torn piece of cloth, usually black in color, over one's heart. In this way, one tears only a small piece of cloth instead of destroying one's clothing. An alternative technique designed to avoid having to discard an otherwise perfectly good garment involves tearing a ribbon (Kolatch 1995, 59–60), which in some cases is actually provided by the funeral parlor for such purposes (Kolatch 1985, 181). An earlier circumvention consisted of "merely making an incision into the seam of one's coat" (Jastrow 1899, 145, 148).

Another instance of circumvention connected with death concerns a custom found among the Ashkenazim (German Jews) as opposed to the Sephardim (Spanish Jews). There is a curse that avoids directly mentioning death: "They should name someone after you!" (Matisoff 1979, 68). This verbal circumlocution refers to a custom whereby the Ashkenazim do not name a newborn baby after a living relative. Since one can, and often does, name a newborn baby after a beloved deceased relative, the curse is a not so subtle way of telling the addressee to "drop dead!" One folk explanation of the logic underlying this custom has to do with the so-called Angel of Death. Apparently, the Angel of Death can be easily confused. If, say, an old grandfather and a newborn baby both have the same name, the Angel of Death who was coming to claim the soul of the grandfather might mistakenly take the soul of the baby who had the same name. This is supposedly the reason why it might be dangerous to name a newborn baby after a living relative. The fallibility of the Angel of Death may also explain another customary form of circumvention. If an older individual were very ill, he or she might assume a new name (e.g., Chayim for a male and Chaya for a female, both names meaning "life"), in order to fool the Angel of Death who in theory might not recognize the sick individual and pass him or her by (Isaacs 1998, 117–118; Kolatch 1995, 297). In some cases, a prospective visitor to a moribund friend bearing his same name might decide not to enter the home for fear that the Angel of Death might take him by mistake (Isaacs 1998, 118).

Another device designed to deceive the Angel of Death comes from a New York Jewish tradition. If a child becomes seriously ill, one can "sell" that child to a neighbor for a nominal sum, say, one dollar. The neighbor should not be related, that is, should not be a family member and should definitely not live under the same roof as the child. The sick child remains at home, but in effect now belongs to the neighbor. The Angel of Death, evidently akin to such folkloristic figures as the stupid ogre or dimwitted giant or jinn, is completely fooled by this deception and leaves the child alone because it now beongs to another household. After the child sufficiently recovers, he can then be "redeemed" by payment to the helpful, obliging neighbor.

Still other examples of circumvention involve marriage rather than death. In Israel, according to Halachic law, a Jew cannot marry a non-Jew, and a Jew with the surname of Cohen (assumed to be of priestly descent) cannot marry a divorcée or a woman converted to Judaism (Zemer 1999, 73–85). A somewhat unusual instance of this prohibition occurred in the United States in 1911. According to a letter written to the Yiddish daily newspaper *Forward*, a couple after being married for nineteen years were not getting along and chose to get a divorce. Three months later, they reconsidered and decided they had made a "grave mistake" and wanted to remarry. The problem was, "My husband is a *kohen*, and no rabbi will perform a religious ceremony for us. The rabbis we went to explained that it is against the Jewish law for a *kohen* to marry a divorced woman" (Metzker 1971, 112–113). In modern Israel, the way around this prohibition is to have the "forbidden" marriage performed in another country (e.g., on the nearby island of Cyprus), and then enter or reenter Israel as a legally married couple (Abramov 1976, 183). This stratagem is just one of the many attempts that "are constantly being made to circumvent the rules of religious law" (Englard 1971, 180). It is of interest that Halakha itself evidently allows this circumvention. Although a civil marriage performed in Cyprus between a Cohen and divorcée is a "religious offense" and the parties are technically obliged to divorce, the validity of the marriage is not in question. As one legal authority remarked, "There is a mockery and an irony in the fact that a religious rule of law should itself become a loophole considering the matter from a viewpoint of a religious Jew" (180n44). But the fact is that the Talmud itself gives detailed tips on how to circumvent legal ordinances: "A person may contrive to bring his produce in whilst still in its chaff so that his animal may eat it without its becoming liable to tithe," and "A person may contrivingly mix his grain with stubble in order to exempt it from tithe" (Shilo 1982, 151; Neusner 1984, 219).

Cyprus is also utilized in other instances of circumvention. For example, modern reproductive technology designed to assist infertile women often requires donations of ova and sperm. According to one 1999 report, in order to circumvent Israeli regulations forbidding the sale of eggs for profit, Israeli doctors established a fertility clinic on Cyprus where women from Russia and elsewhere could go to have their ova harvested for which they received compensation and infertile Israeli women could go to purchase these ova (Kahn 2000, 132). Another curious case of circumvention connected with remedying infertility concerns the donation of sperm. The simplest means of a sperm donor's producing the desired substance is through masturbation. However, the Torah forbids masturbation. It is the sin of Onan (Gen. 38:9–10) who was killed by God for spilling his seed, an act that accounts for the term "onanism." Because of this prohibition, some Orthodox rabbis allow or recommend the use of non-Jewish sperm. "Since non-Jews are not obligated to the same laws that Jews are, it is not of explicit rabbinic concern whether or not they masturbate" (Kahn 2000, 104). Admittedly, another concern of the rabbis is that the multiple progeny of a Jewish sperm donor might marry and thereby unwittingly commit brother-sister incest (Kahn 2000, 97; Kolatch 1985, 156). On the other hand, some Orthodox rabbis have protested the use of non-Jewish sperm on the grounds that such sperm pollutes the purity of the Jewish people (Kahn 2000, 106–107). As we shall discuss later, the obsession with purity is part of a more general pattern in Jewish culture.

Returning to the subject of marriage, we find an even more complex Halachic impediment obstructs widows, especially childless widows, who wish to remarry. The relevant principle of leviratic marriage is set forth in Deuteronomy: "If brethren dwell together, and one of them die, and have no child, the wife of the dead shall not marry without unto a stranger: her husband's brother shall go in unto her, and take her to him to wife, and perform the duty of a husband's brother unto her" (Deut. 25:5). The only way such a widow could be free to remarry whom she wished was if the brother were to renounce officially his obligation and a prescribed ritual was carried out, the ritual consisting of the widow's removing her brother-in-law's shoe and spitting in his face (Deut. 25:8–9; for the Mishnaic details of this ritual called *halitzah* or *halisah*, see Neusner 1988, 364–366; Zemer 1999, 61–72). The ritual has been usefully interpreted as a form of female contempt (Carmichael 1977). The shoe as a symbol of the vagina (Sartori 1894; Schultze-Gallera 1909; Nacht 1915; Levy 1918; Rossi 1976) is removed from the man's foot in dramatic fashion as a public metaphorical *coitus interruptus* and the woman adds insult to injury by spitting, a symbolic equivalent of emitting semen. (A boy who physically resembles his father is often referred to as a "spitten/spitting image" of him.) The hapless shoeless male has been shorn of his "vagina" and rather than being a "spitter," his normal masculine role has been usurped by a female who spits on him.

In modern times, it is simply a matter of the brother-in-law declaring "I do not wish to take her." But problems arose when the brother-in-law was a minor, not old enough to marry or when the brother-in-law forced the widow to pay dearly for his willingness to renounce his privilege. An odd case of circumvention in this regard occurred in Israel in 1967 when a married brother-in-law was willing to participate in the ritual, but he was hearing and speech impaired and therefore could not utter the required verbal formula. "The Chief Rabbis circumvented the difficulty by means of a rabbinically approved marriage, even though the groom already had a wife. They were then taken to a hotel where a room had been reserved for them by the rabbinate. The next morning the couple, having performed Mitzvat HaHityahdut (the act of union), were taken to the rabbinical court, where the husband proceeded to divorce his bride of one day" (Abramov 1976, 184). There was some public protest to the effect that the chief rabbis had facilitated an act of bigamy, but observing Halachic ritual was evidently considered to be more important to the rabbis than violating a civil law banning bigamy. Prior to the marriage, there was a prenuptial agreement stipulating that the brother-in-law would pay her a substantial sum for as long as he remained married to her. This was to ensure that he would not go back on his word and refuse to divorce her. This marriage-for-a-day ruse is certainly reminiscent of the one-day sale of a shop to a Muslim so that a Jew's shop can remain open for business on the Sabbath.

All these examples are illustrations of what we are calling "circumventions" of customs. And it seems reasonable to consider these various devices and ploys as clever often ingenious ways of avoiding Sabbath restrictions. They may not violate the letter of the law, but they do appear to blatantly disregard the spirit of the law. At the same time, these circumventions could themselves, one might argue, legitimately be considered customs. It requires no stretch of the folkloristic imagination to label the unscrewing of a refrigerator lightbulb as a Sabbath custom. The same goes for constructing an *eruv* or wearing a latch-key as a piece of jewelry. All these could properly be construed as forms of traditional behavior, hence qualifying as bona fide customs. Since they were instituted to circumvent other customs, one is tempted to call them "counter customs."

What we have then are two sets of Sabbath customs. The first set is composed of the, so to speak, "official" ones that conform to Halachic doctrine. They stem from the Torah, the Mishnah, and rabbinic pronouncements, among other sources. They represent a type of "ideal" culture. In marked contrast, we have a second set of customs or counter customs that presumably come from the people—though to be sure these practices must eventually be approved by rabbis as being permitted under the restrictions of the first set of customs. This second set of customs might be said to be "real" as opposed to the "ideal," which many Jews would agree are virtually unattainable. There are those who insist that a *minhag* (custom) "can have significance only insofar as it reflects a Torah point of view" (Kalir 1965, 94). Thus *minhag* "may appear to temper the severity of the law with an easier practice," but *minhag* "is not capable of challenging the *halakhah*" (Kalir 1965, 91, 93). One could challenge this view by demonstrating how counter customs would definitely seem to circumvent the strict rules laid down by Halachic authority. Moreover, there are instances in the Talmud when *minhag*'s ability to trump Halacha is acknowledged (Isaacs 2000, 78).

Another way of describing the dichotomous sets of customs would be to employ Gramscian terms. The "official" Sabbath regulations would thereby constitute a form of oppressive hegemonic rule over a "subaltern" community of observant Orthodox Jews. In that light, the counter customs could properly be called counter hegemonic. The excessively repressive "mountains hanging by a hair" that restrict almost all meaningful human activity in modern times—no telephone, no television, no movies, no driving automobiles, no cooking, no bathing with hot water—are circumvented by a second set of customs that facilitates a modicum of freedom from the burden or weight of the "mountains."

A more difficult theoretical issue concerns the significance, if any, of any group of people having two sets of customs such as those practiced by Orthodox Jews. One could well ask if a set of customs is deemed overly oppressive, why not simply repeal them or ignore them? The latter solution would resemble what is termed in legal parlance as desuetude. For example, a law may be technically still on the books, but if a population fails to obey it and if the police fail to enforce it, this law becomes a virtual fossilized survival with little or no impact upon the conduct of daily life. This is certainly not the case of Sabbath laws in the Orthodox Jewish community. Celebration of the Sabbath remains central to Jewish identity, and that celebration consists to some extent of obeying the behavioral norms dictated by Halachic law. From an Orthodox Jewish perspective, repealing or ignoring Sabbath rules is unthinkable. To understand this, it is necessary to realize that for the Orthodox Jew, Halachic law is believed to come directly from God. It is sacred and is divinely ordained, it is considered to be immutable (Abramov 1976, 180, 193) and not subject to man-made tampering. Halachic law is considered to be eternal and everlasting. Even God himself seems to be bound by his own laws. For example, when God tests the faith of Abraham by demanding that Abraham sacrifice his only son Isaac, he does not cancel the sacrifice, which in theory as an omnipotent deity he could certainly do. Instead, God allows Abraham to substitute a ram (Gen. 22:13), which in effect permits Abraham to circumvent the original filicidal command.

The Dutch scholar Van Baaren, in a 1972 paper titled "The Flexibility of Myth," concluded his essay by noting that the invention of writing has wrought havoc inasmuch as it has enabled man to fix the text of myths and other religious ordinances. In a purely oral culture, myths can and do change over time to accommodate different living conditions and thought patterns. In contrast, the existence of a more or less definitive written text inhibits if not precludes such flexibility. Van Baaren comments, "History of religions teaches us that in this situation the flexibility of myth is transferred to its exegesis" (1972, 206). What this means in the present context is that in order for Halachic law to continue to be meaningful and relevant for even the most observant Jews, there needs to be an enormous amount of exegetical energy devoted to interpreting the God-given laws so that modern inventions and crises can be or appear to be covered by these laws.

The fixity and absolute nature of Halachic law is also confirmed by the way it was imposed on the Jews. There is an acknowledged element of coercion implicit in the Orthodox view of Halachic law, which, after all, includes the Torah (Rabinowitz 1996, 33). It is accepted by some Orthodox Jews, for example, that Moses was not really given a choice by God as to whether or not to accept the Ten Commandments. From this vantage point, "the bestowing of the Torah on Mount Sinai can be considered an act of coercion, rather than of free choice" (Abramov 1976, 170, 418n31). To put it another way, the Jews may well regard themselves as the "Chosen People," but they did not choose to be chosen. It was, in theory, God who did the choosing. The Jews in effect had no choice, no choice at all. Chaim Potok in his novel *The Chosen* articulates this Orthodox view in straightforward fashion. Danny, the son of an Orthodox rabbi, tells his friend Reuven what his father told him when studying the Torah together: "He said that man was created by God, and Jews had a mission in life." "What mission is that?" "To obey God" (Potok 1967, 84).

But in fairness, the critical nature of Sabbath observance is not limited to the Orthodox segment of the Jewish community. The majority of Conservative and Reform Jews would not willingly give up their version of the Sabbath, even though by Orthodox standards it is very much watered down. The Sabbath is simply too important a part of a Jewish heritage much valued by nearly all Jews.

What then are we to make of a society that insists, on the one hand, upon retaining a large set of admittedly very restrictive practices but on the other hand has skillfully devised a remarkably imaginative set of ways around these very same practices? Does this tell us anything about Jewish ethnic or national character? Is there a streak of collective masochism that makes Jews bend under the weight of self-imposed Sabbath legislation? If so, how is it that these same Jews go to such lengths to escape from the fetters of their self-imposed prison of the mind? The self-imposition of such all-encompassing restrictions is clearly one of the most astonishing aspects of Sabbath customs. It is one thing for a people to be oppressed by an unwelcome conqueror occupying their land; it is quite another for a people to be oppressed by their own kind.

This is not by any means a new observation. Plutarch, in his essay on superstition, marveled at the Jews' refusal to fight and defend themselves on the Sabbath in the face of a direct attack by the enemy on that day: "But the Jews because it was the Sabbath day, sat in their places immovable, while the enemy were planting ladders against the walls and capturing the defences, and they did not get up, but remained there, fast bound in the toils of superstition as in one great net" (1956b, 481). Jews are caught like hapless fish in a net of superstition, a net of their own making. That is Plutarch's view of one of the dire consequences of observing the Jewish Sabbath. Actually, the Jews themselves had earlier come to realize the folly of not defending themselves when attacked on the Sabbath. In the apocryphal book of 1 Maccabees (Kohlenberger 1997, 716–897), we read of an event that occurred in the second century B.C.E. in which a besieged Jewish group refused to surrender and comply with an enemy king's demands that they forswear their religious beliefs and customs.

> "We will not come out, nor will we do what the king commands and so profane the Sabbath day." Then the enemy quickly attacked them. But they did not answer them or hurl a stone at them or block up their hiding places. . . . So they [the enemy] attacked them on the Sabbath, and they died, with their wives and children and livestock, to the number of a thousand persons. (1 Macc. 2:34–36, 38)

When Mattathias, the father of Judas Maccabaeus, learned of the massacre, he and his friends made an important decision: "Let us fight against anyone who comes to attack us on the Sabbath day; let us not all die as our kindred died in their hiding places" (1 Macc. 2:41). (For a discussion of Josephus's various mentions of the issue of whether Jews could or should fight on the Sabbath, see Weiss [1998].) So Jesus was not the first to rebel against the restraints imposed by Sabbath restrictions. Just as there has been a long history of the evolution of Sabbath rules and regulations, so there is a parallel history of seeking to evade these same rules and regulations. As one scholar described Mattathias's decision, "The Maccabees circumvented the Torah in order to defend themselves on the Sabbath" (Kimbrough 1966, 499; cf. Sharvit 1979, 43).

OBSESSION AND RELIGION ACCORDING TO FREUD

The question of what to make of this strange combination of rules and means of avoiding obeying those same rules remains. It was one of Freud's most brilliant early papers, first published in 1907, "Obsessive Acts and Religious Practices," that provides some help. Freud begins his essay in the first person: "I am certainly not the first to be struck by the resemblance between what are called obsessive acts in neurotics and those religious observances by means of which the faithful give expression to their piety" (1959b, 25). Freud speaks of both "compulsions and prohibitions (that one thing must be done and another may not be done)." Not surprisingly, Freud suggests that obsessive acts "express *unconscious* motives and ideas" (30) and that ceremonial rituals begin "as an act of defence or security—as a protective measure" (31). One analyst distinguishes "compulsion" from "obsession" on the basis that compulsion refers to an act, whereas an obsession refers to a thought. According to this analyst, "A compulsion is an irrational, unavoidable act or persistent drive that must be carried out in order to atone for guilt," whereas "An obsession is an irrational, unavoidable thought which atones for guilt" (Fink 1963, 82).

In any event, for Freud, "the structure of religion seems . . . to be founded on the suppression or renunciation of certain instinctual trends" (1959b, 33). Freud suggests that the renunciation of "instinctual gratification" stems originally from "a dread of external authority" (1957, 112). Finally, Freud speaks of the device of displacement to explain why obsessional behavior seems to concern "petty performances of daily life and are expressed in foolish regulations and restrictions in regard to them" (1959b, 33). In view of Freud's own Jewish identity, one cannot help but wonder if perhaps Freud had Orthodox Jewish "regulations" and "restrictions" in mind when he wrote these words.

One reason for making this assumption is a remark attributed to Freud by Max Eitingon (1881–1943). Eitingon, who was to become one of Freud's most devoted and trusted followers, attended a meeting of the Viennese Psychoanalytic Society on January 30, 1907. Although he was only an invited guest at that time, he gave the principal presentation on "The Etiology and Therapy of the Neuroses." According to the official minutes of those meetings, Eitingon asked in the discussion period whether the "frequency of neurosis is greater among Jews." In recollecting the occasion many years later, he claimed that Freud commented on the frequency of compulsive neuroses among Jews. Freud allegedly said that the very best (*schoensten*) compulsive neuroses were to be found among Jews and furthermore that the Jewish religion was a compulsive neurosis that had persevered for hundreds of years (Eitingon 1950, 78). Others since Freud's day have pointed out the fairly obvious parallels between Jewish rituals and obsessive behavior (Greenberg 1984, 525), although several Orthodox rabbis adamantly insisted to A. A. Roback that "no orthodox Jew suffered from compulsion neurosis" (Roback 1957, 59).

Freud was certainly well aware of Sabbath prohibitions. In a letter dated July 23, 1882, written to his fiancée Martha Bernays, Freud recounted an incident where he went to a stationery shop to purchase some writing paper. The shop-owner was Jewish. Here is Freud's account: "The man from whom I ordered this despotic paper on Friday could supply it only on Sunday; 'for on Saturday,' said he, 'we are not here. It is one of our ancient customs.' (O

I know that ancient custom!)" (Freud, 1960). Freud's parenthetical exclamation commenting on the enforced closure of shops on the Sabbath indicates his basic antipathy to the tyranny of custom and the annoying inconvenience caused thereby.

Freud did speak of the "laws of culture" as being perceived "to be of divine origin" (1949, 32), and that if they were obeyed, "then surely one would be rewarded—at least the only beloved child, the chosen people would be" (34). The phrase "chosen people" certainly suggests Jews in particular, as this epithet continues to be used as an immodest self-referential, self-congratulatory term by contemporary Jews. In any event, Freud concludes by speculating, "In view of these resemblances and analogies one might venture to regard the obsessional neurosis as a pathological counterpart to the formation of a religion, to describe this neurosis as a private religious system, and religion as a universal obsessional neurosis" (1959b, 34). Freud's own studies of religion continued with his remarkably insightful *The Future of an Illusion* ([1927] 1949) and his controversial *Moses and Monotheism* ([1939] 1955).

Freud's approach to religion inspired a spate of psychoanalytic studies of religious phenomena, including the Old Testament and Jewish ritual. (For a helpful entrée to psychoanalytic investigations of religion, see Beit-Hallahmi [1996]; for surveys of psychoanalytic studies of Judaism in particular, see Cronbach [1931–1932]; Ostow [1982]; and Beit-Hallahmi [1994].) Only a few of these considered the Sabbath. Erich Fromm wrote an essay on the subject that was published in *Imago* in 1927. In this essay, he argued along conventional Oedipal lines to the extent that the Sabbath represents a wish for the death of the father—God is depicted as weak insofar as he needs to rest after the work of creation—and at the same time, the restriction against plowing represented the incest taboo against sexual intercourse with "mother" earth. The Sabbath was originally, according to Fromm, "a reminiscence of winning the mother" (1927, 234), with "Sabbath joy, implying a regressing to the intra-uterine state of perfect rest" substituting for the renounced Oedipal gratification (Cronbach 1931–1932, 640). Fromm, in his later discussions of the Sabbath (1951, 241–249; 1966, 152–157), seems to have retreated from his Oedipal position, arguing instead that the Sabbath represents an ideal statement of the proper relationship between man and nature. "A man must not interfere with or change the natural equilibrium and he must refrain from challenging the social equilibrium" (1966, 155). So for Fromm, "we are not dealing with obsessive overstrictness but with a concept of work and rest that is different from our modern concept" (154). This neo-Freudian statement by Fromm is quite far removed from the implications of Freud's 1907 notion that seemingly obsessive religious rituals might have an underlying unconscious basis. Fromm's 1927 Oedipal reading of the Sabbath was given little credence in part because it, like many early Freudian essays, seemed to be based on blind faith and fixed Procrustean applications of Freudian concepts to all subject matter (Clemen 1930, 8–9, 14). Fromm's attempts to analyze the Sabbath are not even mentioned in a 1994 survey of psychoanalytic interpretations of Judaism (Beit-Hallahmi 1996). For that matter, even the apparent parallel between religious ritual and obsessional neurosis has been called into question (Gay 1975).

Perhaps even more important for the study of religion and religious ritual is Freud's thesis in *The Future of an Illusion*, first published in 1927, in which he argues that religion is basically a projection of human familial relationships. Specifically, as man is to god so is infant to parent. Freud describes the infantile prototype of religion as follows: "For once before one has been in such a state of helplessness: as a little child in one's relationship to one's parents" (1949, 29). Earlier, Freud had said something quite similar in his *Totem and Taboo*, first published in 1913: "Psychoanalytic investigation of the individual teaches with especial emphasis that god is in every case modeled after the father and that our personal relation to god is dependent upon our relation to our physical father, fluctuating and changing with him, and that god at bottom is nothing but an exalted father" (1938, 919–920).

It is not hard to imagine the Judeo-Christian deity as a father figure. As one psychotherapist puts it, the Orthodox Jewish God "really serves in loco parentis—God, psychodynamically speaking, is a foster parent" (Strean 1994, 17). Many passages in the Old Testament make this quite explicit. "Like as a father pitieth his children, so the Lord pitieth them that fear him" (Ps. 103:13). "As a man chasteneth his son, so the Lord thy God chasteneth thee" (Deut. 8:5). The parental God is not always male: "Then shall ye suck, ye shall be borne upon her sides, and be dandled upon her knees. As one whom his mother comforteth, so will I comfort you" (Isa. 66:12–13; for a fascinating discussion of the "nursing" father and absent mother in ancient Israel, see Pardes 2000). In the New Testament as well, the heavenly father is addressed as such in the Lord's prayer: "Our Father which art in heaven" (Matt. 6:9). If God is a father figure, then we can better understand why the Jews in Genesis and Exodus are repeatedly referred to as the "children of Israel." Moses as one of the children of Israel would thus be a son vis-à-vis God. Moses received the Ten Commandments directly from God and one of these Commandments concerned the Sabbath. The Commandments represent exalted glorified parental rules for children. The key concept is "Thou shalt NOT," or to put it another way: "Don't!" The majority of the commandments are actually expressed in the form of negative injunctions. Even the one involving the Sabbath contains "thou shalt not do any work" (Exod. 20:10). If one accepts the reasonable premise that any law or rule that forbids a given activity tacitly admits that there is a desire or wish to engage in that activity—otherwise why would there be any necessity to proscribe it?—we can perceive the Ten Commandments as a kind of wish list on the part of children, keeping in mind that adults never cease to be the children of their parents. Incidentally, James George Frazer, in the fourth volume of his *Totemism and Exogamy*, long ago articulated the reasonable premise in question:

> The law only forbids men to do what their instincts incline them to do. . . . Accordingly we may always safely assume that crimes forbidden by law are crimes which many men have a natural propensity to commit. If there was no such propensity, there would be no such crimes, and if no such crimes were committed what need to forbid them? (1910, 97)

As for the coercion factor, we now better appreciate why a rabbi would claim that the coercion involved in demanding obedience to Sabbath regulations is "no more coercion than in a parent forcing his child to behave correctly" (Abramov 1976, 170). Eilberg-Schwartz puts it this way: "As a parental figure, God offers protection and demands obedience" (1994, 85). This facet of the God-parent equation is found in the Bible as well. God may be a strict and demanding disciplinarian, but he promises to reward those who fear and obey him: "And they shall be mine, saith the Lord of hosts . . . and I will spare them, as a man spareth his own son that serveth him" (Mal. 3:17).

What this means is that God recognized that men, in this case, the Jews, had a tendency to kill, steal, commit adultery, bear false witness (lie), covet neighbors' possessions, and so forth. Society, conscience, superego (or whatever one wants to label moral authority) are part of a conspiracy to suppress expressions of the pleasure principle, as Freud termed it. In the face of such restrictions, one of the possibilities for pleasure created by them is to find a way to violate them, preferably without being penalized for so doing. It is basically the forbidden fruit principle. If something is deemed illegal, it becomes per se more enjoyable. I believe this is part of the rationale underlying the undeniable pattern of circumventing custom. It is like a child's outwitting a parent; it is like a lawyer finding a loophole in the law to defend a client; it is, in the words of a proverb, "having one's cake and eating it too." It is obeying a Sabbath rule but at the same time getting around it.

Although Freud tends to regard Moses as a father figure rather than a son—except for the hero pattern discussion in which Moses is clearly the child who conquers his father—he does astutely note (1955, 58) that the breaking of the tables of the law must "be understood symbolically" as "he [Moses] has broken the law." Keep in mind that one of the Ten Commandments being "broken" is the one having to do with the Sabbath. So Moses, soon after receiving the Ten Commandments from God the father, proceeds to break all of them, literally that is. And what is the immediate cause of this rash act? Moses' anger at seeing the golden calf fashioned by his brother Aaron. While Moses was engaged in receiving the Ten Commandments, Aaron had persuaded the people to give him their gold earrings (Exod. 32:2–3) with which to construct the calf as an object of worship. Whether or not the calf represents a competitor religion known as Mithraism, it is surely relevant that it is a calf, not a cow or bull, that is the object of worship. The calf would represent a child as opposed to a parent (cow or bull). In a highly patriarchal world, it is the father god who rules, not a son god. Freud even used this distinction to distinguish Judaism from Christianity. "The Mosaic religion had been a Father religion; Christianity became a Son religion" (1955, 111, 175). The crucial point here is that Moses, a son, broke the Sabbath commandment (along with the rest of the Ten Commandments) within moments of receiving it. Moreover, Moses is not punished for breaking the Sabbath commandment, although one can perhaps detect just a trace of annoyance when God agrees to write down the Ten Commandments for a second time: "And the Lord said unto Moses, 'Hew thee two tables of stone like unto the first: and I will write upon these tables the words that were in the first tables, which thou brakest' " (Exod. 34:1). One could argue that Moses' action in breaking the Sabbath Commandment and getting away with it provides a charter for more than two millennia of Jews finding a way to violate the Sabbath and get away with it. No matter how successful learned rabbis were in managing to contribute new amendments to Sabbath regulations and extending the initial prohibitions to modern technological innovations, such as not being allowed to use electricity, clever Jews have been just as successful in devising "acceptable" ways of avoiding the prohibitions. The process is reminiscent of a kind of game in which the objective is to find a way around an apparently insurmountable obstacle.

Philip Roth in *Portnoy's Complaint* gives a penetrating account of Jewish restrictions in terms of child socialization:

> What else, I ask you, were all those prohibitive dietary rules and regulations all about to begin with, what else but to give us little Jewish children practice in being repressed? . . . Why else, I ask you, but to remind us three times a day that life is boundaries and restrictions if it's anything, hundreds of thousands of little rules

> laid down by none other than None Other, rules which either you obey without question, regardless of how idiotic they may appear (and thus remain, by obeying, in His good graces) or you transgress, most likely in the name of outraged common sense—which you transgress because even a child doesn't like to go around feeling like an absolute moron. (1967, 79–80)

With the help of Freud's insights, we can now better understand how some devout, observant Jews can extol the "joy" of the Sabbath while at the same time others complain bitterly about the burden of the "mountains hanging by a hair." If one reads A. J. Heschel's *The Sabbath: Its Meaning for Modern Man* (1951), one finds a paean in praise of the day; but if one reads other comments on the Sabbath, one discovers more pain than paean: "There are, of course, many for whom the Sabbath is a burden rather than a pleasure. For them, the Sabbath is a host of prohibitions which prevent them from doing what they might otherwise want to do, and they count the hours and minutes until its conclusion" (Waxman 1982, 40). "Not to turn on a light when one is in the dark, not to cook food when it is cold, not to light a cigarette, not to travel become unbearable restrictions" (Danzger 1989, 215). One is reminded of a Yiddish expression, "It's hard to be a Jew," about which one comedic writer comments: "With 613 separate commandments to follow, hundreds of brawkhas [prayers] to say every day, all kinds of delicious food you can't eat and neighborhood louts beating the crap out of you every day, it's easy to see where this saying came from" (Naiman 1983, 147). As for the Sabbath in particular, it has long been argued that the essential idea of the Sabbath is "abstinence" (Toy 1899, 193). If that is so, how can a burden bring about joy?

Freud's answer is what he terms "instinctual renunciation" (1955, 148–153). While "instinctual renunciation," by which he means a refraining from satisfaction because of "external obstacles" or "in obedience to the reality principle," is never pleasurable but is usually painful, it can create "a gain in pleasure" to the ego as a kind of substitute satisfaction. There is pride in renunciation as a kind of achievement intended to please a parent or parent figure. "When the Ego has made the sacrifice to the Super-ego of renouncing an instinctual satisfaction, it expects to be rewarded by being loved all the more" (149). As Freud puts it, "It is the parents' authority—essentially that of the all-powerful father, who wields the power of punishment—that demands instinctual renunciation on the part of the child and determines what is allowed and what is forbidden" (153). Freud applies his insights to the Jews (though without specific reference to Sabbath rules). The Jews, he noted, experienced various difficulties in their history and accordingly they felt guilt because they felt they had not sufficiently observed the laws. Because of this they welcomed God's severity.

> They deserved nothing better than to be punished by him, because they did not observe the laws; the need for satisfying this feeling of guilt, which, coming from a much deeper source, was insatiable, made them render their religious precepts ever and ever more strict, more exacting, but also more petty. (1955, 173)

Some contemporary rabbis insist that Judaism believes "that for healthful living, man must learn the art of subduing, conquering, controlling and repressing" (Amsel 1970, 62).

From this we can understand why Orthodox Jews feel themselves to be more worthy than other Jews by adhering to the strict requirements of Sabbath and other laws (e.g., dietary). The same logic explains why many ascetics find satisfaction, which we might even call "pleasure," in asceticism. This is why there can be what is perceived to be "joy" in the "instinctual renunciation" required by Sabbath rules: no cooking, no bathing with hot water, no television, no telephone, no driving, no leaving home or going beyond the limits of the *eruv*. By strictly observing the Sabbath, the Orthodox Jew successfully renounces both space and time. Remaining within the confines of one's home or within the slightly extended limits provided by an *eruv*, one in theory honors God by not entering the wider space utilized in everyday life. By the same token, the observant Jew every seventh day "renounces his autonomy and affirms God's dominion over him" (Tsevat 1971, 455) and does not use the time span of the Sabbath as he does in the quotidian routine of the other six days.

There is yet another aspect of what Freud terms "instinctual renunciation" that may apply to the Sabbath rules and regulations. Activities forbidden on the Sabbath include the handling of money and writing. The taboo against handling money precludes participating in any recreational activities involving the purchase of admission tickets (e.g., going to the movies) (Gurevitch and Schwartz 1971, 65). The usual explanation of such restrictions has to do with the insistence that regular weekday concerns with business, that is, making money, must be put aside in order to pay homage to God on the Sabbath. Writing too is considered an act of individual indulgence not consonant with devoting oneself entirely to thinking about God on the Sabbath. But there is another possible explanation, although it is one that is likely to strike the reader unfamiliar with Freudian theory as being very bizarre.

ANAL EROTIC CHARACTER

According to Freudian theory, one of the critical developmental stages of infancy involves anality (Fischer and Juni 1981). In fairness, it must be said that not everyone accepts the idea that there is such a thing as an anal stage or anal erotic character. Indeed, the concept has stimulated skeptics to write satirical accounts of purported experiments to test its validity (Levy and Erhardt 1988). It is true that legitimate attempts to scientifically validate the concept have produced mixed results. One representative 1976 survey of the experimental evidence concludes, "It would seem that at present the Freudian concept of an 'anal' character is still awaiting clear and convincing experimental verification" (Hill 1976, 158), while a review first published in 1977 differs considerably: "We would declare with simple directness that the scientific evidence gathered up to this point favors a good part of what Freud said about the anal character" (Fisher and Greenberg 1985, 163). For the sake of argument, we shall take the liberty of assuming that the latter of these statements is closer to the truth.

The infant's initial pleasure in the act of defecation and in the product produced thereby is gradually curbed by parental socialization. The child is eventually taught to control his bowels and to learn to accept the loss of his body products. There is a vast literature devoted to the discussion of what is normally referred to as "anal erotic character" beginning with Freud's 1908 paper "Character and Anal Erotism." It did not take long for other early psychoanalysts to corroborate Freud's insights (e.g., Sadger [1910], and Brill [1912]). Classic delineations of anal erotic character include Ernest Jones' (1918) paper "Anal-Erotic Character Traits," Karl Abraham's (1921) "Contributions to the Theory of the Anal Character," and William Menninger's detailed survey (1943). However, it was Freud who first listed the three supposed anal erotic character traits of "orderly, parsimonious, and obstinate" (1959a, 45) and identified the now well-established "money-feces" equation (49). For Freud, orderly "comprises both bodily cleanliness and reliability and conscientiousness in the performance of petty duties" (45). He defined "order" as: "a kind of repetition-compulsion by which it is ordained once and for all when, where and how a thing shall be done so that on every similar occasion doubt and hesitation shall be avoided" (1957, 55–56). Jones expanded this idea. "Orderliness passes over into the pedantic persistence in the performance of duties" and "The trait of persistence is often related to pedantry and obstinacy, being halfway between the two" (1961, 415, 416). In Jones' view, it is the infant's attempts to "achieve *control* of his sphincters" that lead to an adult's desire for "self-control" (423). Jones speaks of "the pathologically intolerant insistence on the absolute necessity of doing certain things in exactly the 'right' way" (417) as being an anal character trait. Freud in his 1913 paper "The Predisposition to Obsessional Neurosis" praised Jones for pointing out the possible anal erotic elements in obsessive behavior (1959c, 127). Jones also suggests that the desire for self-control explains why individuals pride themselves on giving up pleasures such as "going without sugar in their tea, giving up smoking temporarily . . . and indulging in all sorts of ascetic performances in order to reassure themselves of their power of self-control" (1961, 423). Jones contends that the basis of these "ascetic and self-martyring impulses" or extreme forms of self-control stem from the infant's efforts to control his bowels.

Jones also notes the effect of what is called "reaction formation." Reaction formation refers to an individual's denial of a basic tendency by indulging in the opposite of that tendency. Reaction formation in anal erotic terms would consist in part of a complete denial of any interest in feces or dirt such that one would be obsessed with matters of "cleanliness" (Jones 1961, 416) and purity. Menninger phrases it this way: "Reaction-formations resulting from the soiling and smearing stage in infancy include excessive interest in cleanliness of person and property, excessive hand washing and housecleaning, any of which may become compulsive and aggressive in content" (1943, 175). Karl Abraham confirms Freud's and Jones' findings and comments on some anal erotics' "pedantic observance of fixed forms, so that . . . their preoccupation with the external form outweighs their interest in the reality of the thing" (1953, 380). He also contends that "Pleasure in indexing and classifying . . . in drawing up programmes . . . is well known to be an expression of the anal character" (388). Later studies of the so-called anal character identify such additional traits as meticulousness, feelings of self-importance and superiority, and "a passion for personal autonomy and self-control" (Beloff 1957, 147, 149). With regard to "feelings of self-importance and superiority," we may recall an observation by Isidor Sadger in his 1910 paper "Analerotik und Analcharakter," written just two years after Freud's initial essay on anal erotic character, an observation cited by Abraham that "persons with a pronounced anal character are usually convinced that they can do everything better than other people" (1953, 372). For this reason "they must do everything themselves because no one else can do it as well" (376). There is typically a reluctance to delegate authority. "For, as an executive or a foreman, he does not trust them to do as perfect a job as he does" (Fink 1963, 89). There is even a telling bit of metafolklore (folklore about folklore) that purports to illustrate this alleged Jewish tendency:

> When a Frenchman hears a story, he always laughs three times: first when he hears it, second when you explain it to him, and third when he understands. That is because a Frenchman likes to laugh.
>
> When you tell a joke to an Englishman, he laughs twice: once when you tell it and a second time when you explain it to him. He will never understand it, he is too stuffy.
>
> When you tell a joke to a German, he only laughs once, when you tell it to him. He won't let you explain it to him because he is too arrogant. Also, Germans have no sense of humor.
>
> When you tell a joke to a Jew—before you finish it, he interrupts you. First, he has heard it before; second, you are not telling it right; and third, he ends up telling you the story the way it should be told. (For other versions of this joke, see Ausubel [1948, 15], Rosten [1970, 174], and Pollack [1979, 189].)

Regarding the Jewish propensity to interrupt, we have the report of an anonymous Netherlander writing in the *Jewish Language Review* (1984, 322) who, after a two-month stay in Israel in 1980, noticed "that the concept of turn-taking in conversation is almost absent completely and that interlocutors cut one another off and shout at one another at the same time (it is common to hear the sentence *ten li ligmor*! 'let me finish!')."

A particularly fascinating variant of the joke omits the international comparisons: a passenger on a train in Israel watched in astonishment as the old man across the aisle kept repeating the same pattern. First he would mumble a few words to himself, then he would smile, and finally he would raise his hand and stop talking for a few moments. After observing this unusual behavior for close to an hour, the passenger finally brought himself to address the old man. "Excuse me, sir, but I couldn't help noticing what you were doing. Is anything wrong?" "Not at all," replied the old man. "You see, whenever I take a trip, I get bored, and so I always tell myself jokes, which is why you saw me smiling." "But why did you keep raising your hand?" "Ohhh, that. It's to interrupt myself because I've heard that joke before."

Admittedly one joke can hardly be conclusive, but there is other evidence of the existence of feelings, justified or not, of moral superiority on the part of Jews. For example, it surely borders on hubris for any group to have the temerity to assert that the supreme God of all mankind elected to deliver and entrust his sacred commandments to just one people, one chosen people, out of all those on earth. As to why God should choose to reveal his word to a single people in the first place, most rabbis simply prefer to finesse the question entirely (cf. Rabinowitz 1996, 13). But the Torah makes no bones about God's choice: "For thou art a holy people unto the Lord thy God, and the Lord hath chosen thee to be a peculiar people unto himself, above all the nations that are upon the earth" (Deut. 14:2, 7:6). Peculiar indeed! And as for the burning question of what language God used to communicate with Moses and others, the same arrogance prevails. In the Babylonian Talmud, when one rabbi said that "A person should always ask what he needs in the Aramaic language," another rabbi responded, "Whoever asks for what he needs in Aramaic—the ministering angels don't accede to him, for the ministering angels don't understand Aramaic" (Neusner 1992–1993, IIa, 45; Rosten 1982, 202). The implication seems to be that God and his heavenly crew understand only Hebrew! Rosten puts it this way: "Hebrew, presumably the language God used, is one of the oldest languages on earth" (1970, 531).

In the psychiatric literature, the obsessive-compulsive personality is often referred to as anal character (Ingram 1961; Pollak 1987, 137). The list of traits associated with obsessive-compulsive personality include: orderliness, perseverance, rigidity, and obstinacy (Pollak 1987, 138), as well as "excessive cleanliness" (Ingram 1961, 1035).

Now what has all this to do with Jews and the Sabbath? It is always intellectually risky to raise the issue of possible national or ethnic character. Not everyone is convinced that there is such a thing as "national character" and even if there were such a thing as national character, there is the additional question as to whether it is possible to apply principles that are derived from the study of individuals rather than nations to an entire people.

Anthropologist Alfred Kroeber argued that Jews were not a race but a group "held together by religion" (1917, 294). His mentor Franz Boas, himself of German-Jewish origin, reasoned along similar lines: "There is certainly nothing that would indicate the existence of any definite mental characteristics which are the common property of the Jews the world over, or even of a large part of the Jews of any one community" (1923, 6). Another anthropologist trained by Boas, Melville Herskovits, also Jewish, concurred, saying unequivocally, "I fail to see anything particularly unique in the Jew as Jew" (1927, 117).

Grotjahn claimed, "There is not a Jewish unconscious. In the strictest sense of the word, there also is not a Jewish character type" (1961, 187). Freud, in contrast, believed in the concept of national character and he sought to identify Jewish character in his 1939 *Moses and Monotheism*. But unfortunately Freud's attempt was seriously marred by his obstinate adherence to a Lamarckian notion of the inheritance of acquired characteristics. Specifically, Freud believed in a Haeckelian ontogenetic recapitulation of phylogeny such that an individual possessed at birth a memory of part of the life experience of his forebears. In his words, "the archaic heritage of mankind includes not only dispositions but also ideational contents, memory traces of the experiences of former generations . . . when I speak of an old tradition still alive in a people, of the formation of a national character, it is such an inherited tradition, and not one carried on by word of mouth, that I have in mind" (1955, 127; 1987). I too believe in the concept of national character (Dundes 1989), but unlike Freud, I believe that such character is postnatally acquired through the mediation of culture. If there is such a thing as Jewish character, it is not innate, but rather it is acquired and for that matter, in no small measure by means of oral tradition, that is, by word of mouth. Freud, however, who claimed that he had "set out to explain whence comes the peculiar character of the Jewish people which in all probability is what has enabled that people to survive until today" (1955, 158) asserted that the character of the Jewish people came from the survival of a memory of the religion of Moses (159).

If we can manage to separate the concept of Jewish national character from Freud's rather mystical phylogenetic hypothesis (1987), can a case be made, for example, that the Jews as a population entity do exhibit personality characteristics that, to salvage something helpful from Freudian theory, could conceivably be called anal erotic in nature? It is worth noting that the brilliant psychoanalyst Sandor Ferenczi felt that one could describe whole peoples using such psychoanalytic constructs. He wrote, "Anal characteristics are specially suited for rapid characterological orientation concerning an individual, indeed concerning whole races" (1956, 277n1). To be sure, Ferenczi was speaking generally, not with reference to Jews.

It is especially unwise to attempt to generalize in the case of the Jews for at least two reasons. First of all, Jewish identity has existed in some form for more than three millennia, and, even assuming there is such a thing as a Jewish character or personality, there is no reason to think that it remained stable over such a long period of time. The second reason is that because of the enforced diaspora of the Jews, there have evolved many diverse types of Jews ranging from Ashkenazim and Sephardim to Yemenite or Ethiopian Jews. In that context, can there be any possibility of there being a common thread of character or personality traits? One could argue that to the extent that the Sabbath with its associated rules and regulations has persisted among Jews everywhere to some extent that we might have a basis for seeking some sort of commonality among Jews as a totality.

In the absence of any ethnographic data concerning toilet training in ancient Israel, we can only work inductively, reading back from accounts of projective systems such as religious practices in general and Sabbath rules in particular. We should probably note that not all of those psychologists who accept the notion of anal character necessarily believe it is related to toilet training experiences (Beloff 1957, 170). On the issue of whether one can legitimately apply a twentieth-century theory such as psychoanalysis to an ancient culture, we may adopt a uniformitarian stance. In other words, an insight obtained in one century may well apply to data in centuries past. For instance, in folklore, there is the goose that laid the golden egg, which is one instance of Motif B103.2.1, Treasure-laying bird (Thompson 1955–1958) and donkeys that defecate ducats, which is classified as Motif B103.1.1, Gold-producing ass. Droppings of gold. The use of the term "ass" instead of donkey permits a telling play on words in English. Brill suggested that "The yellow color which is common to gold and feces" may be a factor in this symbolism (1912, 200). One can quite easily adduce cross-cultural data to confirm this insight. In ancient Mexico, for example, gold was called *coztic teocuitlatl*, which translates as "yellow sacred excrement" or alternatively *tonatiuih icuitl*, which translates as "the excrement of the sun." Tonaitiuh, the sun, was a god, "and gold represented the traces of the body wastes he deposited during the night as he passed through the underworld" (Klein 1993, 25).

The money-feces equation noted by Freud (cf. Freud and Oppenheim 1958, 38–39; Borneman 1976; Haight 1977; Fuqua 1986) is also well attested in contemporary folk speech: filthy lucre, to be filthy or stinking rich, to be rolling in it, to have money up the ass, and so forth (Menninger 1943, 172). The underlying symbolic nature of money is additionally signaled by such proverbs as *Pecunia non olet* (Money doesn't smell) (Ferenczi 1956, 276). Why should money smell? Another proverbial aphorism, referring to the use of feces as fertilizer, proclaims that "Money is like shit; you get profit out of it only if you spread it around." (For a version in Hebrew, see Cohen 1961, 345.) Still other illustrative slang items are "paydirt" and "shitload." Consider the following sentence: "I want to get a really good job and earn a shitload of money" (Spears 1997, 57). Then there is the modern idiom to "launder" money (Haight 1977, 624), that is, to make it clean. (Those who are skeptical about Freud's notion of anal character and such related concepts as the feces-money equation have yet to offer a plausible alternative theory to explain the existence of such folk speech and such motifs as geese that lay golden eggs and asses that produce gold!)

In dream symbolism, if one dreams of feces, one is supposedly going to have good fortune or come into wealth. Consider the following passage from the Berakhot tractate of the Babylonian Talmud dating from the second century C.E.: "He who dreams that he is defecating will find that it is a good omen for him. . . . But that is the case only if he in his dreams did not wipe himself" (Neusner 1984, 384). Still, one symbolic equation by itself hardly proves that anal erotic character existed in ancient Israel. And even if the case were made that Jews for the past two millennia have exhibited definite anal erotic characteristics, that should in no way be construed as giving any credence to the stereotypic canard that "Jews are more prone than other people to develop nervous disorders and psychoses" (Lewis 1978, 16; Gilman 1986, 287–289).

Keeping in mind Freud's idea that obstinacy is one of the primary traits of anal erotic character, it may be of interest to note that a prayer in Deuteronomy refers specifically to "the stubbornness of this people" (9:27) and Psalm 78 condemns a generation that was both "stubborn and rebellious." The trait of stubbornness is seemingly confirmed by none other than God: "And the Lord said unto Moses, I have seen this people, and behold, it is a stiffnecked people" (Exod. 32:9). God repeats this accusation: "thou art a stiffnecked people" (Exod. 33:3) and even instructs Moses to "Say unto the children of Israel, Ye are a stiffnecked people" (Exod. 33:7). There are other allusions to the "stiffneckedness" of the Jews (Exod. 34:9; Deut. 9:6, 13; 2 Chron. 30:8). God is unhappy with such stubbornness and wants the Jews to be more compliant. What is fascinating is the language used to recommend a less stubborn attitude: "Circumcise therefore the foreskin of your heart, and be no more stiffnecked" (Deut. 10:16). This same metaphor was employed by Stephen in the New Testament when he chastised a crowd by saying, "Ye stiffnecked and uncircumcised in heart and ears, ye do always resist the Holy Ghost: as your fathers did, so do ye" (Acts 7:51). The inference to be drawn is that just as circumcision signified acquiescence to God the Father's will, so an analogous "cutting" away of the trait of stiffneckedness was required to comply with God's wishes. Psychoanalyst A. Bronson Feldman who claimed that "we are justified in diagnosing devotion to monotheism as a rarefaction of anal erotism," argued that "anal erotic sublimation manifests itself in the obstinacy of the monotheist" (1953, 42) but he did little to document his assertion. Far too often psychoanalysts tend to present unsubstantiated generalized assertions in lieu of data in the form of empirical facts, even when such facts are readily available in the written record.

Patai in *The Jewish Mind* (1977, 375) lists "stubborn" as one of the traits of the "children of Israel," although he also insists "that it is absurd to speak of the "Jewish personality" in general terms (374). However, Patai in his survey of possible Jewish characteristics notes that the Jew "rationalizes and categorizes everything" (377) and he describes the German Jew using such adjectives as "punctual, meticulous, exacting, precise, and thorough" (386), and the Lithuanian Jew with labels such as "sharp-witted . . . stubborn, of a logical bent of mind, rational . . . and insistent on following all the minutiae of the commandments" (384). Obviously there is a danger here of confusing national or ethnic stereotypes with national or ethnic character. The difference is that national or ethnic character refers to the way a people actually are, whereas national or ethnic stereotypes refer to a way a people is perceived to be—either by themselves or by others. Far too often what purports to be an objective delineation of national character turns out to be little more than an exercise in stereotypy. And it is certainly true that it is hard to avoid the problem of perception, whether it is self-perception or perception by others. Perception inevitably entails bias of some kind. There is, to be sure, always the possibility of some overlap. In other words, some features of a stereotype may coincide with actual personality features, even if the stereotype representations are articulated with exaggeration and caricature. In any event, the alleged features listed by Patai for the German and Lithuanian Jews are not inconsistent with the characterological portrait of anal erotic character delineated by Freud, Jones, and Abraham, among others.

The first adjective listed by Patai in his description of the German Jew is "punctual." Dooley (1941, 19–20) discussed a connection between an excessive concern with time and anal erotic character (Fischer and Juni 1981, 61; Mollinger 1980, 471). Just as there is a feces-money equation, so there may be a feces-time equation. One may be accused of "wasting" or squandering time, or being unduly worried about "saving" time (Abraham 1953, 384; Fenichel 1999, 282). In colloquial English, one speaks of "making" time or "passing" time or "passing the time of day." Passing can also refer to acts of anal expulsion such as "passing wind." Certainly, there are clues indicating that Jews are very much concerned with time. Being on time or in time to begin the Sabbath is a case in point. Sabbath preparations must be in place prior to exactly eighteen minutes before sunset on Fridays.

Are there any features of Sabbath regulations that can be said to be directly related to anal topics? One such Sabbath rule is as follows: "A chamber pot may be emptied after use. If the chamber-pot . . . is made of material other than metal or plastic, one should not bring it back to its place after emptying—even if it is clean—unless one is still holding it in one's hand or one puts into it water which is fit to be drunk at least by an animal" (Neuwirth 1989, 293). The fact that one is permitted to handle and remove a chamber pot on the Sabbath provides a convenient metaphor for rabbinical discussions of the disposal of other items. For example, in the Babylonian Talmud, the questions of how to handle dirty plates or the pits of Aramaean dates is answered, "By analogy to a pot of shit" (Neusner 1992–1993, IId, 133; IIe, 83). In other words, it was permitted to remove the dirty plates and to spit out the pits or throw them behind the couch.

One woman complains about the number of Sabbath rules: "Of course there are rules about everything you can think of. There are even rules about what you may think about when you are sitting on the toilet" (Kaye 1987, 17). According to a passage in the Shabbat tractate of the Babylonian Talmud, "In any place it is permitted to conceive an unarticulated thought of Torah except in the bathhouse and toilet" (Neusner 1992–1993, IIe, 114).

In modern times, it is forbidden to erect a partition on the Sabbath, but a partition may be "put around a hospital bed because the presence of uncovered excrement would otherwise prevent the patient from praying or studying Torah" (Neuwirth 1989, 357). However, the partition cannot be opened on the Sabbath unless it has been previously unrolled prior to the Sabbath at least the distance of one *tefach*, a measure of length either 3.15 or 3.8 inches (Neuwirth 1989, 647, 698). A person who is ill should not pray or put on phylacteries in a place where there may be excrement, an uncovered bedpan or the like and it is better not to pray or put on phylacteries at all rather than to do so under such conditions (673). If a folding screen is placed between two hospital beds in a ward, "a patient may subsequently say his prayers, taking advantage of the fact that the screen divides between him and uncovered excrement on the opposite side (as long as the odor does not reach him)" (359–360). Since a person's body must be "clean" when wearing phylacteries, a person suffering from a stomach disorder who cannot control his bowel movements is not allowed to put them on (673; Ganzfried 1961, 1, 33).

A curious contemporary circumvention reported by Kolatch (1995, 232) illustrates the critical importance of keeping any religious activity entirely separate from a place where there may be excrement. Orthodox or observant Jews who take long flights have the possibility of requesting special, that is, kosher, meals. Many airlines offer this option to their Jewish passengers. Accompanying the meal may be a cellophane-wrapped hamburger-type roll with the word *mezonot* printed on it. The word literally means "provisions, food, nourishment," but it is also the name of the prayer recited when one eats food other than bread. Kolatch notes that the word on the wrapper "tells the observant Jew that the roll is not considered bread and that the Hamotzi blessing normally said over bread need not be recited" (1985, 232). Since bread is not being served, the Jewish law that requires a ritual washing of the hands before a meal is inapplicable. "One is not required to wash before eating a meal at which no bread is served" (322). Kolatch remarks that the rabbinic authorities responsible for supervising the kosher meals served by airlines have used the *mezonot* label as a "legal fiction of sorts" because if bread were served, an observant Jew would be obliged to leave his seat in order to wash his hands before eating, but the real difficulty would be because "the only place to wash would be in the lavatory, which would be improper." The proximity of the small sink to the toilet in the plane's cramped lavatory would make a proper ritual cleansing of the hands impossible.

There is a Yiddish proverb that does more than hint that the act of defecation must be kept well apart from any devout religious behavior. "*Kaken is (beim chason) noch far dem dawenen*," which can be rendered "Shitting (in the case of a cantor) must come before davening [praying]." This means that everyone, and especially a cantor, must take care to empty his bowels before praying (Bernstein 1969, 344). A passage in Ecclesiastes (5:1) has been interpreted in much the same way. "Keep thy foot when thou goest to the house of God" supposedly "refers to the orifices that are near the legs." Accordingly, "before praying, it is the duty of every man to ascertain whether he needs to respond to the call of nature. Even if he feels the slightest need for it, he is forbidden to pray or to study the Torah, as long as his body remains impure" (Ganzfried 1961, 1: 39–40).

In one of the documents included in the Dead Sea Scrolls called the Temple Scroll, perhaps dating from the second century B.C.E. (Vermes 1998, 206), there is included in a detailed discussion of "laws of purity" (Yadin 1983, 277–343) an account of how and where to construct latrines: "You shall make for them latrines outside the city where they shall go out, northwest of the city. These shall be roofed houses with holes in them into which the filth shall go down. It shall be far enough not to be visible from the city, (at) least three thousand cubits" (Vermes 1998, 206; Yadin 1983, 294). Inasmuch as one of the most ancient Sabbath rules contained in the Damascus Document insists that a man "shall not walk more than one thousand cubits beyond his town" (Vermes 1998, 139; Kimbrough 1966, 489), one wonders how an observant Jew could reach a latrine located three thousand cubits from the city. Even with the increased allowance amounting to two thousand rather than one thousand cubits as suggested in Numbers (35:5), it would appear that the problem remains. Presumably, there must have been some type of circumvention permitted, even if it has not been recorded in written form. There has even been some question as to whether observant Jews left their homes at all on the Sabbath (Rosenthal 1961, 13). If that were the case, that is, that Jews could not leave their dwellings on the Sabbath, then the location of the latrines issue is moot. Exodus would tend to support the idea that Jews must remain inside their homes: "See, for that the Lord hath given you the Sabbath, therefore he giveth you on the sixth day the bread of two days: abide ye every man in his place, let no man go out of his place on the seventh day" (16:29).

A curious bit of ethnographic data reported by Josephus may be relevant here. Josephus, who considered the Sabbath as a "barometer of piety" (Weiss 1998, 365, 381), gives a fairly detailed account of the lifestyle of the Essenes, a group of Jews he claims "profess a severer discipline" than the Pharisees and the Sadducees (1981, 133). Speaking of the Essenes' Sabbath habits, Josephus notes:

> They abstain from seventh-day work more rigidly than any other Jews; for not only do they prepare their meals the previous day so as to avoid lighting a fire on the Sabbath, but they do not venture to remove any utensil or to go and ease themselves. On other days they dig a hole a foot deep with their trenching-tool . . . and draping their cloak round them so as not to affront the rays of the god, they squat over it; then they put the excavated soil back in the hole. On these occasions they choose the more secluded spots; and though emptying the bowels is quite natural, they are taught to wash after it, as if it defiled them. (1981, 136)

One may well wonder if Josephus's ethnography is accurate. Weiss points out (1998, 385) that "digging a little hole in an isolated spot and refilling it over one's excrement" involves "three problematic activities: traveling to an isolated spot, digging and shoveling" each of which would constitute a Sabbath transgression. Still, the accuracy of Josephus's ethnographic account is partially substantiated by an archaeological report of the apparent discovery in 1956 of the "trenching tool" (De Vaux 1959), as well as a passage in Deuteronomy, although the reference to defecation is couched somewhat euphemistically:

> "Thou shalt have a place also without the camp, whither thou shalt go forth abroad: And thou shalt have a paddle upon thy weapon; and it shall be, when thou wilt ease thyself abroad, thou shalt dig therewith, and shalt turn back and cover that which cometh from thee: For the Lord thy God walketh in the midst of thy camp, to deliver thee, and to give up thine enemies before thee; therefore shall thy camp be holy: that he see no unclean thing in thee, and turn away from thee." (Deut. 23:12–14)

The implication is that God would be mortally offended if he found feces in camp and would "turn away" from the guilty miscreant. Here we are reminded of an insight of Freud made evidently without reference to either the Bible or Jewish custom: "The man who is not clean, i.e., who does not eliminate his excretions, therefore offends others, shows no consideration for them" (1957, 67n1). A formulaic tripartite passage in the Mishnah, repeated in the Babylonian Talmud, would seem to confirm the threat posed by uncovered feces: "They cover a lamp with a dish so that it will not scorch a rafter; and the excrement of a child; and a scorpion, so that it will not bite" (Neusner 1988, 199; 1992–1993, IId, 59). Although the particular danger emanating from uncovered feces is not specified, the parallelism of the rhetoric surely implies that it is something highly negative (e.g., analogous to having a rafter burned and being bitten by a scorpion). Neusner suggests parenthetically that it is only the fear that the defecating child will become defiled by his own feces (1992–1993, IId, 122), but this appears to be little more than an educated guess.

The idea that God might be offended or insulted by being forced to be in the presence of feces may very well explain why Moses was asked to take off his shoes before approaching God in the burning bush episode. God told Moses, "Draw not nigh hither: put off thy shoes from off thy feet; for the place whereon thou standest is holy ground" (Exod. 3:5). A similar incident occurs when Joshua approached a representative of God. After Joshua asked, " 'What saith my lord unto his servant?' And the captain of the Lord's host said unto Joshua, 'Loose thy shoe from off thy foot; for the place whereon thou standest is holy.' And Joshua did so" (Josh. 5:14–15). No explanation is given for this shoe removal order, but it could very well be that since shoes are in direct contact with the earth that may be covered with impurities such as feces, these "dirty" shoes must be removed so as not to defile holy ground.

The same sort of rationale may underlie a statement made by biologist Lewin: "In reading Hebrew scriptures aloud, one is instructed to pronounce neither the Hebrew word for God (*Yahveh*, our Lord) nor that for dung, but should substitute conventional alternatives in order to avoid offending the sensitivities of listeners, if not God" (1999, 5). Many readers will be familiar with the taboo nature of the Tetragrammaton, the four letters, usually transliterated as YHVH, which are not supposed to be uttered. In its place, one is supposed to substitute "Adonai" or "Elohim." Another option is "HaShem," which means "the Name." But they may or may not be aware of the fact that this substitution is part of a longstanding traditional system in which "what is written" (*Kethib*) is not pronounced but replaced by alternative words, often euphemisms, termed "what is read" (*Qere*). So a Hebrew word *har-eihem*, meaning "shit" or "turd" is replaced by a less harsh word *tso'atam*, meaning "filth" or "uncleanness" (Gordis 1937, 167n4). (This is the case, for example, in 2 Kings 18:27, a passage involving the eating of dung, which is repeated in Isaiah 36:12.) This discrepancy between what is written and what is spoken is the opposite of the usual relationship between written and oral tradition. Normally, it is the oral tradition that is uncensored and often crude, while the written tradition is typically expurgated and euphemistic.

With regard to the Sabbath prohibition against writing, one could make a case for an anal component. Writing, that is, putting ink on paper can be construed as a symbolic representation of the act of defecation. The academic formula for success is the proverbial "publish or perish," which may be nothing more than a metaphorical transformation of "shit or get off the pot." Certainly, young academics in the United States seeking tenure are urged to "produce" and to do so "regularly." They are advised not to "sit" on their material, but to get something into print. In this context, writer's block may be nothing more than a form of mental constipation. By the same token, an author's pleasure in seeing his or her work in print is a sublimated form of looking into the toilet after defecation to see what he or she has produced (cf. Jones 1961, 425, 432; Heimann 1962, 411).

The offensive nature of feces is also implicit in the regulations governing the imposition of capital punishment according to the Mishnah. There were four means of carrying out the death penalty, which, listed in order of severity, consist of stoning, burning, decapitation, and strangulation. Instructions for the execution ritual for both burning and strangulation began with "They would bury him in manure up to his armpits" (Neusner 1988, 596).

Returning to Josephus's account, there are two important points. First, it would appear that on the Sabbath, the Essenes did not leave their homes to defecate, this in contrast to other days of the week when they customarily went out to dig an appropriate hole in the ground. Second, according to Josephus, these Jews regarded the contents of their bowels as defiling, so much so that they felt obliged to wash themselves after the act of defecation. The very fact that Josephus bothered to report such a detail in such a fashion suggests that he himself did not regard it necessary to wash after an act of defecation. As for the statement claiming that the Essenes refrained from relieving themselves on the Sabbath, the distinguished Israeli archaeologist Yigael Yadin hypothesized: "They evidently trained themselves, or ate special foods, to enable them to have no recourse to a privy on the Sabbath" (1985, 179). Others have speculated in similar fashion: "Any Jew who refused to defile the camp or break the Sabbath would find it necessary to schedule his consumption so that elimination on the Sabbath was not necessary" (Buchanan 1963, 400). The implied ability to refrain from defecating is referred to in a quite remarkable passage in the Shabbat tractate of the Babylonian Talmud. The allusion is to Rabbi Hanan bar Raba who is quoted: "But lo, Raba is the one who said, 'More numerous are those killed by holding in their shit than by those who died of starvation'? Raba is exceptional, for rabbis forced him against his will [to hold in his shit] because of the fixed times set for his lectures" (Neusner 1992–1993, IIa, 119). The clear implication is that a religious activity (e.g., rabbinical lectures) takes precedence over the need to defecate. This would then seem to be parallel to the Essenes refraining from defecating on the Sabbath. Even if one could defecate on the Sabbath, as was evidently the case with Jews less rigid than the Essenes, there appear to have been other restrictions. According to the Babylonian Talmud, "It is forbidden on the Sabbath to take a shit in a ploughed field" and "It is forbidden to wipe oneself with a sherd on the Sabbath" (Neusner 1992–1993, IIc, 62).

There is one additional piece of ethnographic data that might be germane to the Josephus account of the Essenes' apparent abstention from defecating on the Sabbath. Almost two millennia later at the beginning of the twenty-first century, we learn that some ultra-Orthodox Jews in Israel do not flush their toilets on the Sabbath as evidently the act of pulling a lever or chain is construed as work. There is also the issue of water and its contents flowing from a private to a public domain (Zivotofsky 1995, 125). As far as one can tell, defecation is permitted on the Sabbath—why else would one bother to pretear toilet paper in anticipation of that event? What is not permitted is the flushing of a toilet, a prohibition that has the unfortunate consequence of causing an unpleasant smell to emanate from the bathroom during the Sabbath. Still, a bad odor is evidently preferable to violating the Sabbath by flushing the toilet. In the rabbinical discussion of this question, some authorities have contended that flushing a toilet on the Sabbath is not a problem (Neuwirth 1989, 332; Zivotofsky 1995, 125n105).

If there is any validity to the psychoanalytic claim that "reaction formation is one of the favorite defenses of the Orthodox Jew" (Strean 1994, 155), then we are better positioned to understand why among the hundreds of rituals set down for Orthodox Jews, the ones entailing cleanliness are the most numerous (21). Let's be clear about the reasoning here. Freud noted in *Civilization and Its Discontents* that "The impulse towards cleanliness originates in the striving to get rid of excretions which have become unpleasant to the sense-perceptions" (1957, 66n1). If it is true that anal erotics seek to suppress their initial fixation on feces by becoming compulsively obsessive about cleanliness, then it is not illogical to work backward and assume that a person or persons who evinces a fanatic concern with cleanliness, say by indulging in excessive hand washing, may possess elements of anal erotic character. Let us entertain another highly speculative hypothesis. If there is a money-feces symbolic equation, then the taboo against touching money on the Sabbath might be a sublimated form of not touching feces on the Sabbath.

Even psychiatrists hostile to psychoanalytic theory who consider the notion of "anal-erotic character" to be part of Freudian "mythology" do list "filth" as the first of the most recurrent themes of obsessive behavior and remark on the tendency of obsessives toward "excessive cleanliness" often manifested in repeated hand washing (Lewis 1936, 14–16). While there is apparently no formal medical term for compulsive or ritual hand washing (Lewis 1997), this behavior has long been recognized as an extremely common symptom of obsessional neurosis. In an extended twenty-month case study of a compulsive hand-washer, Goldman described a woman who whenever she thought she had been "soiled" or "contaminated" would wash and scrub her hands, face, and mouth for hours until the skin was sore and red. "Her earliest handwashing, at the age of eight, was associated with a scrupulous regard for the orthodox Jewish religious observances" (Goldman 1938, 101). The woman was also a compulsive prayer. At bedtime, "she had evolved a prayer, which she had to repeat over and over, compulsively, for a period varying from a few minutes to an hour" (100).

In Orthodox Jewish manuals, we are told that children who have reached the age of five or so "should be trained to wash their hands upon rising in the morning" and "Children who wake up during the night and wish to eat or drink must wash their hands (three times on each hand), before eating or drinking" (Cohen 1993, 14–15). In ancient Judaism, hand washing was an important ritual practice (Poirier 1996), and it seems doubtful that a concern about hygiene as a means of not contracting an infectious disease was the primary motivating factor. In Psalm 18, we read "The Lord rewarded me, according to my righteousness; according to the cleanness of my hands hath he recompensed me" (20; also 18:24). It is also curious that the word "hand" is the literal translation of the Hebrew word used in the Bible "for a privy, latrine or lavatory" (Yadin 1985, 178).

Anyone who takes the trouble to read the final lengthy section of the Mishnah, which is a detailed consideration of what are termed "Purities" (Neusner 1988, 893–1137), or *The Book of Cleanness* by Maimonides (1135–1204) cannot possibly doubt the Jews' extreme concern with distinguishing what is "clean" and what is "unclean." It has been pointed out that "Nearly 25% of the laws of the Mishna are related to ritual purity" (Harrington 1993, 35, 178), while Neusner contends that "purity is an essential element in the interpretation of Israel's total religious system over sixteen centuries" (1972, 28; cf. Newton 1985). Milgrom states in no uncertain terms, "Impurity is the most pervasive factor in the cultic laws of the Bible" (1984, 103). The extreme concern with purity and cleanness is by no means confined to the Bible and continues to be a factor in contemporary Jewish life. A personal reminiscence from Leo Rosten's childhood may suffice to demonstrate the abiding preoccupation with cleanliness: "I was greatly impressed as a child, by the obsession with cleanliness in our household, and the scorn with which untidiness was castigated. Cleanliness was not second to godliness; it was second to nothing" (1970, 30). Rosten reports a joke that pokes fun at such an obsession in which two Jews discuss their wives: "My wife is such a great *baleboosteh* [excellent but bossy housekeeper] boasted Frackman, "that she vacuums every room every day and puts a completely clean, empty bag in the Hoover [vacuum cleaner] every night!" "Humph," said Kolchak, "I've got a wife who, whenever I get up in the middle of the night to go to the bathroom, changes the sheets" (1992, 58). In a similar vein, "Have I got a sanitary wife! A real fanatic! She's the only woman in all New York who washes the garbage before taking it outside!" (Spaulding 1969, 149).

It is surely no accident that perhaps the most famous classic joke poking fun at Talmudic reasoning concerns the distinction between coming down a chimney clean and coming down a chimney dirty (Jacobson 1976). Usually, the joke begins with a Catholic priest begging a rabbi to teach him the mechanics of Talmudic reasoning. In Rosten's version, it is the anti-Semitic Nazi Goebbels who occupies the place of the priest:

> Goebbels, the Nazi Minister of Propaganda, came to an elderly rabbi and said, "Jew! I have heard that you Jews employ a special form of reasoning, called Talmudic, which explains your cleverness. I want you to teach it to me."
>
> "Ah, Herr Goebbels," the old rabbi sighed. "I fear you are a little too old for that."
>
> "Nonsense! Why?"
>
> "Well, when a Jewish boy wishes to study *Talmud* we first give him an examination. It consists of three questions. Those lads who answer the questions correctly are admitted to the study of the *Talmud*; those who can't, are not."
>
> "Excellent," said Goebbels. "Give me the exam!"
>
> The old rabbi shrugged. "Very well. The first question: Two men fall down a chimney. One emerges filthy, covered with soot; the other emerges clean. Which one of them washes?"
>
> Goebbels scoffed, "The dirty one, of course!"
>
> "Wrong. The clean one."
>
> "The *clean* one washes?" asked Goebbels in astonishment, "Why?"
>
> "Because as soon as the two men emerge from the chimney, they look at each other, no? The dirty one, looking at the clean one, says to himself, 'Remark-

able—to fall down a chimney and come out clean!' But the clean one, looking at the dirty one, says to himself, 'We certainly got *filthy* coming down that chimney and I'll wash up at once.' So it is the clean one who washes, not the dirty one."

"Ah," nodded Goebbels. "Very clever! Let's have the second question."

"The second question," sighed the rabbi, "is this: Two men fall down a chimney. One emerges filthy, covered with soot, the other emerges clean. Which—"

"That's the same question!" exclaimed Goebbels.

"No, no, Herr Goebbels, excuse me. This is a different question."

"Very well. You won't fool me, Jew. The one who's clean washes!"

"Wrong," sighed the elder.

"But you just told me—"

"That was an entirely different problem, Herr Goebbels. In this one, the *dirty* man washes—because, as before, the two men look at each other. The one who is clean looks at the dirty one and says, 'My! How dirty I must be!' But he looks at his hands and he sees that he is *not* dirty. The dirty man, on the other hand, looks at the clean one and says, 'Can it be? To fall down a chimney and emerge so clean? Am I clean?' So he looks at his hands and sees that *he* is filthy; so he, the dirty one, washes, naturally."

Goebbels nodded. "Clever, Jew; very clever. Now, the third question?"

"Ah, the third question," sighed the rabbi, "is the most difficult of all. Two men fall down a chimney. One emerges clean, the other—"

"But that's the same question!"

"No, Herr Goebbels. The *words* may be the same, but the problem is an entirely new one."

"The dirty one washes!" exclaimed Goebbels.

"Wrong."

"The clean one!"

"Wrong."

"Then what is the answer?" Goebbels shouted.

"The answer," said the rabbi, "is that this is a silly examination. *How* can two men fall down the same chimney and one emerge dirty and the other clean? Anyone who can't see that will never be able to understand *Talmud*." (Rosten 1970, 396–397; for other versions, see Levenson 1946, 51–53; Spaulding 1969, 19–20; Telushkin 1992, 47–48.)

The questioning of the initial premise of the joke is typical of Talmudic reasoning. A short joke included by Freud in his lecture in 1915 to the Vienna chapter of B'nai Brith illustrates this tendency (Freud 1993, 16–17): A son falls off a ladder and lies unconscious. The boy's mother runs to the Rabbi to seek help and advice. "Tell me," asks the Rabbi, "how does a Jewish child come to be on a ladder in the first place?" The rabbi's response shows just how utterly useless such Talmudic logic can be in a time of actual life-

and-death crisis. The chimney joke, however, is of special interest since it ostensibly involves the effort to remain clean in a dirty situation.

Biblical scholars have not failed to comment on what appears to be an obsession with "cleanliness" and "purity" (Paschen 1970; Milgrom 1993; Neusner 1994; Maccoby 1999), but thus far they have been unable to explain it. The best they can do is to suggest that the apparent concern for avoiding contact with "bodily discharges" such as excrement and menstrual blood is nothing more than a desire to avoid contact with a symbolic representation of death (Milgrom 1993, 110). Speaking of death, blood, semen, and scale-disease (often mistranslated as leprosy), Milgrom maintains, "Their common denominator is death" (1984, 106). He is consistently certain that "impurity is symbolic of death" (1991, 924). Another authority calls death "the prototype of defilement" (Feldman 1977, 35). Similarly, Neusner in his extensive survey of "purity" in rabbinic Judaism makes this unequivocal statement, "The principal symbol and generative source of uncleanness is the corpse" (1994, 54). In another articulation, Neusner claims "Uncleanness forms a metaphor for death" (53). Even more interesting is his statement, "The conception of death is that at death something leaves, exudes from, the body" (91).

According to these views of Milgrom and Neusner, fear of body products deemed as polluting is essentially a fear of death. Maccoby rightfully challenges this theory asking a pertinent question: "The theory, however, faces difficulty: in what way, for example, does the impurity caused by emission of semen, or by menstruation, or by childbirth, link with the concept of death?" (1999, 1). Certainly common sense would incline one toward the idea that semen and blood were logical symbols of life rather than death. Still, Mary Douglas, an anthropologist who has devoted much effort to the study of purity (1966), seems to agree with the position taken by Milgrom and Neusner when she says, "The underlying principle is that death and life are opposed." For Douglas, "The biblical idea of purity is simple and coherent. The nature of the living God is in opposition to dead bodies" (1993b, 23, 24), although she does make the comment that "God's violent reaction to impurity seems overdone" (22). Anna Meigs, another anthropologist, in her study of pollution in a society in the Eastern Highlands of Papua, New Guinea, offers a slight modification of this theory. According to Meigs, the revulsion felt by humans is caused by their perception of something "as rotting, decaying, or dying" (1978, 313, 316). But the association of polluting impurity with death remains. Even Freud who considered "pollution rules" (Carroll 1982) as part of his consideration of taboo in his *Totem and Taboo* linked it to fear of the demonic dead, who, in Freud's view, were essentially projections of deceased parents (1938, 854).

What all these scholars fail to realize is that death and feces are equivalent. Feces is the end product of the process beginning with the ingesting and digesting of food just as death is the end result of life. The process of putrefaction is involved in the transformation of food into feces, of a live body into a corpse. Purity implies an absence of putrefaction and that may be why unleavened bread is deemed so essential for Passover. Leaven causes fermentation, which, according to Milgrom (1991, 189) was construed as a symbol of "deterioration and death." The notion of "leaven" as a form of impurity is confirmed by Paul's metaphorical, if not proverbial, dictum "Know ye not that a little leaven leaveneth the whole lump? Purge out therefore the old leaven, that ye may be a new lump, as ye are unleavened" (1 Cor. 5:6–7). Similarly, scale disease (falsely identified as leprosy) could be understood as an instance of bodily putrescence. Certainly both corpses and feces produce unpleasant smells. Both corpses and feces are buried in the ground. Fenichel remarked on the corpse-feces equation in his paper "The Drive to Amass Wealth" first published in 1938 (1954, 105). The equation of corpses and dung is quite clearly stated in the Bible. "They shall die of grievous deaths; they shall not be lamented; neither shall they be buried; but they shall be as dung upon the face of the earth" (Jer. 16:4; cf. 25:33); "They shall not be gathered, nor be buried; they shall be for dung upon the face of the earth" (Jer. 8:2; cf. Ps. 83:10); "Even the carcasses of men shall fall as dung upon the open field" (Jer. 9:22). In Job, we find, "Yet he shall perish for ever like his own dung" (20:7).

There are also passages in the Berakot tractate of the Babylonian Talmud that suggest an equivalence of death and feces, or the acts of corpse burial and defecation. One of the restrictions governing the recitation of the Shema prayer is: "He who digs a burial niche for a corpse in a grave-area is exempt from the requirement to recite the Shema. . . . Once the time for reciting the Shema comes, he comes up [out of the hole], washes his hands, puts on his phylacteries, recites the Shema and says the Prayer." Another is: "He who wants to accept upon himself the yoke of the kingdom of Heaven in a full way should first empty his bowel, then wash his hands, put on his phylacteries, recite the Shema, and say the Prayer" (Neusner 1984, 115–116). The similarity in wording points to the equivalence of digging a grave for a corpse and defecating. Both require identical purification procedures. It is noteworthy that it seems to be a sin to pray to God with one's bowel's full. A passage confirming the necessity of washing before praying in the morning runs as follows: "The Morning Bathers say, 'We bring a charge against you,

O Pharisees, for pronouncing the Divine Name in the morning without prior immersion.' The Phariseees answer, 'We charge you, O Morning Bathers, with uttering the Name from a body containing impurity' " (Sanders 1990, 231).

Similarly, in a rabbinical discussion of the meaning of the phrase "The time of finding" which occurs in Psalm 32:6, one rabbi says " 'The time of finding' refers to burial" while another says " 'The time of finding' refers to finding a toilet" (Neusner 1984, 67). This pair of interpretations suggests an equivalence of burial and toilet that would further imply an equivalence of what is placed in graves and toilets, namely, corpses and feces.

It seems quite arbitrary to claim that fear of pollution is a mask for fear of death. It is not death that is feared, but contact with a corpse. One can be contaminated by contact with a corpse or contact with feces or menstrual blood. It is pollution or defilement or "uncleanness" that is feared. The undeniable emphasis on "clean" and "cleanliness," which borders on obsession, would seem to suggest an anal erotic origin, not a pathological fear of death. It is, in sum, the fear of contact with a defiling substance, not the fear of death, that is primary. In the clinical case of a compulsive hand-washer cited above, the analyst suggested that the function of the hand washing was not really to remove "contamination" but "rather to spread it." The reasoning employed by the analyst was that underlying the compulsion neurosis was a repressed urge. "Under the guise of attempting to remove the contamination, the patient was in reality playing with it, spreading all around dirt, faeces, death, carrying out her most primitive, infantile urges . . . the handwashing had become a substitute for playing with faeces" (Goldman 1938, 120). Similarly, the compulsive praying for the health of her family was, according to the analyst, a counteractant for the latent hostile death wishes toward members of her family. For this patient, the basic fear was allegedly of being contaminated or defiled by "faeces = death" (121).

Can one legitimately generalize about defiling substances? Does a clinical case history recorded in the twentieth century necessarily tell us anything useful about definitions of defiling substances centuries ago? Just what are defiling substances? In Islamic tradition, which is not all that different in this respect from Judaic tradition, "things from the interior of the body, things that have crossed the boundaries of the body, ought not to be outside the body; when they leave their place they become impure" (Reinhart 1990, 7). The only exceptions appear to be tears and mother's milk. Of these body products, it is surely excrement that is the most polluting of all. A body product from the interior once emitted from an orifice becomes instantly impure if not disgusting. It is structurally analogous or equivalent to the

Sabbath prohibition of moving from a private space to a public space, whether the private space be one's domicile or the extended space created by an *eruv*. Most defiling of all would be the reversal of direction such that an emitted body product was used either as fuel in cooking food or as an element in food. In Ezekiel, God orders a punishment for the straying children of Israel: "And thou shalt eat it as barley cakes, and thou shalt bake it with dung that cometh out of man, in their sight." And the Lord said, "Even thus shall the children of Israel eat their defiled bread among the Gentiles, whither I will drive them" (4:12–13).

There is even a passing reference seeming to suggest the ingestion of animal dung: "And there was a great famine in Samaria: and, behold, they besieged it, until an ass's head was sold for fourscore pieces of silver, and the fourth part of a cab of dove's dung for five pieces of silver" (2 Kings 6:25).

Another threat involving feces occurs when God declares his response to priests who insulted his name by offering "polluted bread" and impaired sacrificial animals on his altar: "Behold, I will corrupt your seed, and spread dung upon your faces, even the dung of your solemn feasts; and one shall take you away with it" (Mal. 2:3). If God uses dung as a means of punishment, he also helps the poor by lifting them out of dunghills: "He raiseth up the poor out of the dust, and lifteth the needy out of the dunghill" (Ps. 113:7; 1 Sam. 2:8). But the punishing use of dung is more dramatic. Consider a passage in Isaiah (repeated in 2 Kings): "But Rab sha-keh said, 'Hath my master sent me to thy master and to thee to speak these words? Hath he not sent me to the men that sit upon the wall that they may eat their own dung, and drink their own piss with you?' " (Isa. 36:12; cf. 2 Kings 18:27).

The threat of a divine punishment compelling men to eat their own dung and drink their own urine may strike the reader as being particularly disgusting and extreme. However, it may well be part of an ancient stratum of folk belief. In Egypt, during the Middle Kingdom, which began nearly two thousand years before the Common Era, some wealthy Egyptians were buried in large rectangular wooden coffins. Inscribed in ink on the inside walls of these coffins were apotropaic spells intended to ward off undesirable fates in the afterworld. Among approximately one thousand of these coffin texts transcribed by Egyptologists, quite a large number were concerned with not having to ingest feces or imbibe urine. Not atypical is Spell 173 in this corpus that begins:

> NOT TO EAT FAECES AND NOT TO DRINK URINE IN THE REALM OF THE DEAD. What I doubly detest, I will not eat. Faeces is my detestation, I will not eat it. Filth shall not enter into this mouth of mine, and I will not eat it with

> my mouth, I will not touch it with my finger, I will not tread on it with my toes, because I will not eat faeces for you, I will not drink urine for you. . . . I will not eat for you this filth which issued from the hinder parts of Osiris. (Faulkner 1973, 147)

Spell 174 includes, "My detestation is faeces, and I will not eat it. I will not smell it; urine, I will not drink it. I eat with my mouth, I defaecate with my anus" (Faulkner 1973, 150). This formulaic language is repeated again and again in spell after spell (138–175). The emphasis is on purity and cleanliness: "You are pure! Your front is in purity, your back parts are in cleanness" and "Impurities are my detestation, and I will never eat them, faeces being (cast away) behind the pleasant things which are in the shrine of the gods" (12, 163). There is no guarantee, of course, that these ancient Egyptian coffin texts are necessarily related to the biblical passage cited above, but on the other hand, they could well be. In any case, the connection between "impurities" and "eating" and the longstanding concern for "clean" foods as part of the elaborate Jewish dietary taboos could, in theory, also stem from an anal erotic base.

One of the most prominent of these dietary taboos has to do with the prohibition against eating pork. There has been a vast scholarship devoted to this matter (Milgrom 1991, 649–653), but most of the theories purporting to explicate the underlying rationale seem quite specious. The modern idea, for example, that the taboo stemmed from a hygienic folk preventive medical practice to avoid contracting trichinosis, a disease caused by ingesting the *Trichinella spiralis*, a parasitic nematode often found in undercooked pork, is obviously a post hoc hypothesis. One of the modern experts on food taboos in a long chapter on pork avoidance totally rejects this hypothesis as a possibility (Simoons 1961, 37–39).

A clue as to the real reason for the taboo is suggested in a passage in Isaiah when idolators are castigated for "eating swine's flesh . . . and the mouse" (Isa. 66:17). What, if anything, could a pig and a mouse possibly have in common that would make them off-limits as a food item? The answer could be that they both can be observed eating feces, human or animal in origin. If a pig eats feces, then eating pork would mean eating an animal that ate feces. (That the pig has been observed eating feces is attested by a Yiddish proverb: "The pig swore that he doesn't eat shit" [Kumove 1985, 122].) And that would mean, in effect, that the eater of pork was an eater of feces. We have already seen from the passages cited above that eating feces is considered the ultimate despicable, disgusting act, which is why God reserves it as a punishment for those who disrespect him. As for the linkage between a pig eating feces and Jews being defiled by eating pig, we find that gross image depicted in the anti-Semitic *Judensau* (Jew-pig) iconographic image found throughout German-speaking Europe from the thirteenth century to the present day (Dundes 1989, 121). In that image, a Jew is shown suckling from a pig that is eating feces or in some instances, the Jew is placed beneath the pig's tail about to ingest the pig's feces.

There is also more ancient evidence from the Near East suggesting the association between pigs and feces. In a Hittite document entitled "Instructions for Temple Officials," we find the following: "If a pig (or) a dog somehow approaches the implements of wood or bitumen which you have, and the kitchen servant does not discard it, but gives the god to eat from an unclean (vessel), to such a man the gods will give dung (and) urine to eat (and) to drink" (Pritchard 1969, 209). (The Hittite allusion to a divine punishment consisting of making a sinner eat dung and drink urine confirms the pattern in the ancient Egyptian coffin inscriptions noted above.) Both animals, pigs and dogs, are known to eat feces. The propensity of dogs to eat what is normally considered to be unpalatable is celebrated in a well-known proverb: "As a dog returneth to his vomit, so a fool returneth to his folly" (Prov. 26:11), an image which is repeated in the New Testament: "But it is happened unto them according to the true proverb, The dog is turned to his own vomit again; and the sow that was washed to her wallowing in the mire" (2 Pet. 2:22). Even modern observers of canine behavior can attest to the sniffing greeting etiquette whereby one dog's nose is placed in close proximity to another's anus. In any event, the sense of the Hittite instruction would appear to imply that the very touching of cooking vessels or serving dishes by such unclean animals as pigs and dogs will perforce contaminate, through negative contagious magic, the food offering to the deity (Milgrom 1991, 676). What is of significant import is the particular punishment imposed by the offended god. To such an impious individual, "the gods will give dung (and) urine to eat (and) to drink." It is possibly an instance of "Lex talionis," such that a man who offers pig feces, albeit indirectly, to a deity will be punished by that deity's forcing the man to eat feces.

Incidentally, the notion that a mouse might be impure because it eats fecal material might possibly explain why certain birds were classified as off-limits in terms of diet. Milgrom remarks that the Hoopoe was considered an abomination because of its "dirty habits" (1991, 662), because it "feeds on dunghills" (664; Bulmer 1989, 315). But he offers no plausible explanation for why the eagle, the vulture, the kite, falcons, and owls (Lev. 11:13–19) should be considered unclean other than the fact that they are raptors that consume carrion. Could it be that they are impure because they eat mice and other rodents, which are in direct contact with feces? Bulmer observes that the Hebrews "must have regarded as unclean those small creatures that could readily be contaminated by contact with the unclean products of human activity and with places rendered unclean by human action; and it must follow from this that predators that conspicuously fed upon such creatures should be unclean" (1989, 314). If this is so, then perhaps the distinction between insects that creep and crawl on the ground and those that fly might be seen in a new light (Milgrom 1991, 665). Creatures that crawl on the earth are more likely to come into contact with fecal material than creatures that fly. "And every creeping thing that creepeth upon the earth shall be an abomination; it shall not be eaten" (Lev. 11:41). Rodents and reptiles that remain close to the ground cannot easily avoid touching feces, either those of human origin or those produced by other animals. It is tempting to speculate that a possible reason for the taboo against shellfish is that most mollusks, shrimp, and lobsters are found on the mud bottoms of the sea, ingesting their food, mostly detritus, from that source, as opposed to fish with scales that swim freely well above the mud bottom. In other words, edible fish with scales would be analogous to flying insects, which Milgrom (665) says can be eaten, while shellfish would be analogous to earth-bound insects and other creatures that creep and crawl on the dirty ground. Some Jews even go so far as to refer to the seafood to be avoided as being "bottom feeders" and "scavenger fish" (Diamond 2000, 114). Needless to say, this is a vastly different explanation of why shellfish are taboo from that offered by anthropologist Mary Douglas who inexplicably claimed that such "crawlers" stood for "victims of predation" or poor people treated unjustly (1993, 18, 22). But the explanation proposed here would certainly explain why incorporating "any creeping thing that creepeth" might be thought to defile the body (Lev. 11:43). It would be analogous to the likely rationale underlying the pork dietary restriction. Eating a shit-eating creature, whether it lived on land or under the sea, would be tantamount to eating shit!

It may be of interest to speculate that Jesus himself seems to compare the dangers of defilement by ingestion (e.g., of food) with the dangers of defilement of by excretion. "There is nothing from without a man, that entering into him can defile him: but the things which come out of him, those are they that defile the man" (Mark 7:15). Apparently, his disciples failed to understand his remark so he repeated it: "And he saith unto them, 'Are ye so without understanding also? Do ye not perceive, that whatsoever thing from without entereth into the man, it cannot defile him; Because it entereth not into his heart, but into the belly, and goeth out into the draught, purging all meats?' . . . And he said, 'That which cometh out of the man, that defileth the man' " (Mark 7:18–20). Now it is true that Jesus goes on to say that it is murder, covetousness, blasphemy, and other such sins that constitute the "evil things" that "come from within and defile the man" (Mark 7:21–23), but the basic metaphor with its direct reference to the digestion process is certainly suggestive in the present context. (For a discussion of this passage, see Booth 1986; Maccoby 1999, 155–161.)

Still, with all the pages and pages of the Bible devoted to concerns with purity and cleanness as opposed to uncleanness, there are relatively few explicit references to feces. Menstrual blood and other body emissions from the genital area such as semen, gonorrheally generated fluids, or blood from a parturient female are mentioned (Harrington 1993, 216), often in great detail (e.g., in Leviticus), but discussions of excrement are conspicuously absent. This has led some Bible scholars to claim that feces is not defiling. "The excreta involved in the digestive process . . . are not mentioned as polluting. Defecation is supposed to take place outside the ideal camp . . . but individuals excreting or even touching feces are not considered defiled until evening nor is it prescribed that they must bathe" (Frymer-Kensky 1983, 401). Milgrom, in response to the question of why the Bible fails to label human feces impure, offers the following: "The answer is clear. The elimination of waste has nothing to do with death; on the contrary, it is essential to life" (1991, 767). Harrington, in her thorough study of impurity, makes the unequivocal statement, "Excrement is not impure in the priestly or rabbinic systems" (1993, 25). According to another authority: "It is clear that excretion, unlike emission of semen, is not defiling in the ritual purity sense, for no ritual washing, or waiting until the evening is prescribed for it. Nor is it said anywhere in the Torah that either excrement or urine themselves cause ritual impurity by contact or any other means" (Maccoby 1999, 64–65). Common sense suggests these inferences are counterintuitive. On the contrary, it is much more reasonable to assume that feces is considered defiling in some sense in virtually all human societies. How then to explain the lack of scriptural reference to feces?

One anthropologist has remarked on this lack. "Presumably, like every other human population, the Hebrews had culturally prescribed rules regarding defecation and the disposal of human faeces, but there is hardly any reference to these in the Old Testament. . . . Yet it is inconceivable, for example that defecation was permitted in close proximity to the tabernacle!" (Bulmer 1989, 310). His explanation for the lack of any articulation of such rules: "What was deemed dirty in everyday terms (e.g., human excrement) was *ipso facto* a source of 'ritual uncleanness,' so obviously so that this did not need in most circumstances to be spelt out" (305). Several others have suggested that excrement was regarded as impure in ancient Judaism (Neyrey 1968, 101, 103), but the majority of biblical scholars would disagree with that claim (Harrington 1993, 25).

But the question remains: Can the absence per se of rules governing defecation be in any way significant? A possible answer lies in the possibility that overt references to feces in the Bible were suppressed or repressed. If that were the case, then it would be more understandable why the taboo against even mentioning the word "dung" aloud might be related to a near-fanatic concern with cleanliness and purity.

Actually, the Talmud, as opposed to the Bible, is not nearly so squeamish. In the Shabbat tractate of the Babylonian Talmud, we find details concerning the size and number of pebbles one was permitted to take to a latrine to function as toilet paper. The prescribed size was that "of an olive, a nut, and an egg" and "On the Sabbath it is permitted to take along three rounded pebbles into the privy" (Neusner 1992–1993, IIc, 60). If one selects a pebble on which grass has sprouted, one can use it for toilet paper on the Sabbath as long as one does not take the grass off the pebble (62). A person who fails to defecate is said to smell: "He who has to take a shit but doesn't do it" evokes two separate rabbinical judgments: "He smells like a fart" and "He smells like shit" (63). This would appear to refer to a person who intentionally suppresses his need to defecate: "He who has to take a shit but goes on eating is like an oven that is heated up on top of its ashes, and that is the beginning of b.o. [body odor]" (63). The recommended behavior is to defecate before eating: "He who comes into a house to take regular meal should first walk ten lengths of four cubits—others say, four of ten—and take a shit and then go in and sit in his regular place" (64).

A person who willfully refuses to defecate is one thing. A person who is constipated is quite another. The Babylonian Talmud in its zeal for detail offers some helpful tips for "He who has to take a shit but can't": "Let him stand up and sit down again, stand up and sit down again. . . . Let him shift from side to side" and "Let him fiddle around with a pebble on the anus." A testimonial to the efficacy of these techniques is also included: "I myself saw a Tai-Arab stand up and sit down over and over again, until the shit came out of him as from a pitcher" (Neusner 1992–1993, IIc, 64).

In the Berakhot tractate of the Babylonian Talmud, for example, we find numerous rules forbidding the reciting of the Shema in the presence of excrement. "If a man was standing [and reciting] the Prayer and saw excrement nearby, he should walk forward until it is left four cubits behind him" (Neusner 1984, 166). "He who has to defecate should not say the Prayer. And if, in that condition, he said the Prayer, his Prayer is an abomination" (167).

In a discussion of the latter rule, it is stated that if a person can "hold himself in," the recitation of the Prayer is valid (Ganzfried 1961, 1: 40). There seems to be rabbinical disagreement as to whether it is or is not permissible to recite the Shema "if there is excrement on one's body" (Neusner 1984, 178). As for what to do in the case of excrement passing by in a dung cart, there is again disagreement with one authority stating, "It is permitted to recite the *Shema* [while the stench is going by]" and one indicating that "It is forbidden to recite the *Shema*" (178–179). "A person should not recite the *Shema* in the presence of excrement of man, dogs, pigs, chickens, or of a garbage dump that stinks" (178). The question of the presence of a chamber pot is also raised. "As to a chamber pot for excrement and piss-pot, it is forbidden to recite the *Shema* in their presence, and that is the case even though there is nothing in them" (184).

Chapter 4, "Rules of Decency," and chapter 5, "Cleanness of Places Used for Holy Purposes," in the authoritative *Code of Jewish Law*, compiled by Rabbi Solomon Ganzfried, are quite explicit on these matters. "While in the lavatory, it is forbidden to think of sacred matters. . . . One should be careful to wipe oneself thoroughly, for should even a trace of feces cling to the body, one is not permitted to utter a holy word. . . . If there is excrement on any part of one's body, although it is covered with one's garments, one is not allowed to utter anything that is holy. . . . If there is but a small particle of excrement in the anal orifice, although it is covered, all agree that the covering is of no avail, because excrement in its original place is more loathsome" (1961, 1: 8–9). Even the smell of feces is sufficient to curtail religious activity. "If one had let wind, one is forbidden to utter anything holy until bad odor had ceased; the same applies to a case where the bad odor had issued from his neighbor" (1: 10).

The modern equivalent of these restrictions has to do with dirty diapers. According to one authority, "The area in which one recites a *brocha* must be free of waste substances even if an odor does not emanate from them. . . . If the waste product is behind the individual or to his side, and is not emitting an odor, he may recite a *brocha*, provided he is at least seven feet away from the substance. However, a *brocha* may not be recited while facing waste substances (even if there is no odor), unless they are beyond the range of vision" (Cohen 1993, 25). Since dirty diapers worn by a child three months of age or older are considered "waste," one must "refrain from reciting a *brocha* near a three-month-old child who is wearing a dirty diaper" (25). A person wishing to recite a *brocha* in the presence of a child wearing diapers is not obliged to check the diaper prior to reciting the *brocha*. "However, if he smells an odor, a *brocha* may not be recited" (26).

As for the recitation of prayers in connection with using a toilet, it turns out there is a special set of bathroom blessings. These are clearly set forth in the Berakot tractate of the Babylonian Talmud. "He who goes into a privy says, 'Be most honored, you honored and holy ones, those who serve the Most High. Give honor to the God of Israel. Wait on me until I go in and do what I wish and come back to you. [So guard me from the evil spirits at the privy.]' " (Neusner 1984, 406). Apparently, God or his minions are not supposed to accompany the individual into the latrine, but rather are asked to wait for the person until he or she has completed the act of defecation and exited from the privy. This confirms the idea that God might be offended by the sight or even the smell of feces. He is asked to wait outside, away from the actual site of the act of defecation.

As there is a prescribed predefecation blessing, so is there also a postdefecation blessing. Again, from the Berakot tractate, "When he comes out, he should say, 'Blessed are you . . . who has formed man with wisdom and created in him various sorts of holes and apertures. It is entirely clear before your glorious throne that if one of them [that should remain closed] should open up, or if one of them [that should remain open] should close up, it will not be possible to arise before you who heals all flesh and who does wonders" (Neusner 1984, 404–405). Clearly, the reciter is giving thanks for not being constipated or afflicted with diarrhea. Either condition would make it difficult for the reciter to stand before God and render the requisite obeisance. Supposedly this standard "morning blessing" is said privately by each worshiper rather than recited aloud by the prayer leader in the synagogue (Donin 1980, 186).

There are also rules governing whether it is permissible to wear one's phylacteries when entering a privy. "He who goes into a privy should first remove his phylacteries at a distance of four cubits and only then go in" (Neusner 1984, 167; Donin 1980, 33). "If one forgot and went into the privy while wearing his phylacteries, he puts his hand over them until he completes [his defecation]" (Neusner 1984, 177). It may be of interest that there is clinical data pertinent to keeping religious ritual well away from toilets and anal matters. For example, one twenty-six-year-old male born into an ultra-Orthodox family in Jerusalem had read that "one should be clean at all orifices prior to prayer. To achieve this, he spent twenty minutes before each of the day's three prayers cleaning, washing, and checking his anal region, which always caused him to arrive sufficiently late for prayers to have missed the most important sections. Similarly lengthy cleaning rituals occurred after regular toilet visits" (Greenberg 1984, 527).

Other Berakot regulations dictated where defecation could or should occur, and how it should be carried out. For example, "In Judah, one who defecates should not do so on an east-west axis but on a north-south axis, and in Galilee he should defecate only on an east-west axis" (Neusner 1984, 415). Ideally, one should not be observed while defecating. "If it is behind a fence, one may defecate right away. If it is in an open field, one may do so [as] long as he can fart without his fellow's hearing it." . . . "Who is regarded as modest? It is one who defecates by night in a place in which one would be permitted to defecate by day" (417). In any case, "one wipes not with the right hand but with the left" with a number of reasons given for this including the assertion that the "Torah was given by the right hand" (Deut. 33:2), among others (Neusner 1984, 416; Jacobs 1984b, 196). The latter regulation is strangely reminiscent of a similar practice in India where left and right hands must be kept strictly separate inasmuch as the right hand is used for eating and the left hand for wiping the anus (Dundes 1997a).

The reference to east-west axis and the left-right hand distinction calls to mind a provocative suggestion made by Ernest Jones in his "Anal Erotic Character Traits" essay. He claimed that one of the characterological consequences of anal eroticism was "the tendency to be occupied with the reverse side of various things and situations. This may manifest itself in many different ways: in marked curiosity about the opposite or back side of objects and places—e.g., in the desire to live on the other side of a hill because it has its back to a given place, in the proneness to make numerous mistakes about right and left, east and west; to reverse words and letters in writing; and so on" (1961, 423). If we assume there might be some validity to this suggestion, we might be tempted to speculate about a number of details. One of the striking features of some forms of *shinui* involve reversals (e.g., pouring the milk in the bowl before putting in the cereal, using the left hand instead of the right to write with on the Sabbath, using the handle of the fork or spoon to stir with). It may or may not be relevant that Hebrew is written from right to left, the opposite of the way most modern scripts are read. And it may be too much of a metaphorical stretch to think that the Jews' penchant for looking for "oppositional" positions in *pilpul* or rabbinical debate is yet another reflection of the same basic tendency. Mollinger, not speaking about Jews but about obsessive-compulsives, declares that "the compulsive is torn between obedience and defiance" and characteristic of the style of the obsessive-compulsive is its "antithetical quality." Says Mollinger, "The obsessive-compulsive is full of ambivalence, opposites, and contradictions" (1980, 466).

Abraham, in his 1921 essay on anal character, supports Jones' suggestion that "reversals" are a significant feature of anal erotic personality. Such individuals "tend to act in great and small things in a manner opposite to that of other people. They wear clothes that are as dissimilar as possible from the prevailing fashion. . . . When others ride, they go on foot. . . . The food they enjoy is opposed to the general taste" (1953, 390). Menninger refers to the trait as "contrariness, always on doing the opposite of what everyone else wants to do, or in being stubborn or obstinate" (1943, 183).

American Jews seem to have recognized this trait to the point of naming it. In the 1920s, a Yiddish newspaper, the *Jewish Daily Forward*, published in New York City, featured cartoons with a comic contumacious character named Moishe Kapoyr. Moishe is the Yiddish pronunciation of Moses, while Kapoyr means upside-down (Feinsilver 1970, 116) or "backwards," "reverse," or "the other way around" (Rosten 1970, 257). Hence a "Moishe Kapoyr" is "Anyone who persists in being contrary, opposing, contradicting, putting things exactly opposite to what others do" (257). In the present context, Moishe Kapoyr would seem to be the epitome of a prominent anal erotic character trait!

There is also a Yiddish proverb proclaiming the Jew's penchant for opposites. It depends upon the conventional Jewish greeting formula. When two Jews meet, one normally says to the other, "*Sholem aleichem*" meaning "Peace to you." The ritual response reverses the two words: "*Aleichem sholem*" meaning "To you peace." The proverb in translation says, "A Jew always answers the opposite: greet him with sholem aleichem and he will reply: aleichem-sholem" (Kumove 1999, 177).

The "curiosity about the opposite or back side of objects" mentioned by Jones may even illuminate a puzzling passage in Exodus where God allows Moses to see God's "back parts." "And it shall come to pass while my glory passeth by, that I will put thee in a cleft of the rock, and I will cover thee with my hands while I pass by: And I will take away mine hand, and thou shalt see my back parts; but my face shall not be seen" (Exod. 33:22–23). Eilberg-Schwartz offers an intriguing explanation of this passage. In brief, he argues that if man was created in God's image, "In the day that God created man, in the likeness of God made he him" (Gen. 5:1), then God must have body parts including genitals analogous to those possessed by man. (This, of course, assumes that God is male and must therefore have male sexual parts!) According to Eilberg-Schwartz, God does not want Moses to see his genitals and for this reason, God turns so that only his backside is visible to Moses (1994, 59–80). This fascinating hypothesis in no way precludes the idea that God's decision to show his rear end to Moses is not merely an example of divine "mooning," but is rather an image totally consonant with an anal erotic pattern of behavior and thought.

The anal erotic connection with God himself is by no means limited to his showing his backside to Moses. The particular way God created mankind is very much to the point. "And the Lord God formed man of the dust of the ground, and breathed into his nostrils the breath of life; and man became a living soul" (Gen. 2:7). The stuff or matter from which God formed man is dust. The dusty origin of man is clearly stated. After the expulsion of Adam and Eve from Eden, God tells Adam, "In the sweat of thy face shalt thou eat bread, till thou return unto the ground; for out of it wast thou taken: for dust thou art, and unto dust shalt thou return" (Gen. 3:19). In Hebrew, "Adamah" means soil or dirt.

To appreciate the significance of this, one must recall Ferenczi's brilliant 1914 essay "The Ontogenesis of the Interest in Money." In that essay, Ferenczi traces the gradual evolution of the child's initial interest in his own body product, that is, his excrement, through a series of less "dirty" substitutes: mud (pies), sand, molding clay, and the like. The modern-day equivalents of the later stages of this evolution would be finger painting and handling "silly putty." Ferenczi also links this process with such children's activities as collecting pebbles, glass marbles, and sea shells (1956, 275). Is it only a coincidence that Jewish children who have reached the age of six "must be taught that it is forbidden to play with sand or pebbles" (Cohen 1993, 139) on the Sabbath and that "it is forbidden to play with clay on Shabbos" (140)?

Later in life, adults may continue the process by collecting other waste products such as empty beer bottles, candy wrappers (Muensterberger 1994, 252), or cancelled stamps among other objects, which have no intrinsic worth, other than functioning as "collectibles." In this context, dust or earth is a slightly sublimated, if desiccated, form of feces. In male creation myths, the male deity seeks to emulate female reproduction, but the only substance he can produce from within his body is feces. This is why so many male creation myths tell of gods creating man from mud or earth (Dundes 1962). One psychoanalyst has commented, "According to the Bible man is made of mud (faecal matter) and, moreover, his mate (his first object) is made of a part of himself, which again corresponds to faeces, the part of the body that separates itself from it" (Grunberger 1976, 101n4). To this one could add that there is perhaps more to be said about the creation of Eve from Adam's body. In such a male creation myth, males try to copy female parturition. So as human biology dictates that males are born from females' genital area, so in the myth, a female is created from a male's genital area. The bone used to create Eve was thus not Adam's rib, but rather Adam's *os baculum*. This bone, though found in some mammals, is "missing" in man.

The anal theme in ancient Judaism is also suggested by God's choice of punishments. In Deuteronomy (28:27), the children of Israel are warned that if they do not observe all of God's Commandments and statutes, "The Lord will smite thee with the botch of Egypt, and with the emerods, and with the scab, and with the itch, whereof thou canst not be healed." The term of interest here is "emerods," which are hemorrhoids. But the children of Israel are not the only ones threatened by hemorrhoids. The Philistines who made the mistake of capturing the sacred Ark of God are actually punished by God by this means. "And he smote the men of the city, both small and great, and they had emerods in their secret parts" (1 Sam. 5:9). Evidently, God killed some of the Philistines outright, but the ones not killed were given hemorrhoids. "And the men that died not were smitten with the emerods" (1 Sam. 5:12). This drastic and no doubt painful action fully convinced the remaining Philistines of the seriousness of their offense, and after a period of seven months of possession of the Ark, they finally decided to seek advice from priests and diviners as to what to do. Not only were they obliged to return the Ark, but they had in addition to make a "trespass offering," a fine, so to speak. The offering consisted of "five golden emerods and five golden mice" (1 Sam. 6:4). The reason for five golden hemorrhoids, that is, five gold pieces in the image or shape of hemorrhoids, was that there were five Philistine cities involved (1 Sam. 6:17), and so there was one golden hemorrhoid offered for each city. Incidentally, the very idea of a golden hemorrhoid in and of itself tends to confirm the Freudian feces-money equation. Moreover, one should keep in mind the original Freudian idea that an infant's feces represents a prototypical first "gift" or offering to his parents (Fischer and Juni 1981, 58). Freud states: "Faeces are the child's first *gift*, the first sacrifice of his affection, a portion of his own body which he is ready to part with, but only for the sake of some one he loves" (1959d, 559). This formula is also hinted at by the naughty Philistines offering golden hemorrhoids to placate an angry God. The association of hemorrhoids and gold has continued into modern times. Otto Rank (born Rosenfeld), in his comment on the passages in 1 Samuel, noted that in German folk speech hemorrhoids are referred to as "goldene ader" (1922, 115n2), or "golden vein," presumably carrying the mineralogical sense of golden lode.

In the Shabbat tractate of the Babylonian Talmud, we learn the supposed causes of hemorrhoids or piles: "Ten things cause piles: He who eats leaves of reeds, leaves of vines, sprouts of vines, the rough parts of the meat of an animal, the backbone of a fish, salted fish not properly cooked, he who drinks wine lees, he who wipes himself with lime, potters' clay, or pebbles used by someone else. Some say, He who strains himself in the privy too much" (Neusner 1992–1993, IIc, 61). Hemorrhoids are still part of Jewish folklore as evidenced by the Yiddish proverb: "What do Jews inherit? Troubles and hemorrhoids" (Kumove 1999, 179).

The destruction of the temple of the false god Baal also involved an anal element. "And they brake down the image of Baal, and brake down the housed of Baal, and made it a draught house unto this day" (2 Kings 10:27). "Draught house" is an archaic term for privy. So the ultimate insult to Baal consists of transforming his temple into a latrine.

There is an enigmatic formula in the Torah for removing impurity that may or may not be relevant to the present discussion. The impurity-removing formula involves sprinkling the ashes of a burned red heifer upon an impure individual, which magically removes the impurity. The ritual procedure is set forth rather explicitly in Numbers:

> "This is the ordinance of the law which the Lord hath commanded, saying, Speak unto the children of Israel that they bring thee a red heifer without spot, wherein is no blemish, and upon which never came yoke. . . . And one shall burn the heifer in his sight; her skin, and her flesh, and her blood, with her dung, shall he burn. . . . And he that burneth her shall wash his clothes in water and bathe his flesh in water, and shall be unclean until the even. And a man that is clean shall gather up the ashes of the heifer, and lay them up without the camp in a clean place. . . . it is a purification for sin. And he that gathereth the ashes of the heifer shall wash his clothes, and be unclean until the even." (Num. 19:2, 5, 8, 9, 10)

To my knowledge no one has given a satisfactory explanation of this ritual (cf. Milgrom 1981). Two of the most salient puzzles of the ritual are: (1) why are ashes used as an agent of purification and (2) why do the ashes defile those who do the sprinkling or handling of them? A tentative if admittedly speculative answer might be related to the association of ashes with death and mourning (Jastrow 1899). The phrase "sackcloth and ashes" recurs in the Bible on a number of occasions to signal mourning or behavior akin to it (Esther 4:3), sometimes associated with fasting (Isa. 58:5). Tamar after having been raped by her brother Amnon expressed her grief and disgust as follows: "And Tamar put ashes on her head, and rent her garment of diverse colors that was on her, and laid her hand on her head, and went on crying" (2 Sam. 13:19). The rending of the garment by itself would appear to evoke an image of mourning.

Ashes are not only a symbol of death, but they represent a residue of the burning process, that is, they are a "waste" product! Symbolically speaking, smearing oneself with ashes (or dust or earth or mud) may be a sublimated form of smearing oneself with feces. That would help explain why the individual doing the smearing himself becomes unclean or impure. It would also help answer Milgrom's question (1981, 588) "why were the ashes retained?" Of course, on the practical level, it would be like having "money in the bank" in the case of having a weapon to be used against getting rid of future impurities, but symbolically speaking, saving ashes is a sublimated form of saving feces, a waste product. It is also not insignificant that the red heifer's dung is specifically mentioned as being an essential integral component of what is to go into the prescribed ritual burning process.

For those readers who are understandably dubious about there being any possible connection between red heifer ashes and feces, we might mention a striking rabbinic tradition that may prove relevant. According to this tradition, which was known more than a millennium before Freud was even born, the red heifer was understood to be an appropriate atonement for the golden calf episode. The question addressed in a *midrash* or commentary on Numbers 19:12 contained in the Pesikta Rabbati concerns why a female animal rather than a male was required for this ritual designed to remove uncleanness. Here is the passage from Pisikta Rabbati 14:14: "Why are males specified for all [communal] sacrifices, whereas a female is specified for the rite of the Red Heifer? R. Aibu said: Consider this analogy: There was a maidservant's child who polluted the king's palace. The king said: 'Let his mother come and wipe up the excrement.' In the same way the Holy One, blessed be He, said: 'Let the mother of a calf come and atone for the deed of the [golden] calf' " (Braude 1968, 292).

There is another mystifying ritual having to do with the removal of impurity that we can now explain. An earthen or clay vessel that had been made unclean through contact with an unclean person or by having had an unclean substance fall into it could be purified by breaking it. "And every earthen vessel where into any of them falleth, whatsover is in it shall be unclean; and ye shall break it" (Lev. 11:33). Neusner explains this: "Breaking a clay utensil, meaning, rendering it useless for its former purpose, so changing its character, likewise dissipates the uncleanness that has taken hold of it" (1994, 142). According to one rabbinical school, "it is not because the object is clay, but because the process of *breaking* effects purification" (154). From a symbolic perspective, one is creating a waste product—a formerly useful object has become useless, a valuable object has become valueless. In classic anal erotic theory, the small child comes to realize that his "valuable" body product offered as a "gift" to his or her parents is welcomed by them—the child may be given praise for producing it and in any case, it typically causes a parent to approach the child to remove the "gift" and to cleanse the child's buttocks. At the same time, the parent disposes of the gift, suggesting to the child that the gift is valueless. According to Ferenczi, this may help explain why children grow into adults who become passionate collectors of "valueless" waste products such as cancelled stamps, match covers, empty beer bottles and cans, and so forth. Often these "valueless" products become valuable because of the demand for them by collectors. The paradoxical combination of "valuable" and "valueless" could help explain why breaking an unclean vessel (pot) could be a purification technique. Something useful/valuable is transformed into something useless/valueless and then presumably gotten rid of. This could also be a metaphor for the digestive process whereby food becomes feces. The point is that just as ashes (of a burned red heifer), a waste product, can be an agent of purification, so breaking a clay vessel and destroying it can serve as a mode of purification.

It is tempting to suggest that the Jewish purity fixation might help explain some other aspects of ritual taboos. For example, one odd Sabbath rule has to do with combining or mixing two separate substances (Neuwirth 1989, 80). An example with respect to food: "One may not mix soft cheese into peanut butter on Shabbath, since the two combine to form an even thicker substance than the peanut butter was to start with" (82). In other words, a food must be kept "pure" and not mixed with some other foodstuff that might make it "thick." The prohibition against "mixing" or "commingling" to keep a substance "pure" might be partially explained as a metaphorical expression of the strict rules against intermarriage. God was quite clear about proscribing ethnic intermarriage. Speaking of seven other nations including the Canaanites, God declared: "Neither shalt thou make marriage with them; thy daughter thou shalt not give unto his son, nor his daughter shalt thou take unto thy son" (Deut. 7:3). "Purity" can obviously also refer to breeding, and any group obsessed with maintaining its purity may well apply this obsession to forbidding intermarriage as a necessary means of keeping the group "pure." This is so whether the group is Jewish or whether it is Germans seeking "Aryan" purity. The fear of "contamination" by some "other" ethnic group is a fear that can lead to brutal genocide, or what is termed in modern parlance "ethnic cleansing." The word "cleansing" surely emphasizes the idea that the "other" represents a form of dirt or pollution that might introduce an unwanted sullying element into the supposed racial purity of the dominant group.

One of the most succinct articulations of the prohibition against "commingling" is found in Leviticus 19:19: "Ye shall keep my statutes. Thou shalt not let thy cattle gender with a diverse kind: thou shalt not sow thy field with mingled seed: neither shall a garment mingled of linen and woolen come upon thee." The latter forbidden fusion, called *sha'tnez* (Appel 1977,

296; Ganzfried 1961, 4: 58–59), is apparently based upon the interdiction against combining an animal product (wool from sheep) with a plant product (linen from flax) (Neusner 1992–1993, IIa, 93). Supposedly, strictly Orthodox men will not buy a suit that does not carry a label certifying that the garment's fabric is not a mixture of linen and wool (Feinsilver 1970, 263). "Any garment or apparel, such as a suit, dress, hat, shoes, or socks, which may contain *sha'tnez*, either in the material or in any part of the garment, including the lining and the threads used for the buttons, must be examined before it is worn. The prohibition of *sha'tnez* also applies to material used to cover oneself, such as a blanket or towel, and anything that may tend to cover a part of a person's body" (Appel 1977, 296n1). Reportedly, some Orthodox Jews will buy garments off-the-rack in general clothing stores but then carefully replace "all the threads that are not of the same species as the material itself" (Kolatch 1985, 286).

The idea that the interdiction against commingling is a mask for a taboo against miscegenation is really implicit in the wording of such statutes: "Thou shalt not sow thy vineyard with divers seeds: lest the fruit of thy seed which thou hast sown, and the fruit of thy vineyard, be defiled. Thou shalt not plow with an ox and an ass together" (Deut. 22:9–10). (The latter portion of this image continues to be traditional as in the Yiddish proverb: You don't hitch an ox and a horse to the same wagon [Kumove 1999, 272].)

The agricultural metaphor is frequently used in the Bible to refer to sexual intercourse. Women who cannot conceive are called "barren" and Samson rebukes his wife's people for their pressuring her to reveal the answer to his riddle: "If ye had not plowed with my heifer, ye had not found out my riddle" (Judg. 14:18). (For early enlightening discussions of such sexual symbolism in the Bible and Talmud, see Levy [1914, 1915–1916, 1916–1917, 1917, 1918].)

Carmichael after commenting that "No group of laws has yielded so little meaning as those prohibiting certain mixtures" (1982, 394) does suggest the likely sexual significance of the prohibitions against mixing seed, plowing animals, and wool with linen (1982, 394, 411; 1995). He plausibly proposes that these rules should not be interpreted literally but rather as metaphorical warnings against inter-ethnic marriage (1995, 437). What Carmichael fails to mention is that Orthodox Jews to this day continue to interpret these "laws" literally. "It is forbidden to do any manner of work with diverse kinds of animals, such as ploughing or drawing a vehicle" and in the opinion of some authorities, "it is forbidden to drive two kinds of animals even when they are not harnessed together. Thus, one may not ride a horse and at the same time lead a dog on a leash. He surely may not tie the dog to the rope with which the horse is tied" (Appel 1977, 295). Moreover, Carmichael does not seem to realize a fact that any folklorist knows full well, namely, that one of the standard cross-cultural measures of traditional foolishness is the dogged insistence upon interpreting a metaphor in an exclusively literal sense. In the comprehensive six volume *Motif-Index of Folk-Literature*, the relevant motif, J2470, Metaphors Literally Interpreted, is but one small portion of a much longer section devoted to Literal Fools (Motifs J2450–J2499) (Thompson 1955–58, 4: 214–222). In the present discussion, however, these "forbidden mixtures" may be seen as part of the overall Jewish penchant for "purity," in this case, "racial" purity, which we are arguing is a reflex of basic anal eroticism.

Even the sexual segregation practices of Orthodox Jews may ultimately derive from men's fear of contamination from women. Women menstruate and menstrual blood is considered defiling. There are dozens of purity rules governing *niddah* or the state of impurity women have when menstruating. But there are clues that the imagined female impurity may derive from an anal origin. A statement in the Shabbat tractate of the Babylonian Talmud is to the point: "Though a woman is a pot full of shit and her mouth is full of blood, everybody pursues her" (Neusner 1992–1993, IIe, 123). As for the enforced segregation of Orthodox men and women, there is quite a charming circumvention employed at weddings. Normally, there are separate parties for the men and the women in attendance. The basic rule is that a man is not allowed to touch a woman. However, when the men and women get together to dance, each partner in a couple holds a corner of a handkerchief at arm's length. Even the bride and groom may be seen dancing at an Orthodox wedding with each clasping one end of a handkerchief held in common (Rosten 1992, 233). In this way, Orthodox Jews are able to get around the prohibition against touching such that they can dance together without technically violating a taboo.

Another seemingly strange set of rules concerns smells. It is not easy to make sense of scents, but it is possible that they too may well stem from an anal erotic source. The Berakot tractate includes admonitions regarding passing wind. "If a person was standing and reciting the Prayer and he farted, he should wait until the stink passes and then go back and say the Prayer" (Neusner 1984, 175). Also, "If one was standing and reciting the Prayer and he wanted to fart, he steps four cubits back and farts and then he waits until the stink passes and returns and says the Prayer" (176). The reader may be surprised to learn that the *Code of Jewish Law* provides even more detail: "If a worshiper feels that a bad odor is about to come out of him, and he cannot restrain himself, then if he prays privately at his own house, he should walk four cubits either backwards or to his side, let off wind, wait until the odor vanishes, and then return to his place and say: 'Master of the World! Thou hast created us full of orifices and vessels. Our shame and disgrace are revealed and known unto Thee. We are a shame and a disgrace while we are alive, and worms when we are dead.' After that he may conclude his prayer. If a person lets off wind accidentally at the place where he prays, or when he prays with a congregation and he would be embarrassed to walk backward, then he need not walk away from his place, nor need he say 'Master,' and so forth, but should wait until the odor vanishes and conclude his prayer" (Ganzfried 1961, 1: 61).

According to the same *Code of Jewish Law*, "It is forbidden even to think of anything holy in a place where there is excrement or urine, or anything that produces a bad odor" (Ganzfried 1961, 1: 9). The point is that a bad smell is deemed equivalent to feces. "When praying, we must keep at a distance from the excrement of a human being. . . . Likewise we must keep away from anything that is malodorous, due to decay, such as carrion, and the like. We must also keep away from a chicken coop, evil-smelling water, or water in which flax or hemp is soaked, and which ordinarily emits a bad odor. We must keep at a distance from the aforementioned things just as from excrement" (Ganzfried 1961, 1: 9).

The idea that a divinity might be offended by a disagreeable odor was traditional among other ancient Near Eastern peoples, and passing wind was mentioned specifically (Van der Toorn 1989, 352). This idea of not wanting to offend a deity by offering anything that did not smell good helps explain several details of contemporary Orthodox Jewish Sabbath practice. The Kiddush prayer—Kiddush means sanctity (recited at the beginning of Sabbath)—is required by rabbinical authority to be said over wine. In order not to offend God, it is important that the wine used have a pleasant bouquet. Accordingly, "any wine which has an unpleasant odor (although it still has the taste of wine) is disqualified for Kiddush" (Cohen 1986, 46). The same ritual also involves lighting candles. And, "a candle with a foul odor may not be used if another one is available" (137). The very fact that an authoritative how-to-do-it Sabbath manual specifically mentions that foul-smelling wine and candles might offend or be disrespectful to God is of significance in the present context. Jacobs also mentions the unsuitability of certain gifts to God: "wine with a bad smell cannot be offered as a libation on the altar and wheat kernels found in cows' dung cannot be used in the preparation of a meal offering" (1984b, 40).

It is not just that God might be offended by a foul smell, but also that he would be mightily pleased by a good smell. One of the consistent features of burnt sacrificial offerings to God in the Old Testament is their "sweet savor" or "pleasing aroma" (Milgrom 1991, 162). When Noah wants to give thanks to God for saving him from the flood, he "took of every clean beast and of every clean fowl and offered burnt offerings on the altar. And the Lord smelled a sweet savor" (Gen. 8:20–21). This formula of "sweet savor" is repeated many times in the Old Testament (Exod. 29:18, 41; Leviticus 1:9, 13, 17; 2:2, 9, 12; 3:5, 16; 4:31; 6:15, 21; 8:21, 28; 23:13, 18; Num. 15:3, 7 10, 14, 24; 28:6, 8, 27; 29:2, 8, 13). When God becomes enraged at the thought of the children of Israel disobeying his Commandments, he threatens, "And I will make your cities waste and bring your sanctuaries unto desolation, and I will not smell the savor of your sweet odors" (Lev. 26:31). God's dislike of foul odors and his affinity for "sweet odors" might suggest at least a hint of an anal erotic proclivity. In any event, God's ability to distinguish sweet savors from foul odors certainly suggests anthropomorphism, as presumably God must have something akin to a human nose in order to be able to make such distinctions.

God also exhibits an olfactory predisposition when he chooses to utilize a strong-smelling substance to punish sinners. Brimstone or burning stone is actually the element sulphur, and its combustion produces a strong, acrid, pungent odor. Burning sulphur, that is "brimstone and fire," were "rained" "from the Lord out of heaven" upon Sodom and Gomorrah (Gen. 19:24). Hell was thought to be suffused with the same foul-smelling substance. In Revelation (19:20), we are told that the beast and false prophet were both "cast alive into a lake of fire burning with brimstone" and even "the devil that deceived them was cast into the lake of fire and brimstone, where the beast and false prophet are" (20:10).

Among Jews, even agreeable smells were sometimes prohibited. For example, "There is a rabbinical prohibition against transferring scent onto clothes or similar articles" (Neuwirth 1989, 185). This means that one cannot spray perfume onto a handkerchief or any article of clothing on the Sabbath. In the context of the theory of an anal erotic basis for purity regulations, one can easily understand the concern with smell. With reaction formation, it is not a bad smell, but a good smell, such as the pleasant fragrance of perfume, which is prohibited. On the other hand, there is an interesting Sabbath custom that involves the production of fragrance.

In a long essay first published in 1940, Lauterbach described a custom that he claims seems to have been known in ancient Palestine whereby Jews placed fragrant plants or aromatic herbs on their Sabbath tables (1970, 77–78). Supposedly, they were to provide an aroma or pleasant fragrance in place of the smoke of spices used for the same purpose at the conclusion of the Sabbath meal as mentioned in the Berakot tractate of the Mishnah (Neusner 1988, 10). Lauterbach surveys the various theories proposed to explain the rationale underlying this custom. Perhaps the most relevant one in the present context suggested that "at the end of the Sabbath, the fire in Hell, which was put out during the Sabbath, is started again, issuing a stench. To neutralize this bad odor, the smelling of herbs was introduced for that particular moment of the going out of the Sabbath" (Lauterbach 1970, 93). Often the plant utilized was myrtle, and some authorities suggested that there should be two bunches of myrtle placed on the table at every meal of the Sabbath "for the purpose of enjoying their fragrance" (126). This practice continues among contemporary Orthodox Jews. For example, in the celebration of Havdalah (signaling the end of the Sabbath), each participant is supposed to inhale the fragrance of the spices or flowers or fruits. The *brocha* (blessing) addressed to God consists of "Blessed are you Hashem . . . who creates species of fragrance" or "who has imparted a pleasant fragrance to fruits" (Cohen 1986, 130–132 for a discussion of the benedictions appropriate for thanking God for enjoyable fragrances, see Ganzfried 1961, 2: 24–26). So important is this smelling ritual that "One whose sense of smell is impaired should not recite the *brocha*," and in connection with this stipulation, "One who has a cold and is not sure if he will be able to smell the spices or one who is not sure whether the spices have a pleasant fragrance, may smell the spices before reciting the *brocha* to test his sense of smell or the spices' fragrance" (Cohen 1986, 131–132).

The enjoined presence of myrtle or fragrant spices on the Sabbath could be construed as a type of "deodorizing ritual" (Howes 1987, 411). Such rituals represent a kind of "undoing" of unpleasant smells (Gilman 1986, 180). It has been suggested that bad smells "signify repulsion, corruption, decay, and ultimately death," while good smells "mean attraction, the creation of bonds, sexuality, birth, life" (Rindisbacher 1992, 290). In that light, the use of spices in funerary preparations to conceal the stench caused by the putrefaction of a corpse would be parallel to applying perfumed substances to conceal body odor. This funerary use of spices is well attested in ancient Jewish tradition. The body of Jesus, for example, when claimed by Joseph of Arimathea for burial, was handled as follows: "Then took they the body of Jesus and wound it in linen clothes with the spices, as the manner of the Jews is to bury" (John 19:40). We also know that the malodorous smell caused by the decomposition of a corpse was recognized. When Jesus is about to raise Lazarus from the dead, Lazarus's sister Martha objects. "Jesus said, 'Take ye away the stone.' Martha, the sister of him that was dead, saith unto him, 'Lord, by this time he stinketh: for he hath been dead four days' " (John

11:39). On the other hand, the widespread practice of employing "odoriferous substances to communicate with the gods" (Howes 1987, 400) could well have an anal erotic basis. When anthropologists, in speaking of male puberty rites, note that it is "appropriate that the neophyte makes himself smell dirty" (404), they should realize, as does any parent of a small infant, that it is precisely the smell of that infant's excretion that causes a parent or parent-surrogate to approach (to clean the infant). In other words, there is an infantile precursor of the notion that producing a noticeable odor will serve to summon an all-powerful deity (parent).

Perhaps one of the most intriguing pieces of evidence of an anal erotic basis of the Jewish obsession with purity is etymological in nature. Keeping in mind that violations of Sabbath rules and other "sins" cause a state of uncleanness or defilement, it is not at all illogical for the key term for the removal of such sin to be *kippur*, as in the so-called Day of Atonement, Yom Kippur. Although *kippur* is commonly translated as "atonement" when speaking of Yom Kippur, the word seems to be cognate with an Akkadian verb *kuppuru*, which "has the meaning 'to wipe, rub; purify by wiping' " (Wright 1987, 291). Landsberger's extended discussion of the Akkadian *kuppuru* includes such meanings as "to wipe out" or "to wipe off" (1967, 31) sometimes combined with the sense of magically removing "inner dirt" (30, 33). One passage using the word is "you wipe out the dirt [of his . . .] with a wad of wool" (32n99). Apparently, by magic, "the dirt called *kupirtu* . . . is absorbed by a medium, mostly dough, which is thrown away, buried, or carried to the enemy's land" (32). Levine, who devotes a separate appendix "Observations on K-P-R in Some Semitic Languages" (1974, 123–127) to the term, tries to reconcile two different meanings: "wipe off" and "cover." In the end, he decides that "wipe off" is the primary meaning and the "cover" may be a later semantic development. From the present perspective, it makes sense that after one "wipes off" feces, one then proceeds to bury or cover it. One should keep in mind the specific instruction in Deuteronomy (23:13) that after easing oneself, one should turn back and "cover that which cometh from thee." Levine also notes that "Impurity is viewed as an external force which adheres to a person or object" (1974, 63), a description that could certainly apply to the results of the excretory process. If one accepts the idea that one aspect of obsessive behavior can involve ritual "undoing" (Mollinger 1980, 468), then one can see that purification procedures are in effect a socially sanctioned means of "undoing" acts that resulted in the production of dirt or "uncleanness." In this regard, the fundamental meaning of "wipe off" for *kippur* makes perfect sense. If the removal of impurity can be perceived as a metaphorical extension of parentally imposed toilet training, we can understand such expressions from the Mishnah as "One who desires to purify himself is aided from Above" (Amsel 1970, 65) as an infant who needs a parent (from above) to assist in wiping off the "impurity."

Related to this meaning of *kippur* is Milgrom's persuasive argument that the common Old Testament formula of "sin offering" as a means of expiating an offense is a mistranslation. He suggests that the underlying meaning is rather that of "to cleanse" or "expurgate" or "decontaminate" and that accordingly, "sin offering" should really be translated as "purification offering" (Milgrom 1991, 253). Milgrom states in no uncertain terms that in such contexts "*kipper* means 'purge' and nothing else" (255). It is not without interest that Milgrom, in his magisterial study of Leviticus, chose to end this magnum opus with a short disquisition on the term *kipper* (1079–1084). When we add to this Milgrom's assertion that "impurity was a physical substance" (257) and like the signs of plague on the walls of a house to be taken "out of the city into an unclean place" (Lev. 14:41, 45; Milgrom 1991, 262), we have further support that such purity rituals are sublimated, symbolic forms of the act of defecation and its associated cleansing procedures. Latrines, one must remember, were typically located outside the camp or city at some distance.

This removal of "inner dirt" through a magical disposal of an object to which the dirt has been transferred resonates with an aspect of Yom Kippur ritual. According to Leviticus (16:21), Aaron, functioning as priest, places his hands on the head of a live goat, a scapegoat, and transfers all the iniquities and sins of the children of Israel to the goat, whereupon he sends the goat off into the wilderness. "But the goat, on which the lot fell to be the scapegoat, shall be presented alive before the Lord, to make an atonement with him and to let him go for a scapegoat into the wilderness" (Lev. 16:10), and Aaron "shall make an atonement for the holy place, because of the uncleanness of the children of Israel" (Lev. 16:16). Here we must keep in mind that Yom Kippur, though often translated in English as the Day of Atonement or Expiation, was known in Temple times as the Annual Day of Purgation (Milgrom 1971, 1384).

The dispatching of the sin or dirt-bearing scapegoat to a wilderness area has been shown to be related to other ancient Near Eastern rituals (Hooke 1952, 8–9; Tawil 1980; for the contrary view that the scapegoat ritual is a purely Israelite invention, see Carmichael 2000). Specifically, a scapegoat is sent to a demon named Azazel who is supposed to have emerged from the netherworld. Wright, in his outstanding 1984 doctoral dissertation devoted to the topic of "The disposal of impurity," discusses Azazel at some length and he disputes the alleged connection between "wilderness" and "netherworld" (1987, 25–27). Tawil, however, adduces evidence from other ancient Near Eastern cultures that do place their demons in the netherworld (1980, 48; see also Grabbe [1987, 157] who presents textual evidence of a possible Jewish tradition according to which Azazel is apparently the "ruler over the underworld"). Metaphorically, the netherworld would correspond to the lower part of the body. So sending the "inner dirt" to a "waste" land, to be buried "in a hole" in the ground (Tawil 1980, 52) makes a good deal of sense. The dirt/sin-bearing goat is buried just as any dead body or any feces is properly buried in the ground. This is how one gets rid of the "uncleanness" of the children of Israel!

Apparently, in cognate customs found among other ancient Near Eastern cultures, there are roughly analogous practices. For example, in the Babylonian New Year festival, the priest "literally wipes the sanctuary walls with the carcass of a ram and then throws it in the river" (Milgrom 1991, 1042). In Mesopotamian rituals, the "wiping material" is likewise thrown into a river or other space (1082).

This term *kippuru* for "ritual cleansing" has long been the subject of considerable speculation by scholars (Herrmann 1905; Gerleman 1980; Janowski 1982; Deiana 1994), who, lacking any familiarity with psychoanalytic theory, have been puzzled by it. Why should the basic word for ritual cleaning come from a root meaning to "wipe off"? In the present context, it should be obvious. As an infant is "defiled" so to speak by its own excrement, so a parent or parent-surrogate must come to its rescue by "wiping" it off. Even more interesting is the suggestion by one scholar that the word may be related to a Hebrew and Aramaic cognate *kapar/keper*, which means "to seek release from an obligation surreptitiously . . . to conceal the fact of an obligation by deceit" (Levine 1974, 125). This sounds suspiciously like "circumvention"!

It is a supremely tragic irony of human history that Jews with their near-fanatic concern with remaining "clean" and "undefiled" were victimized by a people with an equally anal character: the Germans. German anti-Semitic folklore insisted that the Jews, despite their actual fastidiousness with respect to cleanness, were "dirty" and that the "dirty Jew" had to be "eliminated" (e.g., by being transformed into soap, a cleansing agent), thereby making Germany *Judenrein* or "clean of Jews" (Dundes 1997b, 103).

SELF-IMPOSED REPRESSION

The idea that Sabbath laws represent a form of strict self-imposed repression whereby Jews are required to renounce virtually all forms of normal bodily activity must be understood in a larger context. In this context, Jews, especially males—as early Judaism, at least as reported in the Old Testament, was highly male-oriented—were obliged to submit to the laws imposed by an all-powerful male God (father figure). This same pattern may be perceived in other key elements of Judaism: circumcision and *kashrut*.

There is a vast literature devoted to the subject of circumcision, but there can be absolutely no doubt that it is one of the principal characteristics of Jewish culture. Interestingly enough, it is described as a "covenant" between God and man just as the Sabbath is similarly described as a "covenant."

> And God said unto Abraham, "Thou shalt keep my covenant. . . . This is my covenant, which ye shall keep, between me and you and thy seed after thee; Every man child among you shall be circumcised. And ye shall circumcise the flesh of your foreskin; and it shall be a token of the covenant betwixt me and you. . . . He that is born in thy house . . . must needs be circumcised; and my covenant shall be in your flesh for an everlasting covenant." (Gen. 17:9–11, 13)

The Sabbath is described in similar terms: "Wherefore the children of Israel shall keep the Sabbath, to observe the Sabbath throughout their generation, for a perpetual covenant. It is a sign between me and the children of Israel for ever" (Exod. 31:16–17). Although the Sabbath and circumcision may both be covenants, it is the Sabbath that is clearly more significant as a marker of Judaism, the reason being that circumcision applies only to males whereas the Sabbath affects both males and females. Whether or not psychoanalysts are correct in regarding circumcision as a form of symbolic castration as Freud said in *Moses and Monotheism* (1995, 186; cf. Rubenstein 1963)—I myself find the argument persuasive—it is patently obvious that it represents a form of male submission to a higher power, just as complying with Sabbath regulations entails submission to that same higher power. The father's guilt caused by his insistence that his infant son be circumcised (symbolically castrated) is only partly assuaged by the curious custom among Orthodox Jews of having the *mohel* (one who performs the ritual) follow the act of cutting by sucking the resulting blood from the infant's penis, "plainly a passive homosexual act" (Malev 1966, 514), no doubt intended to mitigate if not negate the paternal castration of the son by partially resuscitating the injured infant phallus. In any event, Abraham evidently obeyed God's ordinance concerning circumcision "in the selfsame day, as God had said unto him" (Gen. 17:23). Every male in Abraham's household was circumcised including Abraham himself at age ninety-nine. The implication is that Abraham may have circumcised himself (Ostrov 1978, 268). Such an act of self-circumcision is of significance insofar as it could be construed as emblematic of the Jews' masochistic tendency to inflict punishment on themselves.

There is one interesting example of circumvention in connection with circumcision. Among some ultra-Orthodox Jews, it is believed that an uncircumcised Jew, if that is not a contradiction in terms, is somehow unacceptable to God, so much so, that such an individual cannot legitimately be buried in a Jewish cemetery. In that context, we might mention the case of an immigrant to Israel from the former Soviet Union who was killed in a traffic accident in the northern Israeli town of Nahariyya in 1991. For whatever reason, this immigrant had not been circumcised. Most likely it had something to do with the Russian Communists' official policy of antipathy to religion and religious rituals. In any case, the local rabbi with the concurrence of the chief rabbinate arranged to have the corpse circumcised before burial with the explanation that "Halakhah requires that a man be circumcised posthumously if he was not circumcised while alive" (Zemer 1999, 317). Whether or not it is really true that Halachic law forbids the burial of an uncircumcised Jew in a Jewish cemetery is not significant, what is noteworthy here is that the circumvention was employed. Rather than preventing an uncircumcised corpse from being buried in and thereby possibly desecrating sacred ground, one simply circumcises the corpse.

Dietary laws are another major facet of Jewish identity. One of the less well-known taboos prohibits observant Jews from eating the "hindquarters" of an animal. An encyclopedia of kosher foods, for example, includes an illustration of a cow with the words "Hindquarter Not Available for Kosher Consumption" imprinted on its rear end (Eidlitz 1992, 67). Explanations for this taboo range from the practical to the biblical. As it is the fat and especially the sinews in the hindquarters that are forbidden, it is commonly argued that it is simply too much work to remove them (Trepp 1980, 58). An authoritative text says, similarly, "Most of the forbidden fat and the sinew of the thigh vein are found in the hindquarters of the animal. Since their removal is difficult and must be done by one who is highly qualified, the hind quarters are not used for kosher meat in most Jewish communities" (Appel 1977, 239n1). "Thus, the hindquarters of an animal, from which filet mignon is made, are usually separated and sent to a non-kosher meat market" (Greenberg 1983, 99). This is why it is claimed that the steaks served in kosher restaurants are not nearly as good as steaks served in nonkosher restaurants (Kolatch 1995, 94). The alleged reason why it is not permitted to eat the so-called ischiatic nerve of an animal is the episode in Genesis (32:25) where in Jacob's wrestling match with an angel, the angel touches "the hollow of Jacob's thigh" (Gaster 1955, 210). "Therefore the children of Israel eat not of this sinew which shrank which is upon the hollow of the thigh unto this day; because he touched the hollow of Jacob's thigh in the sinew that shrank" (Gen. 32:32). The refusal to eat an animal's rear end may or may not be parallel to a symbolic custom celebrated at the evening meal of Rosh Hashanah, a high holy day, the Jewish new year, when, according to one source, "it is customary to eat the head of a fish, and to exclaim before eating it: 'Let us be the head rather than the tail' " (Himelstein 1990, 76). In the present context, this explicit repudiation of the tails of animals and fish might plausibly be explained as a sign of anal erotic character.

A much more prominent dietary law is the prohibition against mixing "meat" and "dairy" or flesh and milk. One could construe this as another example of a "forbidden mixture," structurally analogous to the taboo against mixing different plow animals or wool with linen. Again, there is a purported passage in the Old Testament that supposedly serves as a charter for this belief and custom. We find three separate but identical iterations of an injunction stating "Thou shalt not seethe a kid in his mother's milk" (Exod. 23:19; 34:26; Deut. 14:21). Note that it is not just that one cannot cook a young kid in milk but specifically in its own mother's milk. So the rule concerns not just the prohibition forbidding mixing meat and dairy products, but interdicting the placement of a young animal in its mother's milk. This curious dietary rule has been said to resemble "an obsessional symptom or rather a compulsive prohibition" (Woolf 1945, 176), but its meaning remains elusive. Explanations proposed range from an attempt to ban a magical cultic practice engaged in by other peoples to an effort to treat animals humanely (Haran 1979; Milgrom 1985). A kid, like a human infant, undergoes a painful process called weaning when its mother no longer allows it to nurse. In that context, one could argue that the rule has to do with the separation of a (male) child from its mother. Or to put it in Oedipal terms, a male child is forbidden to have access to nourishing maternal fluid, that is, to his mother's breast. Whether the rule reflects a defense against a son's Oedipal wish for maternal incest, as Fromm-Reichmann argued (1927, 242), is difficult to prove. A case history reported by Karl Abraham in his correspondence with Freud is suggestive. Abraham wrote that certain cannibalistic fantasies of one of his patients illuminated "the probable roots of the Jewish prohibition against eating milk and meat together." Abraham claimed, "In this analysis the milk proved to be an allusion to the mother and the meat an allusion to the typical biting castration fantasy directed against the father" (Abraham and Freud 1965, 374). If milk is mother and meat is father, then from an Oedipal perspective, a male would want to keep them apart (so as to keep mother/milk for himself). This will no doubt strike the non-Freudian reader as totally implausible. However, it is worth mentioning that there is a modern Jewish joke that does provide an explicit sexual frame for the meat and dairy separation taboo.

> A man woke up one morning and found an unusual growth on his sex organ. Not wanting to alarm his wife, he said nothing about it. Later that day, fearing that it was some kind of cancer, he went to see a doctor. The doctor examined the growth and told the man that it was not serious, and that it was not cancer. He told the man to go home and soak it in a solution of water and baking soda. The man, relieved, went home and began to soak himself in a big kitchen pot. Suddenly his wife came into the room, "Don't worry dear, it isn't cancer!" he said. "Cancer-shmancer!" she yelled. "Nem arois dem shtick flays von milchiken topp!" [Take that piece of meat out of a dairy pot!]. (For other versions in which the punchline is rendered "Nem aroys die fleish fuhn dem milchidicken tup" see Ben Motke der tzig and Ben Pesach 1981, 37; Mr. "P" 1984, 42.)

In this joke, which would likely be unintelligible to a reader unfamiliar with the relevant Jewish dietary restriction or with insufficient knowledge of Yiddish to understand the punchline, we have a direct equation of "meat" or "flesh" with the male organ. The wife wants it kept out of a milk pot in her kitchen. One joke does not a theory make, but it is surely suggestive.

If we consider Orthodox Judaism as part of a larger pattern consisting of a celebration of repressive measures including keeping meat out of dairy pots, male-imposed circumcision, and Sabbath restrictions, we are better able to understand some of the specifics of these restrictions as well as the need to attempt to circumvent them.

What are we to make of the prohibition against lighting a fire and its rabbinical derivative forbidding the use of electricity? Fire has definite sexual connotations (Freud 1957, 50n1) and lighting a fire remains today a common metaphor for sexual excitement. One "burns" with desire and in more vernacular terms, one is "hot" for someone's "bod." An animal, especially a female, in a state of sexual excitement or at a time of sexual readiness, is said to be "in heat." Idioms also attest the fiery imagery (e.g., to be inflamed with passion). To "carry the torch" for someone of the opposite sex signifies being highly enamored of that person (Lewis and Yarnell 1951, 2). In colloquial usage, a former sweetheart may be referred to as an "old flame." There is also the American folk metaphor "to light my fire" referring to someone who arouses the speaker's sexual urges. However, in the Old Testament, fire, as a symbolic representation of sexuality, is strictly a parental prerogative. It is God who appears to Moses in the midst of a burning bush (Exod. 3:2). It is

God who leads the children of Israel "by night in a pillar of fire" (Exod. 13:21), a likely fiery phallus. In the New Testament, we learn "Our God is a consuming fire" (Heb. 12:29). Myths of the origin of fire worldwide typically describe how a mortal man attempts to steal fire that is initially the exclusive property of the gods. Freud discussed such myths in his 1932 paper "The Acquisition of Power over Fire" in which he pointed out that "the acquisition of fire is a crime; it is accomplished by robbery or theft" and he noted the overt phallic symbolism, for example, of Prometheus concealing in a hollow rod the fire he stole from the gods (1959e, 289).

In the present context, we might speculate that a man who lights a fire is acting as though he were a god, clearly a disrespectful if not sacrilegious act. For those who are skeptical of there being any possible relationship between the act of lighting a fire and a genital organ, one has only to consider a curious folk theory of the cause of enuresis. According to a well-known superstition, children who play with matches will wet their beds. Here is direct linkage between lighting a fire and emitting fluid from the genital area. This bit of folklore is supported by empirical data suggesting that juvenile arsonists are not infrequently former bed-wetters (Wax and Haddox 1974; but cf. Quinsey, Chaplin, and Upfold 1989). Whether or not there is an erotic component of pyromania, one finds other evidence of a connection between lighting a fire and sexuality. The fact that the principal primitive means of producing fire consists of rubbing two sticks together or using a fire drill in which an upright stick is twirled rapidly in a hole made in a stick lying flat further supports the underlying symbolic association of fire with sexual activity. Even James George Frazer, hardly a friend of Freudian theory, saw that the process of fire-making symbolized coition, and he thought that might explain why there were myths recounting how "fire was elicited from a woman's body, and particularly from her genital organ" (1930, 220). Grinstein interprets such myths as indicating that it is the mother figure who originally "demanded instinctual renunciation from her children" (1952, 417). Grinstein also suggests that the emphasis on the "control of fire" and, for example, keeping it confined to a particular place so that it does not spread and destroy property or human life, point to anal character (418). Curtailing or inhibiting any aggressive impulse to burn up objects is, according to Grinstein, a derivative of the so-called anal-sadistic phase, and the failure to curb this impulse may be a partial factor in the psychopathology of pyromania. Another psychoanalyst, Wilhelm Stekel, believed that "children find in fire a destructive energy which gives them power over adults" (Lewis and Yarnell 1951, 25).

Assuming that there may be an unconscious erotic component of lighting a fire, and keeping in mind the rabbinical decision to equate electricity with fire, we may legitimately ask if there is any possibility of discovering a similar component in the taboo against using electricity. A curious clinical case reported by A. A. Brill describes a fifty-year-old woman sent to him by the New York City Police Department. She imagined that "fiendish men were injecting electricity into her body during the night. . . . She had only the vaguest idea of who these fiendish men might be, but she was certain that they injected the electricity into her eyes, her nose, her ears, and her mouth" (1955, 70). Brill, after commenting on the fact that the fiendish men injected the electricity into her upper bodily cavities and "never did so into the openings below the waistline," suggests that "in the language of the unconscious she was saying, in effect: 'I have never had any sexual relationship because I consider it fiendish and shocking' " (71).

In a study of the Mennonite and Amish, who also refuse to use electricity, Graber and Forsyth, in addition to citing the Brill case, point out some relevant folk speech (e.g., "A.C.-D.C.," which refers to an individual who is bisexual and can engage in either homosexual or heterosexual activity). They also mention "turn on," which has a definite sexual connotation (1986, 128). If one were a rabid Freudian, one might go so far as to suggest that extending a digit to push a button to make an elevator (a box-like container that goes up and down) come could conceivably have a sexual nuance. In support of this interpretation would be the undeniable sexual slang meanings of "button" referring to either a clitoris or a female breast nipple (Lighter 1994, 336; Richter 1995, 36). Hence to "push someone's buttons" is to stimulate a strong emotional response involving anger or sexual excitement (Lighter 1994, 337). Similarly, the idea of "turning on" a light switch or completing a circuit might have a comparable significance. Inasmuch as "to turn someone on" has a definite sexual connotation, it has been suggested that the sexual meaning in fact may be derived from the act of switching on a light (Richter 1995, 226).

For readers who may still doubt that electricity could possibly have a sexual connection, the following mid-twentieth-century African American joke may be of interest:

> A white man was walking through colored town one day when he heard a Negro woman call her small son, who was playing in the street. "Elec, Elec, come here to me. Elec, Elec, don't you hear me? Electricity! You better come here before I skin you alive."
>
> The white man said, "Did you call the boy Electricity? Isn't that an unusual name for a child?"

"No sah, I don't think it's so unusual. My name is Dinah and my old man's name is Mose. Now don't dynamo's generate electricity?"

"I guess you got something at that," said the white man. (Prange and Vitols 1990, 633)

The play on the word "generate" referring both to a "potent" sexual act and the production of electric power suggests that electricity can indeed have an erotic signification.

If we may summarize, the question of why lighting a fire should be such a criminal offense, punishable by death if one takes literally the Old Testament warning, can now be explained. God who forbids man's lighting a fire is a transformation of a parent who inhibits a child's libidinous proclivities. The rabbinical extension of the fire-lighting prohibition to preclude thereby all activities depending upon the use of electricity is a further attempt to restrict and disable the pleasure principle. The Sabbath is said to be a day of joy—Isaiah (58:13) called the Sabbath "a delight"—but the reality of attempting to suppress most pleasurable activities tends to make it a day of enforced joylessness. No wonder naughty children in the guise of adults do their best to find endless ways to circumvent repressive custom.

The popularity of jokes about circumvention demonstrate its importance in Jewish culture. Here is an example ostensibly treating the subject of childhood rebellion:

Two boys about 12 years old were talking about how difficult home and school were, how no one understood them at either place, and how much they wanted to chuck it all and run away. Finally one of the boys blurted out, "Let's do it. Let's run away!"

"Run away?" asked the second boy, "our fathers will find us and beat the hell out of us."

"So," replied the first youngster, "we'll hit them back."

"What? Hit your father? You must be crazy!" reported the friend. "Have you forgotten one of the most important of the Ten Commandments—always honor your father and mother?"

The initiator of the plot thought silently for a moment and then suggested, "So you hit my father and I'll hit yours." (Strean 1993, 133–134; for another version, see Rosten 1970, 84.)

Another Jewish joke that provides an excellent illustration of circumvention at work goes as follows:

Two woebegone Talmudic students came to their rabbi and made a shamefaced confession. "Rabbi, we've committed a sin."

"A sin? What kind of a sin?"

"We looked with lust upon a woman."

"May God forgive you!" cried the holy man. "That is indeed a serious transgression."

"Rabbi," said the students, humbly, "what can we do to atone?"

"Well, if you sincerely seek penance, I order you to put peas into your shoes and walk about that way for ten days. Perhaps that will teach you not to sin again."

The two young men went home and did as the rabbi had ordered them. A few days later the penitents met on the street. One was hobbling painfully, but the other walked easily, his manner calm and contented.

"Is this the way to obey the rabbi?" asked the first student reproachfully. "I see you ignored his injunction to put peas into your shoes."

"I didn't ignore him at all," said the other cheerfully. "I just cooked them first." (Spaulding 1969, 2–3)

In both these jokes, the Jewish protagonist does not actually violate the literal sense of the commandment or rabbinical instruction, but he certainly does succeed in devising a clever way around it.

THE LOVE OF ARGUMENT

There exists in English a phrase "Talmudic thinking" that may carry a negative connotation suggesting "tricky cleverness as opposed to clear thinking" and a concern with "minutiae" (Halberstam 1997, 53) and "nit-picking logic" (Telushkin 1992, 49). Asher Ginzberg, writing under the pseudonym of Ahad Ha-'Am, believes the phrase may have originated among non-Jews, but that it has been adopted by the Jews themselves: "The Talmudic system of logic has not yet been thoroughly examined by Jewish scholars, who have unquestioningly accepted the non-Jewish idea of Talmudic disputation as a process which violates all the canons of logic and good sense—so much so that we use 'Talmudic reasoning' as a synonym for sophisticated quibbling" (1946, 89; 1912, 274).

Talmudic reasoning is also found in Jewish jokes and in effect is often the subject matter of those jokes. Here is a classic example:

The Scholar

After months of negotiation, a Jewish scholar from Odessa was granted permission to visit Moscow. He boarded the train and found an empty seat. At the next stop a young man got on and sat next to him. The scholar looked at the young man and thought: This fellow doesn't look like a peasant, and if he isn't a peasant he probably comes from this district. If he comes from this district, he must be Jewish because this is, after all, the Jewish district. On the other hand, if he is a Jew where could he be going? I'm the only one in our district who has permission to travel to Moscow. Wait—just outside Moscow there is a little village called Samvet, and you don't need special permission to go there. But why would he be going to Samvet? He's probably going to visit one of the Jewish families there, but how many Jewish families are there in Samvet? Only two—the Bernsteins and the Steinbergs. The Bernsteins are a terrible family, so he must be visiting the Steinbergs. But why is he going? The Steinbergs have only girls, so maybe he's their son-in-law. But if he is, then which daughter did he marry? Sarah married that nice lawyer from Budapest and Esther married a businessman from Zhadomir, so it must be Sarah's husband. Which means that his name is Alexander Cohen, if I'm not mistaken. But if he comes from Budapest, with all the anti-Semitism they have there, he must have changed his name. What's the Hungarian equivalent of Cohen? Kovacs. But if he changed his name he must have special status. What could it be? A doctorate from the University.

At this point, the scholar turns to the young man and said, "How do you do, Dr. Kovacs?"

"Very well, thank you, sir," answered the startled passenger. "But how is it that you know my name?"

"Oh," replied the scholar, "it was obvious." (For other versions of this joke, see Ausubel 1948, 7–8; Rosten 1970, 63–65; Whitfield 1978, 57–58.)

Freud in his remarkable 1905 monograph on *Wit and Its Relation to the Unconscious* included a short joke involving two Jews on a train that parodies the Jewish tendency to make logical, in this case illogical, inferences:

Two Jews met on a train at a Galician railway station. "Where are you traveling?" asked one.

"To Cracow," was the reply.

"Now see here, what a liar you are!" said the first one, bristling. "When you say that you are traveling to Cracow, you really wish me to believe that you are traveling to Lemberg. Well, but I am sure that you are really traveling to Cracow, so why lie about it?" (Freud 1938, 707; for other versions, see Ausubel 1948, 374; Rosten 1970, 335; Eliezer 1984, 77.)

A fuller version of this joke links Freud's text with the preceding one:

Way back in the days when the Czars ruled in Russia, Avram boarded a train for the first time in his life. He sat back in his seat, prepared to gaze out the window and enjoy the rolling countryside. A man came in and sat opposite him. After a moment of silence, Avram was greeted with a big "Shalom, Avram! Do you remem-

> ber me? My name is Muttel. How is your health?" Avram answered, "My health? Ehhhh!" nodding his head as he spoke. There was a long pause. Muttel broke the silence. "So where are you going, Avram?" "Ehhhh . . . I'm taking a little ride to Minsk." Muttel went into a strange interlude. He began to reason to himself: Avram tells me he's taking a little ride to Minsk. If he was going to Minsk, would he tell me, practically a perfect stranger? No! So if he's not going to Minsk, where could he be going? One place. Pinsk! So what is he going to do in Pinsk? Only one thing. After all, a bachelor he still is, so he's going to Pinsk to get married. So whom could he be marrying in Pinsk? In Pinsk, there are only three Jewish families he could possibly know . . . the Pitzicks, the Rabinowitzs and the Pupkowitzs. To the Pitzicks, he wouldn't be going. Pitzick has only sons. The Rabinowitzs have two daughters but they're both married. But the Pupkowitzs, ah! They have three daughters . . . Sonia, Tanya and Luba. Sonia is too young; Tanya, well not so good looking; ah! But Luba, a living doll! So, one thing . . . he's going to marry Luba Pupkowitz. Muttel called across to Avram, "Avram, my friend, allow me to congratulate you on your forthcoming marriage to Luba Pupkowitz!" Avram, startled, stammered, "Well, well . . . how do you know that?" "How did I know that?" replied Muttel. "Why, you practically told me!" (Blumenfeld, 1969, 17–18; for other versions, see Pollack 1979, 52–53; Rosten 1982, 31; Telushkin 1992, 51–52.)

It is not hard to make fun of talmudic reasoning as these joke texts attest.

Some of the best parodies of talmudic reasoning are to be found in the many beloved Yiddish folktales recounted that purport to illustrate the would-be wisdom of the inhabitants of Chelm. In a good many of these celebrated stories, the false premises or false inferences drawn through the manipulation of "typical Chelmic logic" (Spaulding 1969, 115) are clearly meant to poke fun at rabbinical thought processes. In one text, a young cobbler of Chelm takes a bride of eighteen but is surprised when three months after the marriage, she gives birth. He rushes to the rabbi saying that his own mother had told him that it takes nine months to make a baby.

> The rabbi stroked his beard and reflected upon this strange occurrence. When he had meditated long and earnestly, he spoke to the young man, his voice unusually kind. "We will solve this mystery with talmudic logic, through the asking of questions. First, my son, you say you have been married for three months?"
>
> "Yes, Rabbi."
>
> "Your wife has lived with you for three months?"
>
> "Yes, she has."
>
> "And you have lived with your wife for three months?"
>
> "Yes."
>
> "There you have it, young man, add up the total: three months plus three months plus three months. How much is that?"

"Nine months, Rabbi."

"Correct," said the rabbi gently. "Peace be with you and yours. Now go home to your wife and nine-month baby." (Spaulding 1969, 116)

Freud, early on in *Moses and Monotheism*, made a specific allusion to his hope that readers would not deem his reasoning overly Talmudic: "It is not attractive to be classed with the scholastics and Talmudists who are satisfied to exercise their ingenuity, unconcerned how far removed their conclusions may be from the truth" (1955, 17). On the other hand, it is reported that Freud, acknowledging that the Jewish penchant for overintellectualization may have been a good thing for the development of psychoanalysis, saw this trait as a positive one: "Certainly the Jews have a strong tendency to rationalize—that is a very good thing" (Wortis 1963, 146). Actually, as early as 1908, psychoanalyst Karl Abraham wrote a letter to Freud in which he remarked that he felt they shared in common a "Talmudic way of thinking." Abraham continued by commenting, "Some days ago a small paragraph in *Jokes* strangely attracted me. When I looked at it more closely, I found that, in the technique of apposition and in its full structure, it was completely Talmudic" (Abraham and Freud 1965, 36). One rabbi suggested that Talmudic logic "delves beneath the surface to find logical connection where none would seem at first sight, to exist" (Rabinowitz 1996, 116). And in a brilliant essay, Handelman shows in convincing fashion that Freud's technique in interpreting dreams is identical in structure to rabbinic reasoning. "Both rabbinic hermeneutics and psychoanalysis attain unity by expansion and dilation of meaning, by making manifest the hidden unseen *connections between* phenomena" (1981, 210). Freud and the host of rabbis interpreting the Oral Torah did not claim to be creators of meaning but rather that they were merely uncovering or discovering inherent latent truths (214). Ostow phrases the matter in similar fashion, observing that biblical exegesis and psychoanalytic interpretation "resemble each other in that both infer concealed meaning from manifest text, by the application of a set of rules" (1982, 10). It should, however, be noted that there have been detailed criticisms of so-called Talmudic logic on the grounds of its possibly specious assumptions and reasoning (Sion 1997, 222), criticisms that have also been leveled at psychoanalytic interpretation.

The self-imposition of stringent restrictions may or may not be related to the themes of self-hate and masochism, which others have claimed are part of Jewish ethnic character (Raskin 1992, 78). However, the attempt to circumvent these self-imposed restrictions, often by means of tortuous casuistry, whether correctly labeled Talmudic or not, cannot be denied. Whether it is wearing one's door-key or pretearing toilet paper or constructing an *eruv*, the observant Jew has successfully managed to find a way around repressive laws of his own making. The observant Jew is regressing to the point of being a naughty child, willfully and somewhat gleefully violating a parental injunction. God the parent says, "Thou shalt NOT," but the observant Jewish "child" says, "Okay, I'll obey, but at the same time, I will do something else which is legally permissible." The behavior of the Orthodox Jew is essentially a compromise between "compliance" and "disobedience" (Strean 1994, xix). The delight in disputation and a definite penchant for argument are unquestionably part of this process.

There seems little doubt that Jews like to argue. They argue with God and they argue with one another. As one essayist felicitously phrased it, "The Jews are not the only people to claim to have talked to God but are, I think, the only people to have talked *back* to God, to have attempted to bargain and negotiate" (Whitfield 1978, 56). The pattern of arguments with God has certainly been well documented (Laytner 1990; Olsvanger 1921), but this pattern has not to my knowledge been understood as a projection of a child's argument with his or her parents. Just think of a child's attempt to negotiate with a parent concerning how late he or she can stay up before going to bed: ten more minutes, how about twenty more minutes, how about thirty more minutes? And then reread Abraham's dialogue with God concerning the imminent destruction of Sodom and Gomorrah. Abraham asks if God will spare the cities if there are fifty righteous souls there. God agrees whereupon Abraham counters with, "Peradventure there shall lack five of the fifty righteous: wilt thou destroy all the city for lack of five?" and God replies, "If I find there forty and five, I will not destroy it" (Gen. 18:28). Abraham continues to bargain much as a merchant might do in a market transaction. He persuades God to spare the cities if there are forty, then thirty, then twenty, and finally ten righteous souls (Gen. 18:32).

Moses too argues with God. When God commands Moses to speak to the Pharaoh to demand the release of the children of Israel, Moses demurs, mentioning his speech impediment: "And the Lord spake unto Moses, saying, 'Go in, speak unto Pharaoh king of Egypt, that he let the children of Israel go out of his land.' And Moses spake before the Lord, saying, 'Behold, the children of Israel have not hearkened unto me; how then shall Pharaoh hear me, who am of uncircumcised lips?' " (Exod. 6:11–12). God is evidently somewhat swayed by Moses' protestations and orders Moses' brother Aaron to assist in the effort to convince the Pharaoh to release the enslaved Jewish population.

There is another incident in which Moses takes issue with God. When

God learns that his people have made a molten calf to worship, he becomes angry. He says to Moses, "Now therefore let me alone, that my wrath may wax hot against them, and that I may consume them" (Exod. 32:10). Moses unhesitatingly voices his strenuous opposition to God's decision. "And Moses besought the Lord his God, and said, 'Lord, why doth thy wrath wax hot against thy people. . . . Turn from thy fierce wrath, and repent of this evil against thy people' " (Exod. 32:11, 12). Moses wins the argument: "And the Lord repented of the evil which he thought to do unto his people" (Exod. 32:14). Moses' victory is celebrated in the Psalms: "Therefore he said that he would destroy them, had not Moses his chosen stood before him in the breach, to turn away his wrath, lest he should destroy them" (Ps. 106:23).

There is another striking incident when Moses dares to oppose God's announced plans to destroy the children of Israel. During the exodus from Egypt, Moses sends a scouting party ahead to reconnoiter and these spies return with alarming reports of "a land that eateth up the inhabitants thereof" and inhabited by fearsome giants (Num. 13:32). The people begin to grumble, "Would God that we had died in the land of Egypt! Or would God we had died in this wilderness! . . . Were it not better for us to return into Egypt?" (Num. 14:2, 3). God becomes enraged at the people's lack of faith in him and he threatens to destroy them. "And the Lord said unto Moses, 'How long will this people provoke me? And how long will it be ere they believe me, for all the signs which I have showed among them? I will smite them with the pestilence, and disinherit them' " (Num. 14:11–12). God is clearly capable of feeling anger and displaying his temper. A passage in Isaiah confirms this: "Hear, O heavens, and give ear, O earth: for the Lord hath spoken; I have nourished and brought up children, and they have rebelled against me. . . . Ah sinful nation, a people laden with iniquity, a seed of evildoers, children that are corrupters: they have forsaken the Lord, they have provoked the Holy One of Israel unto anger, they are gone away backward" (1:2, 4). Moses, acting as a defense attorney, again takes issue with God who decides to take Moses' advice: "Pardon, I beseech thee, the iniquity of this people according unto the greatness of thy mercy, and as thou hast forgiven this people, from Egypt even until now. And the Lord said, 'I have pardoned according to thy word' " (Num. 14:19–20).

Still another instance of an argument with God is when, in a passage cited earlier, He orders Ezekiel to act the part of the children of Israel about to be punished for their iniquity with particular reference to the fuel to be used for baking bread: "And thou shalt eat it as barley cakes, and thou shalt bake it with dung that cometh out of man, in their sight" but Ezekiel protests against this use of human feces, claiming that he has never in his life violated

God's laws. God is evidently persuaded by this and he relents by allowing Ezekiel to substitute cow dung. "Then he said unto me, 'Lo, I have given thee cow dung for man's dung, and thou shalt prepare thy bread therewith' " (Ezek. 4:12, 15). It is not altogether clear whether God's command involves merely using human excrement as fuel (Lewin 1999, 124) or rather actually ingesting it as a component of a cake mixture (Maccoby 1999, 65).

Throughout the Old Testament, various leaders and prophets complain bitterly to God about his treatment of his "Chosen People," the "children of Israel." The Book of Job is a classic example of a righteous man complaining to God about the suffering he has to endure, which includes the loss of his wealth, children, and health (Laytner 1990, 32–38; Leamon 1995, 19–32). As one modern astute observer remarks with respect to the Jews being the "chosen people," "What in the world were they chosen for, suffering and yet more suffering?" (Feinsilver 1970, 276). A folk version of this sentiment asks: "Dear God, if you really loved the Jews why did you make them the chosen people?" (Rosten 1982, 170), or "Thou hast chosen us from among all the nations—but why did You have to pick on the Jews?" (Rosten 1992, 47). Some Jews feel that the whole idea of their being "the" "Chosen People" should be totally abandoned inasmuch as it carries an unfortunate connotation of smugness if not outright arrogance (Kolatch 1985, 24–25).

Quite a remarkable dialogue illustrating the Jewish resentment at what they consider to be their unfair treatment by God is found in an anecdote cited by Immanuel Olsvanger in a fascinating paper originally presented to the Swiss Folklore Society in Basel in 1919.

> The soul of a Jew standing at the gates of Heaven was asked by God, "Has thou been honest in thine earthly deeds?" The Jew answered this challenge by the Lord of the Universe: "And Thou, O Lord, has Thou dealt honourably with Thy People?" "What wrong then have I done?" asked God of him, and the Jew replied: "That would I not say, because Thou wouldst then have to be ashamed." But on God's loudly exclaiming, "I order thee to speak," the Jew said, "Thy command must I obey. Hearken then: The Jews, who serve Thee faithfully and adore Thee alone, go through life in abject poverty; but the Christians who assign to Thee a wife and a son, enjoy wealth and even luxury. And I am a poor Jew. Is it to be wondered at, that I should now and then be led to do unworthy acts in my affairs? Why dost Thou not have a care for my welfare as Thou didst promise. I should like to see what would be Thy course, if Thou were in reality burdened with a wife and children and had a God who cared for Thee as Thou carest for us." And there was silence on the part of the Lord of the Universe. (Olsvanger 1921, 24–25)

It is precisely God's seeming silence, if not obdurate indifference, in response to acute Jewish suffering that makes some Jews angry. Rabbis ask God,

"Who like you hears the humiliation of His children and remains silent?" (Wolpe 1990, 144).

There are other equally powerful complaints. Here is one that Rosten calls the most memorable story he knows.

> On the eve of Yom Kippur, that most solemn and sacred day, an old Jew looked up to heaven and sighed: "Dear God, listen: the butcher in our village, Shepsel, is a good man, an honorable man, who never turns away the needy; yet Shepsel himself is so poor that he and his wife sometimes go without meat! . . . Or take Fishel, our shoemaker, a model of piety and kindness—yet his beloved mother is dying in terrible pain. . . . And Reb Label, our *melamed* [teacher], who loves all the lads he teaches and is loved by all who know him—he just developed an eye disease that may leave him blind! . . . So, on the eve of this most holy night, I ask You directly, God: Is this *fair*? I repeat: *Is this fair*? . . . So, tomorrow, O Lord, on Yom Kippur—if You forgive us, we will forgive You!" (1992, 519)

This is strikingly reminiscent of Freud's observation of the occasional transposition of the parent-child relationship: "If I were father and you my child, I would treat *you* badly" (1957, 115).

A similarly strong statement is expressed in the proverb, "When a Hassid becomes enlightened, he curses God" (Kumove 1985, 190). (For additional examples of Old Testament figures arguing with God, see Olsvanger 1921; Blank 1953; Gemser 1955; Huffmon 1959; and Kaplan 1980. For a list of other debates and arguments in the Old Testament, see Jacobs 1984, 3.)

Arguments and disputes also occur in the Old Testament between brothers. This is the case of Cain and Abel, Jacob and Esau, Moses and Aaron, Joseph and his brothers, among others. All these instances are clearly examples of sibling rivalry that again confirm the familial framework of the Old Testament. Cain, the first-born of Adam and Eve, is a farmer while his younger brother Abel is a shepherd. Both make offerings to God who favors Abel's offering over Cain's. Cain is so incensed at this slight that he kills Abel (Gen. 4:1–8). When God asks Cain, "Where is Abel thy brother?" Cain pleads ignorance and answers curtly with a flip impertinent, "Am I my brother's keeper?" (Gen. 4:10), which is hardly an appropriate reverential response to God. This is another example of the Jewish habit of treating God in an overly familiar fashion.

The folkloristic pattern of the younger son triumphing over or displacing the older is quite common (e.g., in the case of Jacob who lived in tents cheating his older brother Esau the hunter, "a man of the field," out of his birthright [Gen. 25:27, 33]). The desire of Cain to be "chosen" by God over his brother Abel and Jacob's trickster-like deceit to become senior to his brother Esau reflect this sibling rivalry pattern. Jacob, blind in his old age, is asked by his son Joseph to bless his sons, that is Jacob's grandsons Ephraim and Manasseh. Manasseh is the older, and Joseph positions him to receive the blessing from Jacob's right hand. But Jacob in placing his right hand upon Ephraim's head and his left hand on Manasseh's head overturns the rule of seniority. Manasseh was Joseph's first-born and should have received the favored "right-hand" blessing of Jacob, but Jacob literally crossed up Joseph's placement of the two boys, and as a result Ephraim is favored. Joseph protests and argues with his father, but Jacob explains that he knows what he is doing and says Manasseh "shall be great: but truly his younger brother shall be greater than he" (Gen. 48:19). The vying for a father figure's preferred blessing is almost certainly related to Jews' repeated declaration that they are God's "Chosen People." In sibling rivalry, children typically compete for their parent's blessing. Each child wants to be his or her parents' favorite and favored one.

The Jews' delight in dispute is by no means confined to the Bible. Indeed, one could say that much of the basis of the Halacha was determined by Talmudic arguments between various rabbis. According to the author of a book entitled *The Talmudic Argument*, "The Babylonian Talmud consists almost entirely of arguments. . . . Theories are advanced and then contradicted" (Jacobs 1984a, 1). After rules with respect to various situations are presented in the Mishnah, two or more rabbinical judgments will conclude with one saying "permitted" and the other saying "not permitted" or one saying "valid" and the other saying "invalid" or one saying "clean" and the other saying "unclean." One account describes the process of arguing over Talmudic interpretation as follows: "It accumulates rebuttal on top of dissent on top of opinion" (Kahn 1968, 121). On the other hand, Neusner in his ambitious 2500-page, five volume overview of halachic law sees it as basically coherent and systematic despite the apparent sets of contradictory propositions (2000, I: 16n9).

There is even a technical term *pilpul*, which denotes "various methods of talmudic study and exposition, especially by the use of subtle legal, conceptual, and casuistic differentiation" (Breuer 1972, 524). Jews skilled in the art of *pilpul* were masters of hair-splitting disputation, with particular reference to minute details of Halachic issues. The *pilpul* tradition was strong in the Middle Ages (Ehrentreu 1905) and thereafter (Pollack 1971, 77–78), but in one sense it has never really died out. Rabinowitz offers a positive definition: "The essential use of logical argument in the Talmud lies in the investigation of the truth of assertions and opinions, testing them and discussing them critically. This dialectic is called *pilpul*" (1996, 128). In contrast, Potok describes *pilpul* as: "empty discussions about matters that had no practical connection with the desperate needs of the masses of Jews. *Pilpul*, these discussions are called—empty, nonsensical arguments over minute points of the Talmud that have no relation at all to the world" (1967, 107). Rosten tends to agree with this assessment: "An inflated form of analysis and debate used in Talmudic study, i.e., unproductive hair-splitting that is employed not so much to advance clarity or reveal meaning as to display one's own cleverness" (1970, 202; 1982, 254). Gilman documents the idea of *pilpul* as "representative of Talmudic aggressiveness" and the "source of all error among modern Jews. . . . By its manner of understanding and presentation, its faulty logic, and its superficial analysis, it corrupts Jews, and at such an early age that their entire lives are warped" (1986, 93).

Even in modern times, there are serious disagreements as to what the proper interpretation of a given law is or should be. The love of argument and disagreement is well documented in Jewish folklore. A popular proverb proclaims: "Two Jews, three opinions" (Spaulding 1969, 174). An old joke claims that "the only thing two Jews can agree on is how much a third Jew should give to charity" (Feinsilver 1970, 222). Anything and everything can be subject to debate, can be questioned. In one old chestnut, a Jew is asked, "Why do Jews always answer a question with a question?" His answer, "Why not?" (Feinsilver 1970, 298; Naiman 1983, 117). Sometimes, it happens that the differences of opinion degenerate into shouting matches. Here is an excellent Jewish joke that comments on this tendency:

> Yeshiva University decided to field a crew team. Unfortunately, they lost race after race. They practiced for hours every day, but never managed to come in any better than dead last. The Yeshiva coach finally decided to send Yankel to spy on the Harvard team. So Yankel shlepped off to Cambridge and hid in the bullrushes along the Charles River from where he carefully watched the Harvard team as they practiced. Yankel finally returned to Yeshiva and reported to the crew coach: "I have figured out their secret," he announced. "They have eight guys rowing and only one guy shouting." (For another version, see Cohen [1999, 42].)

Very often, the dispute or argument concerns religious practice. Here is a somewhat detailed version of a very common Jewish joke:

> There is a Jewish story that starts with a shipwreck and a Providential rescue on a desert island for twenty male survivors, of mixed faiths. The men take stock as rapidly as possible. They find plentiful food and water. The native women are

amiable and pleasingly pale. After a month, the survivors decide to thank God and meet in three separate groups to plan their houses of worship.

Seven are Roman Catholics. They say a Hail Mary, and build a church.

Nine are Protestants. They talk briefly and build two churches, one with a dirt floor for Fundamentalists.

The three Jews argue for a week before they can agree on what to do. Then they build four synagogues. Three cover specific branches of religious Judaism. The fourth gives them each a synagogue not to be caught dead in. (Kahn 1968, 49; cf. Spaulding 1969, 102)

In this version of the joke, the Jews argue for a week before reaching any kind of decision. In many versions, it is a single Jew stranded on a desert island. When a ship finally appears, one of the rescuers notices that the Jew has built two synagogues. When the rescuer asks, "Why are there two synagogues?" The Jew says, "Well, this one I go to, and that one I wouldn't set foot in!" In another version, the punchline is: "This one I go to and that one, feh, is the one I used to belong to." In yet another version (Kramer 1994, 162), the punchline is: "But this one, here, is where I pray, and the other I wouldn't go into if you paid me."

One of the finest examples of a joke illustrating the Jewish penchant for arguing about religious practice is surely the following:

A new rabbi comes to a well-established congregation. Every week on the Sabbath, a fight erupts during the service. When it comes time to recite the *Sh'ma Yisra'el*, "Hear, O Israel, the Lord is Our God, the Lord is One," half of the congregation stands and the other half sits. The half who stand say, "Of course we stand for the *Sh'ma Yisra'el*: It's the credo of Judaism. Throughout history, thousands of Jews have died with the words of the *Sh'ma* on their lips." The half who remain seated say, "No. According to the *Shulkhan Aruch*, if you are seated when you come to the *Sh'ma*, you remain seated." The people who are standing yell at the people who are sitting, "Stand up!" while the people who are sitting yell at the people who are standing, "Sit down!" It's destroying the whole decorum of the service, and driving the new rabbi crazy.

Finally, it's brought to the rabbi's attention that at a nearby home for the aged is a ninety-eight-year-old man who was a founding member of the congregation. So in accordance with Talmudic tradition, the rabbi appoints a delegation of three, one who stands for the *Sh'ma*, one who sits, and the rabbi himself, to go interview the man. They enter his room, and the man who stands for the *Sh'ma* rushes over to the old man and says: "Wasn't it the tradition in our congregation to stand for the *Sh'ma*?"

"No," the old man answers in a weak voice. "That wasn't the tradition."

The other man jumps in excitedly. "Wasn't it the tradition in our congregation to sit for the *Sh'ma?*"

"No," the old man says, "That wasn't the tradition."

At this point, the rabbi cannot control himself. He cuts in angrily. "I don't care what the tradition was! Just tell them one or the other. Do you know what goes on in services every week—the people who are standing yell at the people who are sitting, the people who are sitting yell at the people who are standing—"

"That was the tradition," the old man says. (Telushkin 1992, 97–98)

It turns out that the issue of whether to sit or stand when a portion of the Torah is read during a service is a genuine one (Brooks 1990, 36). According to one source, the debate goes back to the seventh century if not before. Supposedly Babylonian Jews sat down when reading the Shema while the Jews remaining in Palestine stood up (Finkelstein 1938, 181; Donin 1980, 148). Moreover, the debate about whether to sit or stand during the Shema is reminiscent of the difference of opinion as to whether to sit or stand during the declaration of the Sabbath Kiddush or Sanctification (Pick 1998, 31; Kolatch 1995, 227). According to one source, "Different customs prevail on whether everyone stands or sits during the Kiddush. Either way is correct" (Donin 1972, 76; Cohen 1986, 39). The same variation is found with respect to the recitation of the Havdalah, the blessing marking the formal end of the Sabbath (Cohen 1986, 125–126). The comment "Either way is correct" serves as a reminder that although Jews tend to disagree, they seem content to accept disagreements and contradictions as a matter of course. This attitude is reflected in another standard Jewish joke:

There was once a rabbi who was so open-minded that he could see every side of a question. One day a man came to him with the request that he grant him a divorce. "What do you hold against your wife?" asked the rabbi gravely. The man went into a lengthy recital of his complaints. "You are right," he agreed when the man finished. Then the rabbi turned to the woman, "Now let us hear your story," he urged. And the woman in her turn began to tell of the cruel mistreatment she had suffered at her husband's hands. The rabbi listened with obvious distress. "You are right," he said with conviction when she finished. At this the rabbi's wife, who was present, exclaimed, "How can this be? Surely both of them couldn't be right!" The rabbi knitted his brows and reflected. "You're right, too!" he agreed. (Ausubel 1948, 22; for many other versions see Raskin 1992, 33–44.)

What is so extraordinary is that it is one thing for scholars to say, "The frequency of quarrelling in the life of the ancient Hebrews is reflected on many pages of the Old Testament" (Gemser 1955, 120); it is quite another to suggest that this propensity to argue about everything, even with God, has been a consistent characteristic of Jewish mentality for the past two millennia (Kaplan 1980, 43; Laytner 1990, 238).

One of the reasons why Jews argued, especially with God, was because they often felt God was being unfair or unjust. The debates with God by Abraham and Moses cited above illustrate this. In some instances, God's seemingly callous behavior made the Jews angry. As one authority phrased it: "Anger has a long and noble pedigree in Judaism, directed against a God who so often seems less protective, less good, than we have been promised" (Wolpe 1990, 145). It is partly a problem of reconciling theophany with theodicy (Crenshaw 1970, 1983). A people who believe that God appeared in person to Moses cannot understand why such a God would allow the existence of evil. The horrors of the Holocaust in Nazi Germany in the twentieth century surely exacerbated this dilemma (Leamon 1995, 185–219). As one writer put it: "Many Jews were stunned into silence, some into the religious rebellion of Job: God has allowed to happen what has happened; where is God?" (Maybaum 1965, 21). How could a merciful God have so utterly abandoned his "Chosen People" and allowed such mass murder and suffering to occur? Chaim Potok in *The Chosen* puts the question in the mouth of an Orthodox rabbi: "Master of the Universe, how do you permit such a thing to happen?" (1967, 191). Much the same sentiment is expressed in a Yiddish proverb: "Master-of-the-Universe, look down from Your heaven and take a good look at Your world!" (Kumove 1985, 197; Feinsilver 1970, 138). Jewish criticism of God, however, antedates the Holocaust. A Jewish joke that first appeared in print in the mid-1920s and has often been reprinted in anthologies (Raskin 1992, 61–69) illustrates this point:

> The rabbi ordered a pair of new pants for the Passover holidays from the village tailor. The tailor, who was very unreliable, took a long time finishing the job. The rabbi was afraid that he would not have the garment ready for the holidays. On the day before Passover, the tailor came running all out of breath to deliver the pants. The rabbi examined his new garment with a critical eye. "Thank you for bringing my pants on time," he said. "But tell me, my friend, if it took God only six days to create our vast and complicated world, why did it have to take you six weeks to make this simple pair of pants?" "But, Rabbi!" murmured the tailor triumphantly, "Just look at the mess God made, and then look at this beautiful pair of pants!" (Ausubel 1948, 16; cf. Spaulding 1969, 14–15; Emmes 1998, 86; and especially Raskin 1991.)

Jews have a great deal of difficulty in reconciling all the trials and tribulations they have suffered with their consistent and loyal worship of God.

Another traditional joke offers a weak divine explanation: "A religious Jew prays: 'Dear God, why is it that I suffer though I pray every day while my neighbors prosper though they are not at all religious?' A wrathful voice booms from the sky, 'Because you *nudgied* me!' " (Rosenberg and Shapiro 1958, 78; cf. Rosten 1970, 260; 1982, 348; Pollack 1979, 107; Naiman 1983, 103–104). *Nudge* or *nudzh*, as a verb means "to bore, to pester, to nag" (Rosten 1970, 274). Here God appears to have a strain of anti-Semitism. One is reminded of the old definition of an anti-Semite as "someone who hates Jews more than he should" (Rosenberg and Shapiro 1958, 75). Even in the Old Testament we find evidence that God takes umbrage at the Jews' propensity to complain: "And the Lord spake unto Moses and unto Aaron, saying, 'How long shall I bear with this evil congregation, which murmur against me? I have heard the murmurings of the children of Israel, which they murmur against me' " (Num. 14:27). His punishment is severe: "Your carcasses shall fall in this wilderness, and all that were numbered of you, according to your whole number, from twenty years old and upward, which have murmured against me, Doubtless ye shall not come into the land, concerning which I sware to make you dwell therein" (Num. 14:29–30). God's decision to punish the "murmurers" by not allowing them to enter into the Promised Land is also found in his response to a blatant act of disobedience by Moses. There are two versions of God's instructions to Moses as to how to obtain much-needed water for his charges. In the first Moses is told to strike a rock (Exod. 17:6), but in the second, God tells Moses to speak to the rock (Num. 20:8). In the second account, Moses fails to do so and instead, he hits the rock twice, an act that does produce water. However, God is angry: "And the Lord spake unto Moses and Aaron, 'Because ye believed me not . . . therefore ye shall not bring this congregation into the land which I have given them" (Num. 20:12). But the issue here is not so much God's being angry with the Jews as the Jews being angry with God.

Sometimes the level of frustration and the degree of anger reached the breaking point. The suppressed anger is evident in such a proverb as "If God lived on earth, all His windows would be broken" (Kumove 1985, 107). In a version of this same proverb cited by famed anthropologist Margaret Mead in her foreword to *Life Is With People*, we have "If God lived in the *shtetl*, He'd have His windows broken" (Zborowski and Herzog 1962, 13). The anger is less suppressed on those occasions when rabbis actually put God on trial for what was considered the undeserved suffering of "His" Chosen People (Raskin 1992, 55; Rosten 1982, 362). Noted author Elie Wiesel, survivor of Auschwitz and Buchenwald, saw such a trial held in a concentration camp. It inspired him to later write a three-act play *The Trial of God*, set in the seventeenth century. Wiesel explained the play's genesis: "Inside the kingdom of night, I witnessed a strange trial. Three rabbis—all erudite and pious men, decided one winter evening to indict God for allowing his children to be massacred. I remember: I was there, and I felt like crying. But there nobody cried" (1979, 1).

Undeserved suffering is a theme that is of considerable antiquity (Crenshaw 1983, 4). Consider the Old Testament passage, "O Lord, how long shall I cry, and thou wilt not hear! Even cry out unto thee of violence, and thou wilt not save!" (Hab. 1:2). God's seeming callousness in the light of Jewish needs is also reflected in a modern Yiddish proverb: A mentsh trakht un got lakht (Man makes plans and God laughs) (Matisoff 1979, 46; Emmes 1998, 51; Kumove 1999, 142). Avner Ziv in the introduction to his edited book *Jewish Humor* offers this insight: "The suffering of the Jews is, after all, like everything else in the world, an outcome of God's will. Since man cannot be angry at God and show aggression towards him, this aggression is directed inward, that is, towards ourselves" (1986, 8).

A psychotherapist who has treated many Orthodox patients says much the same thing. According to him, the anger initially directed at God is usually re-channeled toward the self. "Though infuriated at God for not granting permanent peace on earth and good will toward people, the Orthodox have a propensity to turn their venom against themselves and become even more devout, subservient to, and masochistic with their God" (Strean 1994, 13, 152). This psychotherapist explains: "Because many of their prayers and wishes are frequently ungratified . . . Orthodox Jews have an angry relationship with God. However, when children feel anger and hatred towards parents whom they desperately need, they turn their anger inward and feel like 'bad children' " (18), and "Orthodox Jews would rather maintain their punitive superegos, feel guilty much of the time, and not aggress toward their God" (35). Another analyst puts it this way: "We repress anger directed toward God and redirect it against ourselves, in the hope of retaining or increasing God's protection" (Ostow 1980, 22). Here we find an echo of Freud's formulation in the concluding section of *Moses and Monotheism* in which he suggested that the Jews' feelings of guilt (for not having sufficiently observed God's laws) stemmed from "the repressed hostility to God" and that this guilt was endless as is typical "in the reaction-formations of obsessional neurosis" (1955, 173). Freud also remarked that when a "father fosters the development of an over-strict super-ego . . . the child has no other way of disposing of its aggressiveness than to turn it inwards" (1957, 117n1). Interestingly enough, another psychoanalyst has made a parallel observation with respect to masochistic tendencies often expressed in Jewish jokes. According to Grotjahn, "Aggression turned against the self seems to be an essential feature of the truly Jewish joke" (1961, 186). There is a Jewish joke that articulates and confirms the portion of this theory that reflects the Jew's disappointment with what he or she perceives to be a unfeeling, uncaring God, indifferent to human pain and suffering:

> An American Jew visiting Israel is living in a flat with a view overlooking the Wailing Wall. Each day, he can see out of his window a little old man, dressed in black Orthodox clothing, davening at the Wall, three times a day, morning, noon, and night. One day, he happens to encounter the man on the street and he comments that he has seen him praying faithfully every single day and that he is curious about one thing: What exactly does he pray for? The man replies that first of all he prays for world peace and the end of warfare; second, he prays that life-threatening diseases will be wiped out and that good health will prevail everywhere on earth; and finally, he prays there will be an end to poverty and hunger for all mankind. The American Jew responds, "Those are worthy goals all right, but tell me, when you look at the world as it is today with its violence, plagues, and poverty, what do you think?" The little old man answers, "It's like talking to a wall!" (For another version, see Rosten 1992, 202–203.)

The traditional idiom of "I might as well be talking to the wall" as an ironic expression of extreme exasperation or frustration from futility may well have come from a Yiddish phrase "*Red tsum vant!*" (Talk to the wall!) (Feinsilver 1970, 88, 340–341; Rosten 1982, 141, 321), or "*Gey red tsu der vant*" (Go talk to the wall) (Kumove 1999, 137). This fact plus the setting of the joke in Jerusalem emphasize its quintessential Jewishness.

There is another Yiddish proverb that not only confirms the God-father equation but also expresses a complaint against the various afflictions God sees fit to impose. "God is a father: If He doesn't give you a boil, He gives you a blister" (Kumove 1999, 143).

There have been other explanations offered for the Jew's alleged propensity to direct his anger and aggression inward toward himself and his own group. Lewin, for example, in his pioneering 1941 essay titled "Self-Hatred Among Jews," suggested that assimilation was a factor. Specifically, he claimed that the Jew had internalized the values of the dominant, majority culture and consequently saw himself through Christian, often anti-Semitic, eyes (1941, 225–226). One of his observations: "The feeling of inferiority of the Jew is but an indication of the fact that he sees things Jewish with the eyes of the unfriendly majority" (1941, 230; for earlier articulations of this theory of Jewish self-hate, see Gilman [1986, 286–308]).

Freud also wondered about the Jewish response to God's harsh treatment of them. In *Moses and Monotheism*, he raised the issue: "Why the people of Israel, however, adhered to their God all the more devotedly the worse they were treated by him—that is a question which we must leave open for the moment" (1955, 143). He gave a partial answer in *Civilization and Its Discontents*:

> The people of Israel believed themselves to be God's favourite child, and when the great Father hurled visitation after visitation upon them, it still never shook them in this belief or caused them to doubt his power and his justice; they proceeded instead to bring their prophets into the world to declare their sinfulness to them and out of their sense of guilt they constructed the stringent commandments of their priestly religion. (1957, 111)

But the thrust of my argument in this extended essay is that Jews once having constructed so many "stringent commandments" have managed to cleverly find ways around obeying them. Their unmitigated delight in dispute has served them well in looking for loopholes.

It is my contention that there is such a thing as Jewish character and furthermore that one of the consistent traits of that character is a type of *cacoethes carpendi*. I maintain, furthermore, that Jews themselves recognize this tendency to criticize and find fault and that this recognition is overtly acknowledged in Jewish jokes. The idea that the "Jewish joke reveals the Jewish character" is not new (Gilman 1986, 253), and that is one reason why I have not hesitated to cite jokes on numerous occasions in this essay. As for the tendency to offer unsolicited criticism, consider the wording in the following three versions of the same joke. First, from the kibbutz Kfar Blum in the Upper Galilee region in 1985: "Why don't Israelis have sex on the lawn? Because their neighbors would tell them how to do it." An earlier version from Tel Aviv in 1959: "Why don't Jews make love in the street? They don't want advice from the neighbors." Finally, from a small anthology of Jewish jokes published in 1984: "Why don't people make love on the pavement in Israel? Because passers-by would point out what they were doing wrong" (Eliezer 1984, 45). Sometimes the penchant for giving advice has a sexist slant:

> Student: Rabbi, why did God make man before woman?
> Rabbi: Because He didn't want any advice on how to make man!

Another revealing bit of data supporting the notion that Jews themselves recognize this tendency comes from folk speech. The term *kibitzer*, as defined by Rosten, is one who "Comments from the sidelines, Offers unasked-for advice, Sticks his nose into the business of others" (1992, 265).

This endless propensity to critique, to take issue, and to offer unsolicited advice not surprisingly results in a definite penchant for argumentation as well as a delight in finding legalistic loopholes. It is not entirely clear whether the numerous examples of circumvention discussed in this essay technically meet the definition of "legal fiction" as described by legal scholars (Fuller 1967). One such scholar even goes so far to as to insist that "the jurists of the ancient Middle East did not employ the legal fiction in its proper sense" (Olivier 1975, 4). On the other hand, the author of a prize-winning essay on the subject that appeared in the *Harvard Law Review* in 1893 offers the following apt definition: "A legal fiction is a device for attaining a desired legal consequence, or avoiding an undesired legal consequence" (Mitchell 1893, 253). He further refines the definition: "A legal fiction is a device which attempts to conceal the fact that a judicial decision is not in harmony with the existing law" (262). By the terms of this definition, the circumventions of custom enumerated in this essay would surely seem to fall under the rubric of "legal fiction." Mitchell claims that legal fictions "obtain what vitality they have originally from the people" (252) and that they serve as a corrective force to satisfy popular needs when the official reigning legal system proves too rigid or inflexible to do so. With a perfect legal system, there would be no need for legal fictions (265). The relevance of this to the current discussion seems obvious. The high incidence of circumventions among Orthodox Jews is a prima facie indication that Halachic law is perceived as being too restrictive. Inasmuch as Halachic law is deemed sacred, deriving directly from God himself or the sages and rabbis who were inspired by him, it simply cannot be amended by ordinary men, no matter how inconvenient or oppressive this law might appear to be. As one writer phrased it, "Halacha relates itself to the changing social reality but in so doing is guided by transcendental prior values" (Englard 1968, 258). Hence the only solution possible is through the creation of circumventions, which, often through devious if ingenious reasoning, provide essential legal loopholes. It seemingly gives credence to the maxim: "The longest way round is the shortest way found."

Even in discussions of the topic of circumvention itself, there is clever argument used to create such a legalistic loophole that amounts to a form of circumvention. Chaim Friedberg, in a concluding summary to Rabbi Halperin's monograph *Shabbat and the Modern Kitchen*, takes up the whole question of circumvention and its ethics. No doubt the reason he did so was because the whole rationale for the existence of the Institute for Science and Halacha of which Halperin was the leading light was at stake. The principal work of the institute was to devise novel forms of elevators, electrical outlets, water heaters, and the like that would allow observant Jews to get around Sabbath restrictions. Friedberg raises the question in an unadulterated fashion: "Doesn't this approach circumvent Torah observance and create a breach in the fortress of religious law? Didn't our sages forbid circumvention of Torah law in several places in the Talmud and adopt preventive measures against its use?" (1986, 195).

Friedberg worries because most of the inventions achieved by the institute do not involve life-threatening situations that as such would automatically allow for breaking a Halachic law. Certainly the creation of a Shabbat elevator could not possibly be classified as having anything to do with a life-saving situation. It is a device designed to allow Orthodox Jews to use an elevator instead of climbing countless numbers of stairs in modern buildings such as luxury hotels. (It is also frequently found in Jewish hospitals but even there it is not necessarily a matter of life and death.)

Friedberg distinguishes two types of circumvention. The first consists of cases of evasion, and as they are tantamount to deceit and lying, they are forbidden. The second, "characterized by cunning and inventiveness only—which circumvent a prohibition without coming into contact with it" is permissible (Friedberg 1986, 201). As Friedberg phrases it, "When an evasive action is done in accordance with halachah, it is clearly not forbidden at all" (202). In the introduction to *Kashrut and the Modern Kitchen*, Rabbi Oratz boasts, "A unique quality of this book is that it explains the halakhic basis for modifications that permit actions that would otherwise be prohibited" (Halperin and Oratz 1994, 9).

Now listen to the logic presented by Friedberg summarizing Halperin's views:

> The 613 commandments were given to the people of Israel in view of their special virtue as the chosen people of the Creator. The performance, or lack of performance of a commandment by a Jew, therefore, relates to the doer, rather than to its having been done. . . . The prohibition is, then, against a Jew *doing* work on Shabbath; the intent of the Torah is not that work not be done on Shabbath. For, according to Torah law, it is permissible for a Jew to have a gentile do all types of work for him on Shabbath. (1986, 199–200)

By this reasoning, Friedberg concludes "that in the approach adopted by the Institute for Science and Halacha there is no exploitation of a breach or loophole in halachah" (1986, 200–201). In justifying the search for technological means to circumvent Sabbath restrictions, Orthodox Jews are simply extending the concept of the *Shabbes Goy*. In Israel, non-observant Jews often fulfilled the role of the *Shabbes Goy*, but an even better solution was to have ingeniously designed mechanical devices such as a Shabbat elevator replace the need for a *Shabbes Goy*. In this way, science and technology can eventually replace the *Shabbes Goy* (Abramov 1972, 9), and these new inventions can make it possible for Orthodox Jews to avoid desecrating the Sabbath (Halkin 1980–1981, 25).

CONCLUSIONS

The circumvention of custom by creating "counter-customs" documented in this essay has had at least two significant consequences for Jews—one positive, one negative. The positive consequence is that the practice of finding loopholes has generally prepared Jews well for the difficulties inevitably encountered by them during the many long centuries of surviving in the diaspora. Until the establishment of the State of Israel in 1948, the Jews of the world were by definition a minority group living in a culture or country dominated by a majority of some kind, a majority not always sympathetic or hospitable to Jews. The Jews living in Germany just prior to World War II made a serious miscalculation, one that cost many of them their lives. These Jews wrongly self-identified themselves as Jewish Germans, whereas it turned out that the majority culture, the Germans, saw these individuals as German Jews. To put the matter another way, it was a question of whether "German" was a noun or an adjective. The Jews considered themselves German, using the word as a noun, but the Germans considered them as Jews, using the word as an adjective.

A similar situation with respect to noun and adjective obtains in the United States. What is the difference, if any, between an American Jew and a Jewish American? An American Jew is a Jew first and an American second, at least grammatically speaking. The adjective modifies the more important noun; the noun does not modify the adjective! In contrast, a Jewish American is an American first, and a Jew second. Some Jews use both labels, depending upon where they are. If such a Jew were visiting Israel, he would be likely to call himself an American Jew, in part to show his solidarity with the other Jews in Israel. The same Jew at home might prefer to call himself a Jewish American to show solidarity with his fellow Americans.

One could argue that the shift from American Jew to Jewish American is a movement toward assimilation, a movement that is of concern to many

Jews who fear that Jewish culture is in danger of disappearing. At the same time, it could also be contended that the shift indicates that Jews are becoming more mainstream, even if still remaining a self-identified minority. In any case, the shift from American Jew to Jewish American is part of a larger pattern to be found among other minority groups. American Negro (with American as an adjective) has shifted to African American (with American as a noun) just as American Indian has become Native American.

In any event, whether American Jew or Jewish American, the Jew in the United States as elsewhere has had to learn to accommodate the customs and mores and especially the laws of the majority culture. In cases, where these customs, mores, and laws interfered with or threatened Jewish life, as was obviously the situation in prewar Germany, the Jews have had to find a way around them in order function or even to survive. The ability to find a clever way of avoiding conscription into the military or getting around unfair restrictions imposed upon Jews as a group is surely related to the Sabbath circumvention techniques.

A serious negative consequence of the Jewish penchant for circumvention is that it has no doubt contributed to the anti-Semitic stereotype of the Jew as a devious, crooked, wily, untrustworthy individual who will find a sneaky or tricky way to cheat a non-Jew, especially in business dealings. Once again, there are Jewish jokes that demonstrate that Jews are well aware of this stereotype: One Jew meets another on the street and says: "So, Abe, I hear you had a fire in your store last week." "Quiet, quiet," Abe replies, "it's *next* week." The resort to arson to defraud insurance companies is a common theme, so common in fact as to have inspired an American slang phrase "Jewish lightning" to refer to such deliberate burning of insured property. Two retired Jewish businessmen meet in Miami. "So, how were you able to retire?" "My store caught fire; I lost everything, but fortunately I was fully covered by insurance. How about you?" "There was a terrible flood which completely destroyed my shop, but I too was fully covered by insurance." "How do you start a flood?" In another version, a rich man settled in southern California shows his poor brother his newly purchased mansion in Bel Air. "You'll never guess how much I paid for this place," he boasted. "In fact, I had to protect my investment by taking out insurance: fire, burglary, and earthquake." The poor brother's response, "Fire and burglary I can understand, but how do you start an earthquake?" (Spaulding 1969, 412).

The term "shyster" often applied to lawyers, Jewish lawyers, refers to unethical behavior that typically involves the utilization of legal loopholes. One scholar contends that the word comes from a Yiddish word apparently related to the German *scheiss* (shit) or *scheisser* (shitter) (Feinsilver 1970,

340), an etymology not out of line with the anal erotic thesis advocated in this essay. (For further discussion of "shyster," see G. Cohen 1982; 1984; Gold 1989, 35–41.) The fact that most individuals who use the term "shyster" are almost certainly totally unaware that it may derive from *scheisser* does not negate its possible significance. One wonders if it is just phonetic coincidence that the name of the unscrupulous Jewish money-lender in Shakespeare's *Merchant of Venice* begins with the same set of initial consonants: Shylock. Rosten goes so far as to suggest that the aural effect of the numerous Yiddish expressions that begin with "sh" point to an anal linkage (1982, 275).

It might be worth remarking that there are plenty of other modern Yiddish words that refer directly or obliquely to *scheiss* activities. A crotchety old man is called an *alter kocker*, which translates literally as "old defecator" (Rosten 1970, 14). A slang term *bupkes* refers to "an insignificant quantity, bordering on nothing" and supposedly comes from Russian for "beans," but in Yiddish it means "goat droppings" (Rosten 1982, 65) or "rabbit turds" (Naiman 1983, 16), which look like beans. A reliable informant reported a phrase learned from his grandfather used to chasten a bored child when he complains that there is nothing to do. The child may be told to *kak in di hand un shmeer an di vand* (to shit in one's hand and smear it on the wall). There is also a Yiddish proverb, "If you don't have enough to do, shitting is also work" (Kumove 1984, 149; Bernstein 1969, 334). In fact, there are quite a few Yiddish proverbs that refer directly to the act of defecation. In 1908, the great Jewish paremiologist Ignaz Bernstein published not only his major collection of Yiddish proverbs, *Jüdische Sprichwörter und Redensarten*, but also a separate limited edition of some 227 obscene proverbs titled *Erotica and Rustica*. This valuable collection has been included as an appendix to the 1969 reprint edition of the Bernstein proverb corpus and has also been translated from Yiddish into English (Weltman and Zuckerman 1975).

Interestingly enough, the maverick psychologist A. A. Roback, in a postscript to a letter written to Freud on March 10, 1930, called Freud's attention to Bernstein's "little book," suggesting that if Freud looked at it, he "would probably be able to infer that anal eroticism is quite frequent among the Jews as a class" (1957, 31). Roback said no more than this and did not cite any of the numerous examples of proverbs concerned with urination and defecation (e.g., *Winschen ün kaken is alz ejns* [Wishing and shitting is all one]), to which Bernstein added an annotation suggesting that the people knew that it was not true that wishing and shitting were the same thing, citing another proverb, "If a man wishes in one hand and shits in the other, only the second hand stays full" (Bernstein 1969, 156), a proverb that is still to be found in contemporary oral tradition. Another Yiddish proverb concerned with wishing observes, "If one needs [either] to wish or to fart, one doesn't have to get out of bed" (Bernstein 1969, 344). Another proverb seems to allude to constipation: *As men ken nit kaken, is a forz alejn auch güt* (If a person can't shit, a solitary fart is also good) (Bernstein 1969, 334). Another proverb uses constipation in a metaphorical fashion: *Kak, as der tuchoss is zü!* (Go shit when your ass is closed up), which Bernstein explains as referring to a situation when someone has something to do but lacks the means to do it. One anal erotic proverb mentions the Sabbath: *A jüd kakt schaboss mit blei* (A Jew shits lead on the Sabbath), which Bernstein explains as resulting from the fact that Sabbath dishes tend to be quite indigestible fare, hence as heavy as lead. The alleged linkage between feast-day diet and anal discomfort is alluded to by Freud in a letter of September 18, 1874, written to his boyhood chum Eduard Silberstein. "It is most remarkable how certain holidays are distinguished by a very special effect on the abdominal organs. Thus the Passover has a constipating effect due to unleavened bread and hardboiled eggs. Yom Kippur is so lugubrious a day not so much through God's wrath as through the plum jam and the evacuation it stimulates" (Boehlich 1990, 63). Anal themes are also found in tongue twisters. One cited by Bernstein: *Klejne kinder kaken klejne küpkelech,* which has been cleverly rendered in English as "Tiny tots make tiny turds" (Bernstein 1969, 344; Weltman and Zuckerman 1975, 4). Of course, not all Jews know Yiddish. Sephardic Jews, for instance, are more likely to speak Ladino. Still, this kind of proverbial evidence does suggest that anal erotic elements continue to be a significant part of Jewish life.

Let me cite two final jokes that combine themes of both survival and deception, with the implication that some deception may very well be necessary in order to survive.

> A Jewish businessman was in a great deal of trouble. His business was failing. He had put everything he had into the business. He owed everybody—it was so bad he was even contemplating suicide. As a last resort, he went to a rabbi and poured out his story of tears and woe. When he had finished, the rabbi said, "Here's what I want you to do: Put a beach chair and your Bible in your car and drive down to the beach. Take the beach chair and the Bible to the water's edge, sit down in the beach chair, and put the Bible in your lap. Open the Bible; the wind will riffle the pages, but finally the open Bible will come to rest on a page. Look down at the page and read the first thing you see. That will be your answer, that will tell you what to do."
>
> A year later, the businessman went back to the rabbi and brought his wife and children with him. The man was in a new custom-tailored suit, his wife in a mink

> coat, the children shining. The businessman pulled an envelope stuffed with money out of his pocket, gave it to the rabbi as a donation in thanks for his advice. The rabbi recognized the benefactor and was curious.
>
> "You did as I suggested?" he asked.
>
> "Absolutely."
>
> "You sat in a beach chair with the Bible in your lap?"
>
> "Absolutely."
>
> "You let the pages riffle until they stopped?"
>
> "Absolutely."
>
> "And what were the first words you saw?"
>
> "Chapter 11."

This joke is of interest for several reasons. First of all, it is a striking use of the ancient divination custom known as bibliomancy, whereby a book, typically the Bible, is opened at random to reveal a verse or passage that is presumed to have predictive value in recommending a course of action. Second, it reminds us that one of the options in federal bankruptcy law, namely "chapter eleven," is a perfectly legal way to avoid the payment of debts. It could certainly be construed as a legal fiction designed to place an individual's property beyond the reach of creditors. It thus qualifies as a modern form of circumvention, in this case one that in part resulted from rabbinical instruction.

The second joke also involves money and business.

> Two beggars are sitting on a park bench in Mexico City. One is holding a Cross and one a Star of David. Both are holding hats to collect contributions. People walk by, lift their noses at the man with the Star of David and drop money in the hat held by the man with the Cross. Soon the hat of the man with the Cross is filled while the hat of the man with the Star of David is empty. A priest watches and then approaches the men. He turns to the man with the Star of David and says, "Young man, don't you realize that this is a Catholic country? You'll never get any contributions in this country holding a Star of David." The man with the Star of David turns to the man with the Cross and says, "Moishe, can you imagine, this guy is trying to tell us how to run our business?"

Like most jokes, many important issues are touched upon. There is the "ubiquitous Jew" who in many texts is shown to unexpectedly appear in the strangest contexts. There is the "indignant Schnorrer" (professional mendicant or moocher) who considers he is doing his would-be benefactor a favor by allowing him to give alms and who furthermore chastises this same benefactor for having previously criticized him (Rosten 1976; 1982, 302–304;

for a useful discussion of the distinction between an ordinary beggar and a Schnorrer, see Heilman 1975). But in this case, we have Jews, living in an alien land, carrying out a deception in order to make a living. The idea that a Jew has to pretend to have converted to Catholicism to do so is part of the history of Jews in Spain and Portugal among other countries. In this case also, the Jew is well aware of the existence of anti-Semitism but he uses it to his own advantage. The two Jewish beggars are partners in a "business," even if the business involves deceiving the public.

The study of the circumvention of custom is a topic that ranges far beyond that of the particulars of Orthodox Judaism. For example, we find comparable instances among the Mennonite and Amish populations. These groups also object to the use of automobiles and electricity though not just on one day a week, the Sabbath, but rather every day (Graber and Forsyth 1986). But in some of these groups, a member may not own an automobile but is free to ride in one. In other groups, a member may own a tractor "only if its wheels are steel instead of rubber" (122). So the thesis in this extended essay is certainly not that Jews are the only people on earth who practice some form of circumvention. It is likely that all peoples indulge in some kinds of activity that could properly be called circumvention. However, it would seem that Jews are particularly adept at devising ingenious techniques of circumvention. In short, Jews are good at it. There is just no way around coming to this conclusion! In this respect, there may be some truth in the aphorism: "The Jews are just like everyone else—only more so" (Rosten 1970, xxxix).

There is one final point to be made about the connection between Sabbath and circumvention, albeit admittedly a somewhat speculative one. The reader may recall that the Ten Commandments charter for the Sabbath used the terms "Remember" and "Observe," which suggests that the Sabbath must have already been known prior to Moses' receiving the Commandments. The stated raison d'être for the Sabbath regulation, that is, to commemorate God's resting on the seventh day after creating the world and its contents, is not entirely satisfactory as a causal explanation for the observance. Why should an omnipotent deity have had to rest at all? Is it merely a divine instance of male couvade, where men imitate the actions of women giving birth (i.e., resting after the creative act of parturition)? We know that the Sabbath has something to do with the symbolic significance of the number seven, and we also suspect that the Jewish Sabbath may be related to the Babylonian *sabbatu.* The additional clue to the possible origin of Sabbath is provided by an observation made by biblical scholar Julian Morgenstern concerning the number seven. "There is some reason," he maintained, "for believing that among the ancient Semites, as is the case still today in certain Semitic localities, seven was regarded as an unlucky number" (1966, 24).

> The evidence, scanty though it may seem, perhaps justifies the hypothesis that among the ancient Semites seven was originally considered an unlucky, ill-omened number, rather than lucky and holy. It was definitely associated with evil spirits. Consequently, its mention, use, or association with any person or object was calculated to attract the evil spirits and commit the person or object into their power. (1996, 26)

We did note earlier that the number seven did not always carry a positive connotation, referring to the seven-day period of impurity resulting from touching a dead body. According to Morgenstern, a form of circumvention was practiced by the Babylonians with respect to the number seven. "In Babylonian religious literature, while the seven evil spirits were frequently spoken of as a group, no more than six were ever mentioned together by name" (1996, 25).

Morgenstern is speaking only about the number seven, but in an interesting footnote, he remarks that this may account for the institution of the Sabbath every seventh day. As a day of ill omen, belonging to the evil spirits, it may have been regarded as expedient to do no work on that day (Morgenstern 1966, 202n25). The dangers thought to be associated with a "seventh day" might also possibly be related to the traditional practice of circumcising male infants on the *eighth* day after their birth (Gen. 17:12), a practice perhaps parallel to the one according to which a new lamb was supposed to remain with its "mother" for seven days before being sacrificed "on the eighth day" (Exod. 22:30). According to one source, a custom reported in the thirteenth century entailed a vigil on the eve of a circumcision. "There was a common superstition that evil spirits seek to harm a child on that night to prevent the circumcision from taking place" (Bloch 1980, 3). Certainly if the seventh day was regarded as a day when evil spirits were about, then it would make perfect sense to take precautions to avoid doing anything on that seventh day that might attract the attention of those spirits. This might help answer the question raised by some scholars (e.g., Delaney 1998, 98) as to why circumcision was required to be performed on the eighth day after a male infant's birth.

If the seventh day were a day of danger because of prowling demonic spirits, then one might well desist from doing any normal routine work of any kind on that day, and one might well decide to stay close to the protective walls of home, to remain inside a safe area. In other words, to find a way around exposing oneself to the potential maleficent powers of evil spirits, one observed a day of seclusion and rest, perhaps appealing to one's deity for shelter and security. If there is any validity to this speculation, this would make the institution of the Sabbath itself a sacred form of circumvention. Origins of customs are always problematic and difficult to ascertain and in one sense, such questions tend to be of interest primarily to historians or scholars in other disciplines concerned with history. The Sabbath, whatever its origins, is a *fait accompli*. Called by one author "the supreme symbol of Judaism" (Dresner 1970, 14) the Sabbath is frequently extolled in the most extravagant manner. Early rabbis claimed, "The Sabbath is equal to all the other precepts of the Torah combined" (Kolatch 1985, 44). A modern writer had this to say: "If we were to condense all of Judaism—its faith, thought, life, poetry and dreams—into a single word, there is but one word which could be used—*Shabbat*, or as it is referred to in English, the 'Sabbath' " (Peli 1988, 1). So the Sabbath has for the Jew existed and persisted for more than two millennia and is likely to continue to endure for the foreseeable future.

Given the likely continuation of the Jewish Sabbath, one may well ask if the pattern of Sabbath circumventions is also likely to continue in decades if not centuries to come. The answer to this question in my opinion is yes. One reason for the continuation of Sabbath circumventions has to do with the undoubted importance of the Sabbath for Jewish identity. Even if a Jew elects to circumvent a Sabbath restriction through what a Gentile might perceive as being a somewhat devious if ingenious subterfuge, the fact is that the counter custom does per se acknowledge the existence and sacred nature of the Sabbath. The very act of avoiding a Sabbath rule in effect confirms the perpetuation of the power of that rule. If one grants the premise that so long as Judaism exists, so also will some form of Sabbath observance, then it seems inescapable that the scores of circumventions, or shall we say circum-inventions, are bound to increase in number and force. It would be a serious mistake to peremptorily dismiss the various circumventions detailed in this essay as mere Jewish non-sins (pun intended!). Their very existence and continuation constitute a kind of Sabbath glue that provides a critical adhesive basis for Jewish identity, at least among some elements in the Jewish community. As one writer phrased the issue, "Yes, all the various prohibitions serve to make the Jews a 'strange people,' and hence are a bulwark against assimilation. But we *need* the prohibitions" (Weinberger 1991, 18). Another writer claims that "the litmus test of Orthodoxy is not Passover or any other festival, not *kashrut*, not even prayer, but Shabbat" (Danzger 1989, 215) and, as we have amply demonstrated, Shabbat includes circumventions.

There is another possible reason why Sabbath circumventions will continue to play a significant role in Jewish life, and that has to do with the anal erotic hypothesis proposed in this essay. Ernest Borneman, in his thoughtful introduction to a collection of essays in *The Psychoanalysis of Money*, made the following astute observation: "Since the anal character wishes to retain, keep, guard, protect his excreta, he also 'conserves' his property, maintains traditions, clings to what has been 'tested,' upholds what is traditional and of long standing. He is 'conservative,' which means he is so keen on property that he even wishes to 'conserve' his excreta" (1976, 40). The preservation of Halacha and other forms of Jewish heritage to the extent that they become virtual obsessions among ultra-Orthodox Jews would appear to exemplify Borneman's insight.

There is yet another reason why some form of circumvention customs are likely to continue and it is a very practical one. It concerns the concept of limited time on earth for individuals. Early on, classical writers criticized the notion of the Jewish Sabbath on the grounds that Jews were obliged to "lose" one whole day every week for the duration of their lives. In sum, one-seventh of their earthly existence had to be consecrated to God, and normal productive activity had to be suspended for that day. This adds up over the course of a lifetime. As one writer phrased it, "when adding up all the Sabbaths in an average life of seventy years, we find to our amazement that there are no less than *ten years of Sabbath* in our life" (Peli 1988, 111). If the Sabbath were considered to be a lost opportunity for productive activity, that would certainly amount to a considerable chunk of precious time. If we compound the issue by noting that a normal individual is expected to sleep for approximately eight hours in a twenty-four-hour day, we see that one-third of one's life is already "lost" as far as waking-hour creativity and productivity are concerned. The one-third fraction applies independently of whether or not one observes the Sabbath. In this context, it is no wonder that some Jews resent the strict restrictions imposed by Halachic law with respect to allowable activities on the Sabbath, and that is surely one reason why circumventions were introduced in the first place and why they are very likely to continue in the future.

What is the likely response to this essay on circumvention and Jewish character? First of all, it is unlikely that many Orthodox Jews will even read it. Nor for that matter will many Conservative Jews. Reform Jews might find some of the details of interest as they have their own agenda with respect to being castigated by the Orthodox Jewish community. Orthodox Jews do not consider Reform Jews to be real Jews. Some secular Jews will probably learn about facets of Orthodox Jewish culture that they were not previously aware of. Those readers unfamiliar with or hostile to Freudian theory (often the same individuals) will no doubt reject the whole notion of "anal erotic character," not to mention the always controversial concept of ethnic or national character in general. Historians will surely object to what they consider to be the unapologetic and cavalier marshaling of source materials covering a period of 2,500 or more years. Legal scholars will quibble over what they perceive to be an unnecessary confusion of "law" and "custom." I should probably not indulge in any further attempt at prolepsis as it will surely do nothing more than help reviewers to write devastatingly negative reviews of this unusual odyssey that started from a Shabbat elevator and proceeded to refrigerator lights, *eruvs*, and *Shabbes Goys* to finally identifying what seems to me to be an abiding facet of Jewish character or mentality over a very long time span. On the other hand, if I'm fortunate enough to elicit any comments from Jewish reviewers, and if these reviewers just cannot resist arguing at length and in minute detail with my thesis, either by pointing out all my many mistakes or better yet by indicating to their readers what I really should have said, then I will be immensely pleased to see that perhaps my argument does have some merit after all.

Bibliography

Abraham, Hilda C., and Ernst L. Freud, eds. 1965. *A Psycho-Analytic Dialogue: The Letters of Sigmund Freud and Karl Abraham, 1907–1926*. New York: Basic Books.

Abraham, Karl. 1953. Contributions to the Theory of the Anal Character. In *Selected Papers on Psychoanalysis*, Karl Abraham, ed., 370–392. New York: Basic Books.

Abramov, S. Zalman. 1972. The Halachah and the Requirements of a Modern State. *Central Conference of American Rabbis Journal* 19 (1): 2–18.

———. 1976. *Perpetual Dilemma: Jewish Religion in the Jewish State*. Cranbury, N. J.: Associated University Presses.

Amsel, Abraham. 1970. Judaism and Psychology. *Tradition* 11 (2): 60–73.

Andreasen, Niels-Erik. 1972. *The Old Testament Sabbath: A Tradition-Historical Investigation*. Missoula, Mont.: Society of Biblical Literature.

———. 1974. Recent Studies of the Old Testament Sabbath: Some Observations. *Zeitschrift für die Alttestamentliche Wissenschaft* 86: 453–469.

Andrian, Ferdinand von. 1901. Die Siebenzahl im Geistesleben der Völker. *Mittheilungen der Anthropologischen Gesellschaft in Wien* 31: 225–274.

Appel, Gersion. 1977. *The Concise Code of Jewish Law*. New York: KTAV Publishing House.

Asheri, Michael. 1978. *Living Jewish: The Lore and Law of the Practicing Jew*. New York: Everest House.

Ausubel, Nathan. 1948. *A Treasury of Jewish Folklore*. New York: Crown Publishers.

Bacchiocchi, Samuele. 1977. *From Sabbath to Sunday: A Historical Investigation of the Rise of Sunday Observance in Early Christianity*. Rome: Pontifical Gregorian University.

———. 1998. *The Sabbath under Crossfire: A Biblical Analysis of Recent Sabbath/Sunday Developments*. Berrien Springs, Mo.: Biblical Perspectives.

Back, Sven-Olav. 1995. *Jesus of Nazareth and the Sabbath Commandment*. Åbo: Åbo Akademi University Press.

Barack, Nathan A. 1965. *A History of Sabbath*. New York: Jonathan David.

Beare, F. W. 1960. The Sabbath Was Made for Man? *Journal of Biblical Literature* 79: 130–136.

Bechhofer, Yosef Gavriel. 1998. *The Contemporary Eruv: Eruvin in Modern Metropolitan Areas*. Jerusalem: Feldheim Publishers.

Beit-Hallahmi, Benjamin. 1994. The Foundations of Judaism: Psychoanalytic Interpretations. *Israel Journal of Psychiatry and Related Sciences* 31: 200–210.

———. 1996. *Psychoanalytic Studies of Religion: A Critical Assessment and Annotated Bibliography*. Westport, Conn.: Greenwood Press.

Beloff, Halla. 1957. The Structure and Origin of the Anal Character. *Genetic Psychology Monographs* 55: 141–172.

Ben Motke der Tzig, Pesach, and Dan Ben Pesach. 1981. *Mostly Vulgar Yiddish Humor*. Stony Creek, Conn.: Yiddish Archivist Press.

Benedict, Ruth. 1929. The Science of Custom. *Century Magazine* 117: 641–649.

Berkovits, Eliezer. 1983. *Not in Heaven: The Nature and Function of Halakha*. New York: KTAV Publishing House.

Bernstein, Ignaz. 1969. *Jüdische Sprichwörter und Redensarten im Anhang Erotica und Rustica*. Hildesheim: Georg Olms Verlagsbuch-Handlung.

Biggs, Charles R. 1975. Exposition and Adaptation of the Sabbath Commandment in the OT. *Australian Biblical Review* 23: 13–23.

Bishai, Wilson B. 1963. Sabbath Observance from Coptic Sources. *Andrews University Seminary Studies* 1: 25–31.

Blank, Sheldon H. 1953. Men Against God: The Promethean Element in Biblical Prayer. *Journal of Biblical Literature* 72: 1–13.

Bleich, J. David. 1986. Use of Disposable Diapers on Shabbat. *Journal of Halacha and Contemporary Society* 12 (Fall): 27–49.

———. 1995. Use of Crockpots on *Shabbat*. *Tradition* 29 (4): 43–46.

Bloch, Abraham P. 1980. *The Biblical and Historical Background of Jewish Customs and Ceremonies*. New York: KTAV Publishing House.

Blumenfeld, Gerry. 1969. *Some of My Best Jokes Are Jewish*. New York: Paperback Library.

Boas, Franz. 1923. Are the Jews a Race? *The World Tomorrow* 6 (1): 5–6.

Boehlich, Walter, ed. 1990. *The Letters of Sigmund Freud to Eduard Silberstein 1871–1881*. Cambridge: Harvard University Press.

Booth, Roger P. 1986. *Jesus and the Laws of Purity: Tradition History and Legal History in Mark 7*. Sheffield: JSOT Press.

Borneman, Ernest. 1976. On the Psychoanalysis of Money. In *The Psychoanalysis of Money*, Ernest Borneman, ed., 1–70. New York: Urizen Books.

Bracciolini, Giovanni Francesco Poggio. 1968. *The Facetiae of Giovanni Francesco Poggio Bracciolini*. New York: Award Books.

Brandes, Stanley. 1985. *Forty: The Age and the Symbol*. Knoxville: University of Tennessee Press.

Braude, William G., trans. 1968. *Pesikta Rabbati: Discourses for Feasts, Fasts, and Special Sabbaths*. 2 vols. New Haven, Conn.: Yale University Press.

Breuer, Mordechai. 1972. Pilpul. *Encyclopaedia Judaica*, Vol. 13., 524–527. Jerusalem: Encyclopaedia Judaica.

Brill, A. A. 1912. Anal Eroticism and Character. *Journal of Abnormal Psychology* 7: 196–203.

———. 1955. *Lectures on Psychoanalytic Psychiatry*. New York: Vintage Books.

Bronner, Leila Leah. 1993. From Veil to Wig: Jewish Women's Hair Covering. *Judaism* 42: 465–477.

Brooks, Roger. 1990. *The Spirit of the Ten Commandments: Shattering the Myth of Rabbinic Legalism*. San Francisco: Harper & Row.

Broyde, Michael, and Howard Jachter. 1991. The Use of Electricity on Shabbat and Yom Tov. *The Journal of Halacha and Contemporary Society* 21 (Spring): 4–47.

———. 1993. Electrically Produced Fire or Light in Positive Commandments. *Journal of Halacha and Contemporary Society* 25 (Spring): 89–126.

———. 1995. The Use of Elevators and Escalators on Shabbat and Yom Tov. *Journal of Halacha and Contemporary Society* 29 (Spring): 62–88.

Budde, Karl. 1928. The Sabbath and the Week: Their Origin and Their Nature. *Journal of Theological Studies* 30: 1–15.

Buchanan, George Wesley. 1963. The Role of Purity in the Structure of the Essene Sect. *Revue de Qumran* 4: 397–406.

Bulmer, Ralph. 1989. The Uncleanness of the Birds of Leviticus and Deuteronomy. *Man* 24: 304–320.

Caplan, Philip J. 1996. *The Puzzle of the 613 Commandments*. Northvale, N.J.: Jason Aronson.

Carmichael, Calum M. 1977. A Ceremonial Crux: Removing a Man's Sandal as a Female Gesture of Contempt. *Journal of Biblical Literature* 96: 321–336.

———. 1982. Forbidden Mixtures. *Vetus Testamentum* 32: 394–415.

———. 1995. Forbidden Mixtures in Deuteronomy XXII 9–11 and Leviticus XIX 19. *Vetus Testamentum* 45: 433–448.

———. 1999. The Sabbatical/Jubilee Cycle and the Seven-Year Famine in Egypt. *Biblica* 80: 224–239.

———. 2000. The Origin of the Scapegoat Ritual. *Vetus Testamentum* 50: 167–182.

Carroll, Michael P. 1982. Totem and Taboo, Purity and Danger . . . and Fads and Fashion in the Study of Pollution Rules. *Behavior Science Research* 17: 271–287.

Carson, D. A., ed. 1982. *From Sabbath to Lord's Day: A Biblical, Historical, and Theological Investigation*. Grand Rapids, Mich.: Zondervan.

Celada, Benito. 1948. Numeros sagrados derivados del siete (Contribucion a la historia de siete, la semana y el sabado). *Sefarad* 8: 48–77, 333–356.

Cicero. 1951. *De Finibus Bonorum et Malorum*. Cambridge: Harvard University Press.

Clemen, Carl. 1930. Die Anwendung der Psychoanalyse auf die Erklärung der israelitisch-jüdischen Religion. *Archiv für die Gesamte Psychologie* 77: 1–14.

Cohen, Alfred S. 1995. Minhag. *Journal of Halacha and Contemporary Society* 29 (Spring): 30–61.

Cohen, Boaz. 1977. The Shulhan Aruk as a Guide for Religious Practice Today. In *Conservative Judaism and Jewish Law*, Seymour Siegel, ed., 80–110. New York: Rabbinical Assembly.

Cohen, Gerald Leonard. 1982. *Origin of the Term "Shyster."* Frankfurt am Main: Peter Lang.

———. 1984. *Origin of the Term "Shyster": Supplementary Information*. Frankfurt am Main: Peter Lang.

Cohen, Israel. 1961. *Dictionary of Parallel Proverbs in English, German and Hebrew*. Tel Aviv: Machbarot Lesifrut Publishers.
Cohen, Simcha Bunim. 1986. *The Radiance of Shabbos*. Brooklyn: Mesorah Publications.
———. 1988. *The Sanctity of Shabbos*. Brooklyn: Simcha Graphic Associates.
———. 1991. *The Shabbos Kitchen: A Comprehensive Halachic Guide to the Preparation of Food and Other Kitchen Activities on Shabbos or Yom Tov*. Brooklyn: Mesorah Publications.
———. 1993. *Children in Halachah*. Brooklyn: Mesorah Publications.
———. 1995. *The Shabbos Home: A Comprehensive Halachic Guide to the Laws of Shabbos as They Apply Throughout the Home*. Brooklyn: Mesorah Publications.
Cohen, Ted. 1999. *Jokes: Philosophical Thoughts on Joking Matters*. Chicago: University of Chicago Press.
Colson, F. H. 1926. *The Week: An Essay on the Origin & Development of the Seven-Day Cycle*. Cambridge: Cambridge University Press.
Cotton, Paul. 1933. *From Sabbath to Sunday*. Bethlehem, Pa.: Times Publishing Company.
Crenshaw, James L. 1970. Popular Questioning of the Justice of God in Ancient Israel. *Zeitschrift für die alttestamentliche Wissenschaft* 82: 380–395.
———, ed. 1983. *Theodicy in the Old Testament*. Philadelphia: Fortress Press.
Cronbach, Abraham. 1931–32. The Psychoanalytic Study of Judaism. *Hebrew Union College Annual* 8–9: 605–740.
Danby, Herbert. 1958. *The Mishnah*. London: Oxford University Press.
Danzger, M. Herbert. 1989. *Returning to Tradition: The Contemporary Revival of Orthodox Judaism*. New Haven, Conn.: Yale University Press.
De Vaux, Roland. 1959. Une Hachette Essénienne. *Vetus Testamentum* 9: 388–407.
Deiana, Giovanni. 1994. *Il Giorno dell'Espiazione: Il* kippur *nella tradizione biblica*. Bologna: Edizioni Dehoniane.
Delaney, Carol. 1998. *Abraham on Trial*. Princeton, N.J.: Princeton University Press.
Delitzsch, Friedrich. 1903. *Babel and Bible*. Chicago: Open Court.
Deshen, Shlomo. 1979. The Kol Nidre Enigma: An Anthropological View of the Day of Atonement Liturgy. *Ethnology* 18: 121–133.
Diamant, Anita. 1985. *The New Jewish Wedding*. New York: Summit Books.
Diamond, Etan. 2000. *And I Will Dwell in Their Midst: Orthodox Jews in Suburbia*. Chapel Hill: University of North Carolina Press.
Donin, Hayim Halevy. 1972. *To Be a Jew: A Guide to Jewish Observance in Contemporary Life*. New York: Basic Books.
———. 1980. *To Pray As a Jew*. New York: Basic Books.
Dooley, Lucille. 1941. The Concept of Time in Defence of Ego Integrity. *Psychiatry* 4: 13–23.
Douglas, Mary. 1966. *Purity and Danger: An Analysis of Concepts of Pollution and Taboo*. New York: Praeger.
———. 1993a. The Forbidden Animals in Leviticus. *Journal for the Study of the Old Testament* 59: 3–23.
———. 1993b. *In the Wilderness: The Doctrine of Defilement in the Book of Numbers*. Sheffield: JSOT Press.

Dresner, Samuel H. 1970. *The Sabbath*. New York: Burning Bush Press.

Dressler, Harold H. P. 1982. The Sabbath in the Old Testament. In *From Sabbath to Lord's Day*, D. A. Carson, ed., 13–41. Grand Rapids, Mich.: Zondervan.

Dundes, Alan. 1962. Earth-Diver: Creation of the Mythopoeic Male. *American Anthropologist* 64: 1032–1051.

———. 1971. A Study of Ethnic Slurs: The Jew and the Polack in the United States. *Journal of American Folklore* 84: 186–203.

———. 1989. *Life Is Like a Chicken Coop Ladder: A Study of German National Character Through Folklore*. Detroit: Wayne State University Press.

———. 1997a. *Two Tales of Crow and Sparrow: A Freudian Folkloristic Essay on Caste and Untouchability*. Lanham, Md.: Rowman & Littlefield.

———. 1997b. Why Is the Jew Dirty? In *From Game to War and Other Psychoanalytic Essays on Folklore*, 92–119. Lexington: University Press of Kentucky.

———. 1999. *Holy Writ as Oral Lit: The Bible as Folklore*. Lanham, Md.: Rowman & Littlefield.

Eder, Asher. 1997. The Sabbath Commandment: Its Two Versions. *Jewish Bible Quarterly* 25: 188–191.

Ehrentreu, H. 1905. Ueber den 'Pilpul' in den alten Jeschiboth. *Jahrbuch der Jüdisch-Literarischen Gesellschaft* 3: 206–219.

Eider, Shimon D. 1968. *Halachos of the Eruv*. Lakewood, N.J.: Eider.

———. 1970. *Halachos of Shabbos*. Lakewood, N.J.: Eider.

Eidlitz, Eliezer. 1992. *Is it Kosher? Encyclopedia of Kosher Foods: Facts and Fallacies*. Jerusalem: Feldheim Publishers.

Eilberg-Schwartz, Howard. 1994. *God's Phallus*. Boston: Beacon Press.

Eisenstein, Ira. 1970. Jewish Law and the Ways of Judaism in Our Time. In *Tradition and Contemporary Experience: Essays on Jewish Thought and Life*, Alfred Jospe, ed., 249–256. New York: Schocken.

Eitingon, Max. Aus der Frühzeit der Psychoanalyse. In *Max Eitingon In Memoriam*. Moshe Wulff, ed., 73–79. Jerusalem: Israel Psycho-Analytical Society.

Eliezer, Ben. 1984. *The World's Best Jewish Jokes*. London: Angus & Robertson.

Emmes, Yetta. 1998. *Drek! The Real Yiddish Your Bubbe Never Taught You*. New York: Plume.

Englard, Izhak. 1968. The Problem of Jewish Law in a Jewish State. *Israel Law Review* 3: 254–278.

———. 1971. The Relationship Between Religion and State in Israel. In *Jewish Law in Ancient and Modern Israel*, Haim H. Cohn, ed., 168–189. New York: KTAV Publishing House.

Faulkner, R. O. 1973. *The Ancient Egyptian Coffin Texts*. Vol. I. Warminster: Aris & Phillips.

Feinsilver, Lillian Mermin. 1970. *The Taste of Yiddish*. New York: Thomas Yoseloff.

Feldman, A. Bronson. 1953. Freudian Theology, Part 2. *Psychoanalysis* 1 (4): 37–53.

Feldman, Emanuel. 1977. *Biblical and Post-Biblical Defilement and Mourning: Law as Theology*. New York: KTAV Publishing House.

Fenichel, Otto. 1954. The Drive to Amass Wealth. In *The Collected Papers of Otto Fenichel*, 2nd Series, 89–108. New York: Norton.

———. 1999. *The Psychoanalytic Theory of Neurosis*. London: Routledge.

Ferenczi, Sandor. 1956. The Ontogenesis of the Interest in Money. In *Sex in Psycho-Analysis*, Sandor Ferenczi, ed., 269–279. New York: Dover.

Fink, Harold Kenneth. 1963. Guilt and the Obsessive-Compulsive Neurotic Personality. *Samiksa* 17: 82–96.

Finkelman, Shimon. 1991. *Shabbos: The Sabbath—Its Essence and Significance*. Brooklyn: Mesorah Publications.

Finkelstein, Louis. 1938. The Persistence of Rejected Customs in Palestine. *Jewish Quarterly Review* 29: 179–186.

Fischer, Richard E., and Samuel Juni. 1981. Anality: A Theory of Erotism and Characterology. *American Journal of Psychoanalysis* 41: 57–71.

Fisher, Seymour, and Roger P. Greenberg. 1985. *The Scientific Credibility of Freud's Theories and Therapy*. New York: Columbia University Press.

Frank, Gelya, et al. 1997. Jewish Spirituality Through Actions in Time: Daily Occupations of Young Orthodox Jewish Couples in Los Angeles. *American Journal of Occupational Therapy* 5: 199–206.

Frazer, James George. 1910. *Totemism and Exogamy*. Vol. 4. London: Macmillan.

———. 1930. *Myths of the Origin of Fire*. London: Macmillan.

Freud, Ernst L., ed. 1960. *The Letters of Sigmund Freud*. New York: Basic Books.

Freud, Sigmund. 1938. *The Basic Writings of Sigmund Freud*. New York: Random House.

———. 1949. *The Future of an Illusion*. London: Hogarth Press.

———. 1955. *Moses and Monotheism*. New York: Vintage.

———. 1957. *Civilization and Its Discontents*. London: Hogarth Press.

———. 1959a. Character and Anal Erotism. In *Collected Papers*, Vol. II, 45–50. New York: Basic Books.

———. 1959b. Obsessive Acts and Religious Practices. In *Collected Papers*, Vol. II, 25–35. New York: Basic Books.

———. 1959c. The Predisposition to Obsessional Neurosis. In *Collected Papers*, Vol. II, 122–132. New York: Basic Books.

———. 1959d. From the History of an Infantile Neurosis. In *Collected Papers*, Vol. III, 471–605. New York: Basic Books.

———. 1959e. The Acquisition of Power over Fire. In *Collected Papers*, Vol. V, 288–294.

———. 1987. *A Phylogenetic Fantasy*. Cambridge, Mass.: Harvard University Press.

———. 1993. Death and Us. In *Freud and Judaism*, David Meghnagi, ed., 11–39. London: Karnac Books.

Freud, Sigmund, and D. E. Oppenheim. 1958. *Dreams in Folklore*. New York: International Universities Press.

Friedberg, Chaim. 1986. Bridging the Gaps and Reinforcing the Wall. In *Shabbat and the Modern Kitchen*, L. I. Halperin, ed., 195–206. Woodbridge, Conn.: Gefen Books.

Friedlander, Yehuda. 1986. Halachic Issues as Satirical Elements in Nineteenth Century Hebrew Literature. In *Jewish Humor*, Avner Ziv, ed., 135–147. Tel Aviv: Papyrus.

Fromm, Erich. 1927. Der Sabbath. *Imago* 13: 223–234.

———. 1951. *The Forgotten Language: An Introduction to the Understanding of Dreams, Fairy Tales and Myths*. New York: Grove Press.

———. 1966. *You Shall Be As Gods: A Radical Interpretation of the Old Testament and Its Tradition*. New York: Fawcett.

Fromm-Reichmann, F. 1927. Das jüdische Speiseritual. *Imago* 13: 235–246.

Frymer-Kensky, Tikva. 1983. Pollution, Purification, and Purgation in Biblical Israel. In *The Word of the Lord Shall Go Forth*, Carol J. Meyers and M. O'Connor, eds., 399–414. Winona Lake: Eisenbrauns.

Fuller, Lon L. 1967. *Legal Fictions*. Stanford, Calif.: Stanford University Press.

Fuqua, Paula B. 1986. Classical Psychoanalytic Views of Money. In *The Last Taboo: Money as Symbol and Reality in Psychotherapy and Psychoanalysis*, David W. Krueger, ed., 17–23. New York: Brunner/Mazel.

Gandz, Solomon. 1948–49. The Origin of the Planetary Week or the Planetary Week in Hebrew Literature. *Proceedings of the American Academy for Jewish Research* 18: 213–254.

Ganzfried, Solomon. 1961. *Code of Jewish Law*. 4 vols. Trans. Hyman E. Goldin. New York: Hebrew Publishing Company.

Gaster, Theodor H. 1955. *Customs and Folkways of Jewish Life*. New York: William Sloane.

Gay, Volney Patrick. 1975. Psychopathology and Ritual: Freud's Essay "Obsessive Actions and Religious Practises." *Psychoanalytic Review* 62: 493–507.

Gemser, B. 1955. The *Rîb*-or Controversy-Pattern in Hebrew Mentality. In *Wisdom in Israel and in the Ancient Near East*, M. Noth and D. Winton Thomas, eds., 120–137. Leiden: E. J. Brill.

Gerleman, Gillis. 1980. Die Wurzel *kpr* im Hebräischen. In *Studien zur Alttestamentlichen Theologie*, 11–23. Heidelberg: Verlag Lambert Schneider.

Gilat, Y. D. 1963. Regarding the Antiquity of Several Sabbath Prohibitions. *Annual of Bar-Ilan University* 1: xxiv–xxvii.

Gilman, Sander L. 1986. *Jewish Self-Hatred*. Baltimore: Johns Hopkins University Press.

Gils, Félix. 1962. "Le Sabbat a été fait pour l'homme et non l'homme pour le Sabbat." *Revue Biblique* 69: 506–523.

Ginsburg, Elliot K. 1989. *The Sabbath in the Classical Kabbalah*. Albany: State University of New York Press.

Gold, David L. 1989. *Jewish Linguistic Studies*. Haifa: Association for the Study of Jewish Languages.

Goldenberg, Robert. 1991. The Place of the Sabbath in Rabbinic Judaism. In *The Sabbath in Jewish and Christian Traditions*, Tamara C. Eskenazi, Daniel J. Harrington, William H. Shea, eds., 31–44. New York: Crossroad.

Goldman, George E. 1938. A Case of Compulsive Handwashing. *Psychoanalytic Quarterly* 7: 96–121.

Goldman, Solomon. 1956. *The Ten Commandments*. Chicago: University of Chicago Press.

Gordis, Robert. 1937. *The Biblical Text in the Making: A Study of the Kethib-Qere*. Philadelphia: Dropsie College for Hebrew and Cognate Learning.

Grabbe, Lester L. 1987. The Scapegoat Tradition: A Study in Early Jewish Interpretation. *Journal for the Study of Judaism* 18: 152–167.

Graber, Robert Gates, and Dan W. Forsyth. 1986. Psychoanalytic Speculations on Horse-and-Buggy Sectarianism. *Journal of Psychoanalytic Anthropology* 9: 121–142.

Graus, Yekutiel Zeev. 1999. *The Complete Eruv Chatzeiros Guide*. Weehawken, N.J.: Maven Quality Printers.

Greenberg, Blu. 1983. *How to Run a Traditional Jewish Household*. New York: Simon and Schuster.

Greenberg, David. 1984. Are Religious Compulsions Religious or Compulsive? A Phenomenological Study. *American Journal of Psychotherapy* 38: 524–532.

Grinstein, Alexander. 1952. Stages in the Development of Control over Fire. *International Journal of Psycho-Analysis* 33: 416–420.

Grollman, Earl A. 1965. *Judaism in Sigmund Freud's World*. New York: Appleton-Century.

Grotjahn, Martin. 1961. Jewish Jokes and Their Relations to Masochism. *Journal of the Hillside Hospital* 10: 183–189.

Grunberger, Béla. 1976. Study of Anal Object Relations. *International Review of Psychoanalysis* 3: 99–110.

Grunveld, I. 1972. *The Sabbath: A Guide to Its Understanding and Observance*. Jerusalem: Feldheim Publishers.

Gurevitch, Michael, and Gila Schwartz. 1971. Television and the Sabbath Culture in Israel. *Jewish Journal of Sociology* 13: 65–71.

Ha-'Am, Ahad. 1912. *Selected Essays*. Philadelphia: Jewish Publication Society of America.

———. 1946. *Essays, Letters, Memoirs*. Oxford: Phaidon Press.

Haight, David F. 1977. Is Money a Four-Letter Word? *Psychoanalytic Review* 64: 621–629.

Halberstam, Joshua. 1997. *Schmoozing: The Private Conversations of American Jews*. New York: Perigee Books.

Halkin, A. S. 1980–81. The Shabbes Goy. *Forum on the Jewish People, Zionism and Israel* 40: 23–27.

Hallo, William W. 1977. New Moons and Sabbaths: A Case-Study in the Contrastive Approach. *Hebrew Union College Annual* 48: 1–18.

Halperin, Levi Yitzhak. 1983. *Maaliot B'Shabat (Elevators on the Sabbath)*. Jerusalem: Institute for Science and Halacha.

———. 1986. *Shabbat and the Modern Kitchen*. Woodbridge, Conn.: Gefen Books.

Halperin, Levi Yitzchak, and Dovid Oratz. 1994. *Kashrut and the Modern Kitchen*. Jerusalem: Feldheim Publishers.

Handelman, Susan. 1981. Interpretation as Devotion: Freud's Relation to Rabbinic Hermeneutics. *Psychoanalytic Review* 68: 201–218.

Haran, Menahem. 1979. Seething a Kid in Its Mother's Milk. *Journal of Jewish Studies* 30: 23–35.

Harrington, Hannah K. 1993. *The Impurity Systems of Qumran and the Rabbis: Biblical Foundations*. Atlanta: Scholars Press.

Hehn, Johannes. 1907. *Siebenzahl und Sabbat bei den Babyloniern und im Alten Testament*. Leipzig: J. C. Hinrichs'sche Buchhandlung.

———. 1925. Zur Bedeutung der Siebenzahl. In *Vom Alten Testament: Karl Marti zum Siebzigsten Geburtstage*, Karl Budde, ed., 128–136. Giessen: Verlag von Alfred Töpelmann.

Heilman, Samuel C. 1975. The Gift of Alms: Face-to-Face Almsgiving Among Orthodox Jews. *Urban Life and Culture* 3: 371–395.

Heimann, Paula. 1962. Notes on the Anal Stage. *International Journal of Psycho-Analysis* 43: 406–414.

Herrmann, Johannes. 1905. *Die Idee der Sühne im Alten Testament: Eine Untersuchung über Gebrauch und Bedeutung des Wortes* kipper. Leipzig: J. C. Hinrichs'sche Buchhandlung.

Herskovits, Melville J. 1927. When Is a Jew a Jew? *Modern Quarterly* 4: 109–117.

Heschel, A. J. 1951. *The Sabbath: Its Meaning for Modern Man*. New York: Farrar, Straus and Giroux.

Hill, A. B. 1976. Methodological Problems in the Use of Factor Analysis: A Critical Review of the Experimental Evidence for the Anal Character. *British Journal of Medical Psychology* 49: 145–159.

Himelstein, Shmuel. 1990. *The Jewish Primer*. New York: Facts on File.

Hirschfeld, H. 1896. Remarks on the Etymology of Sabbath. *Journal of the Royal Asiatic Society of Great Britain and Ireland* 353–359.

Hoenig, Samuel N. 1993. *The Essence of Talmudic Law and Thought*. Northvale, N.J.: Jason Aronson.

Hoenig, Sidney B. 1978. The Designated Number of Kinds of Labor Prohibited on the Sabbath. *Jewish Quarterly Review* 68: 193–208.

Hooke, S. H. 1952. The Theory and Practice of Substitution. *Vetus Testamentum* 2: 2–17.

Howes, David. 1987. Olfaction and Transition: An Essay on the Ritual Uses of Smell. *Canadian Journal of Sociology and Anthropology* 24: 398–416.

Huffmon, Herbert B. 1959. The Covenant Lawsuit in the Prophets. *Journal of Biblical Literature* 78: 285–295.

Hultkrantz, Åke. 1960. *General Ethnological Concepts*. Copenhagen: Rosenkilde and Bagger.

Ingram, I. M. 1961. Obsessional Personality and Anal-Erotic Character. *Journal of Mental Science* 107: 1035–1042.

Isaacs, Ronald H. 1998. *Divination, Magic, and Healing: The Book of Jewish Folklore*. Northvale, N.J.: Jason Aronson.

———. 2000. *Every Person's Guide to Jewish Law*. Northvale, N.J.: Jason Aronson.

Jachter, Howard, and Michael Broyde. 1993. Electrically Produced Fire or Light in Positive Commandments. *Journal of Halacha and Contemporary Society* 25 (Spring): 89–126.

Jacobs, Louis. 1981. *Teyku: The Unsolved Problem in the Babylonian Talmud*. London: Cornwall Books.

———. 1984a. *The Talmudic Argument: A Study in Talmudic Reasoning and Methodology*. Cambridge: Cambridge University Press.

———. 1984b. *A Tree of Life: Diversity, Flexibility, and Creativity in Jewish Law*. Oxford: Oxford University Press.

———. 1999. *Ask the Rabbi*. London: Vallentine Mitchell.

Jacobson, Sol. 1976. The Logic of the Talmud. *Midstream* 22 (6): 50.

Janowski, Bernd. 1982. *Sühne als Heilsgeschehen: Studien zur Sühnetheologie der Priesterschrift und zur Wurzel KPR im Alten Orient und im alten Testament*. Neukirchen: Neukirchener Verlag.

Janssens, P. 1958. Het Getal Zeven in Het Volksgeloof. *Volkskunde* 59: 14–36.

Jastrow, Morris. 1898. The Original Character of the Hebrew Sabbath. *American Journal of Theology* 2: 312–352.

———. 1899. Dust, Earth, and Ashes as Symbols of Mourning Among the Ancient Hebrews. *Journal of the American Oriental Society* 20: 133–150.

Jones, Ernest. 1953. *The Life and Work of Sigmund Freud*. Vol. I. New York: Basic Books.

———. 1961. Anal-Erotic Character Traits. In *Papers on Psycho-Analysis*, 413–437. Boston: Beacon Press.

Josephus, Flavius. 1981. *The Jewish War*, G. A. Williamson, trans. London: Penguin Books.

Jungk, Peter Stephan. 1985. *Shabbat: A Rite of Passage in Jerusalem*. New York: Random House.

Kahn, Roger. 1968. *The Passionate People: What It Means to Be a Jew in America*. New York: William Morrow.

Kahn, Susan Martha. 2000. *Reproducing Jews: A Cultural Account of Assisted Conception in Israel*. Durham, N.C.: Duke University Press.

Kalir, Joseph. 1965. The Minhag. *Tradition* 7 (2): 89–95.

Kapelrud, Arvid S. 1968. The Number Seven in Ugaritic Texts. *Vetus Testamentum* 18: 494–499.

Kaplan, Abraham. 1980. The Jewish Argument with God. *Commentary* 70 (4): 43–47.

Katz, David. 1991. The Live-In Maid. *Journal of Halacha and Contemporary Society* 22 (Fall): 4–30.

Katz, Jacob. 1989. *The "Shabbes Goy": A Study in Halakhic Flexibility*. Philadelphia: Jewish Publication Society.

Kaye, Evelyn. 1987. *The Hole in the Sheet: A Modern Woman Looks at Orthodox and Hasidic Judaism*. Secaucus, N.J.: Lyle Stuart.

Kelley, Donald R. 1990. "Second Nature": The Idea of Custom in European Law, Society and Culture. In *The Transmission of Culture in Early Modern Europe*, Anthony Grafton and Ann Blair, eds., 131–172. Philadelphia: University of Pennsylvania Press.

Kertzer, Morris N. 1993. *What Is a Jew?* New York: Collier Books.

Kimball, Bruce A. 1978. The Origin of the Sabbath and Its Legacy to the Modern Sabbatical. *Journal of Higher Education* 49: 303–315.

Kimbrough, S. T. 1966. The Concept of Sabbath at Qumran. *Revue de Qumran* 5: 483–502.

Klein, Cecelia F. 1993. Teocuitlatl, "Divine Excrement": The Significance of "Holy Shit" in Ancient Mexico. *Art Journal* 52 (3): 20–27.

Kohlenberger, John R., ed. 1997. *The Parallel Apocrypha*. New York: Oxford University Press.

Kolatch, Alfred J. 1985. *The Second Jewish Book of Why*. New York: Jonathan David Publishers.

———. 1995. *The Jewish Book of Why*. Rev. ed. New York: Jonathan David Publishers.

Kraeling, E. G. 1933. The Present Status of the Sabbath Question. *American Journal of Semitic Languages* 49: 218–228.

Kraemer, David. 1997. The Spirit of the Rabbinic Sabbath. *Conservative Judaism* 49 (4): 42–49.

Kraft, Robert A. 1965. Some Notes on Sabbath Observance in Early Christianity. *Andrews University Seminary Studies* 18: 18–33.

Kroeber, A. L. 1917. Are the Jews a Race? *The Menorah Journal* 3: 290–294.

Kramer, A. Stanley. 1994. *World's Best Jewish Humor*. New York: Citadel.

Kumove, Shirley. 1985. *Words Like Arrows: A Collection of Yiddish Sayings*. New York: Schocken Books.

———. 1999. *More Words More Arrows: A Further Collection of Yiddish Folk Sayings*. Detroit: Wayne State University Press.

Landsberger, Benno. 1967. *The Date Palm and Its By-Products According to the Cuneiform Sources*. Graz: Archiv für Orientforschung.

Lauterbach, Jacob Z. 1970. The Origin and Development of Two Sabbath Ceremonies. In *Studies in Jewish Law, Custom and Folklore*, Jacob Z. Lauterbach, ed., 75–132. New York: KTAV Publishing House.

———. 1973. The Sabbath in Jewish Ritual and Folklore. In *Rabbinic Essays*, 437–470. New York: KTAV Publishing House.

Laytner, Anson. 1990. *Arguing with God: A Jewish Tradition*. Northvale, N.J.: Jason Aronson.

Leamon, Oliver. 1995. *Evil and Suffering in Jewish Philosophy*. Cambridge: Cambridge University Press.

Leiser, Burton M. 1971. Custom and Law in Talmudic Jurisprudence. *Judaism* 20: 396–403.

Levenson, Sammy. 1946. *Meet the Folks: A Session of American-Jewish Humor*. New York: Citadel.

Levi, Leo. 1966. On the Use of Electrical Equipment on Shabbath and Yom Tov. *Proceedings of the Associations of Orthodox Jewish Scientists* 1: 31–51.

Levine, Baruch A. 1974. *In the Presence of the Lord: A Study of Cult and Some Cultic Terms in Ancient Israel*. Leiden: E. J. Brill.

Levy, David A., and Drew D. Erhardt. 1988. Stinks and Instincts: An Empirical Investigation of Freud's Excreta Theory. *Journal of Irreproducible Results* 35 (5): 8–9.

Levy, Ludwig. 1914. Die Sexualsymbolik der Bibel und des Talmuds. *Zeitschrift für Sexualwissenschaft* 1: 273–279, 318–326.

———. 1915–16. Die Sexualsymbolik des Ackerbaus in Bibel und Talmud. *Zeitschrift für Sexualwissenschaft* 2: 437–444.

———. 1916–17. Sexualsymbolik in der Simsonsage. *Zeitschrift für Sexualwissenschaft* 3: 256–271.

———. 1917. Sexualsymbolik in der biblischen Paradiesgeschichte. *Imago* 5: 16–30.

———. 1918. Die Schuhsymbolik im jüdischen Ritus. *Monatsschrift für Geschichte und Wissenschaft des Judenthums* 62: 178–185.

Lewin, Kurt. 1941. Self-Hatred Among Jews. *Contemporary Jewish Record* 4: 219–232.

Lewin, Ralph A. 1999. *Merde: Excursions in Scientific, Cultural, and Sociohistorical Coprology*. New York: Random House.

Lewis, Aubrey. 1936. Problems of Obsessional Illness. *Proceedings of the Royal Society of Medicine* 29: 325–336.

———. 1978. Psychiatry and the Jewish Tradition. *Psychological Medicine* 8: 9–19.

Lewis, Nolan D. C., and Helen Yarnell. 1951. *Pathological Firesetting (Pyromania)*. New York: Nervous and Mental Disease Monographs.

Lewis, Richard Alan. 1997. Ritual Handwashing. *American Journal of Psychiatry* 154: 1172–1173.

Lighter, J. E., ed. 1994. *Random House Historical Dictionary of American Slang*. Vol. 1, A–G. New York: Random House.

Linke, Stuart. 1999. *Psychological Perspectives on Traditional Jewish Practices*. Northvale, N.J.: Jason Aronson.

Lowenstein, Steven M. 2000. *The Jewish Cultural Tapestry: International Jewish Folk Traditions*. New York: Oxford University Press.

Maccoby, Hyam. 1999. *Ritual and Morality: The Ritual Purity System and its Place in Judaism*. Cambridge: Cambridge University Press.

McKay, Heather. 1991. New Moon or Sabbath. In *The Sabbath in Jewish and Christian Traditions*, Tamara C. Eskenazi, Daniel J. Harrington, and William H. Shea, eds., 12–27. New York: Crossroad.

———. 1992. From Evidence to Edifice: Four Fallacies about the Sabbath. In *Text as Pretext: Essays in Honour of Robert Davidson*, Robert P. Carroll, ed., 179–199. Sheffield: JSOT Press.

———. 1994. *Sabbath and Synagogue: The Question of Sabbath Worship in Ancient Judaism*. Leiden: E. J. Brill.

Mahler, Eduard. 1908. Der Sabbat: Seine etymologische und Chronologisch-historische Bedeutung. *Zeitschrift der Deutschen* Morgenländischen *Gesellschaft* 62: 33–79.

Maimonides, Moses. 1954. *The Book of Cleanness (The Code of Maimonides, Book 10)*. New Haven, Conn.: Yale University Press.

Malev, Milton. 1966. The Jewish Orthodox Circumcision Ceremony. *Journal of the American Psychoanalytic Association* 14: 510–517.

Malinowski, Bronislaw. 1967. *Crime and Custom in Savage Society*. Totowa, N.J.: Littlefield, Adams & Co.

Marchant, Dovid. 1986. *Understanding Shmittoh and Halochos of Shmittoh*. Jerusalem: Feldheim Publishers.

Matisoff, James A. 1979. *Blessings, Curses, Hopes, and Fears: Psycho-Ostensive Expressions in Yiddish*. Philadelphia: ISHI.

Maybaum, Ignaz. 1965. *The Face of God After Auschwitz*. Amsterdam: Polak and Van Gennep.

Meek, Theophile James. 1914. The Sabbath in the Old Testament (Its Origin and Development). *Journal of Biblical Literature* 33: 201–212.

Meier, Samuel A. 1991. The Sabbath and Purification Cycles. In *The Sabbath in Jewish and Christian Traditions*, Tamara C. Eskanazi, Daniel J. Harrington, and William H. Shea, eds., 3–11. New York: Crossroad.

Meigs, Anna S. 1978. A Papuan Perspective on Pollution. *Man* 13: 304–318.

Meinhold, Hans. 1909. *Sabbat und Sonntag*. Leipzig: Quelle & Meyer.

Menninger, William C. 1943. Characterologic and Symptomatic Expressions Related to the Anal Phase of Psychosexual Development. *Psychoanalytic Quarterly* 12: 161–193.

Metzger, Joshua. 1989. The Eruv: Can Government Constitutionally Permit Jews to Build a Fictional Wall Without Breaking the Wall Between Church and State? *National Jewish Law Review Annual* 4: 67–92.

Metzker, Isaac. 1971. *A Bintel Brief*. New York: Ballantine Books.

Milgrom, Jacob. 1984. Rationale for Cultic Law: The Case of Impurity. *Semeia* 45: 103–109.

———. 1985. "You Shall Not Boil a Kid in Its Mother's Milk." *Bible Review* 1 (3): 48–55.

———. 1991. *Leviticus 1–16*. New York: Doubleday.

———. 1993. The Rationale for Biblical Impurity. *Journal of the Ancient Near Eastern Society* 22: 107–111.

Mirsky, Yehudah. 2000. New York Diarist: Openings. *New Republic* 223 (8): 50.

Mitchell, Oliver R. 1893. The Fictions of the Law: Have They Proved Useful or Detrimental to Its Growth. *Harvard Law Review* 7: 249–265.

Mollinger, Robert N. 1980. Antithesis and the Obsessive-Compulsive. *Psychoanalytic Review* 67: 465–477.

Morgenstern, Julian. 1966. *Rites of Birth, Marriage, Death and Kindred Occasions Among the Semites*. Cincinnati, Ohio: Hebrew Union College Press.

Muensterberger, Werner. 1994. *Collecting: An Unruly Passion*. Princeton, N.J.: Princeton University Press.

Nacht, Jacob. 1915. The Symbolism of the Shoe with Special Reference to Jewish Sources. *Jewish Quarterly Review* 6: 1–22.

Nádor, G. 1962. Some Numeral Categories in Ancient Rabbinical Literature: The Numbers *Ten, Seven* and *Four*. *Acta Orientalia* 14: 301–315.

Naiman, Arthur. 1983. *Every Goy's Guide to Common Jewish Expressions*. New York: Ballantine Books.

Naron, G. 1984. Fact & Folklore of Familiar Jewish Things or How the Fish Became Gefilte. *Jewish Monthly* 98 (March): 8–14.

Negretti, Nicola. 1973. *Il Settimo Giorno*. Rome: Biblical Institute Press.

Neulander, Arthur H. 1950. The Use of Electricity on the Sabbath. *Proceedings of the Rabbinical Assembly of America* 14: 165–171.

Neumann, Yechiel. 1983. Passenger Responsibility for Descent: A Halakhic Analysis. In *Maaliot B'Shabbat (Elevators on the Sabbath)*, Levi Ylitzhak Halperin, ed., 24–29. Jerusalem: Institute for Science and Halacha.

Neusner, Jacob. 1973. *The Idea of Purity in Ancient Judaism*. Leiden: E. J. Brill.

———. 1984. *The Talmud of Babylonia: An American Translation. I. Tractate Berakhot*. Chico, Calif.: Scholars Press.

———. 1988. *The Mishnah: A New Translation*. New Haven, Conn.: Yale University Press.

———. 1991. *Studying Classical Judaism: A Primer*. Louisville, Ky.: Westminster/John Knox Press.

———. 1992. *Decoding the Talmud's Exegetical Program*. Tampa: University of South Florida.

———. 1992–93. *The Talmud of Babylonia: An American Translation. II. Tractate Shabbat*. 5 vols. Atlanta: Scholars Press.

———. 1994. *Purity in Rabbinic Judaism: A Systematic Account. The Sources, Media, Effects, and Removal of Uncleanness*. Atlanta: Scholars Press.

———. 2000. *The Halakhah: An Encyclopedia of the Law of Judaism*. 5 vols. Leiden: Brill.

Neuwirth, Yehoshua Y. 1989. *Shemirat Shabbath: A Guide to the Practical Observance of the Sabbath*. 2 vols. 2nd ed. Jerusalem: Feldheim Publishers.

Newton, Michael. 1985. *The Concept of Purity at Qumran and in the Letters of Paul*. Cambridge: Cambridge University Press.

Neyrey, J. 1968. The Idea of Purity in Mark's Gospel. *Semeia* 35: 91–128.

North, Robert. 1954. *Sociology of the Biblical Jubilee*. Rome: Ponteficio Istituto Biblico.

———. 1955. The Derivation of Sabbath. *Biblica* 36: 182–201.

Olivier, Pierre J. J. 1975. *Legal Fictions in Practice and Legal Science*. Rotterdam: Rotterdam University Press.

Olsvanger, Immanuel. 1921. *Contentions with God: A Study in Jewish Folk-Lore*. Cape Town: T. Maskew Miller.

Oratz, Dovid. 1993. *Shabbat and Electricity: Electrical and Electronic Devices on Shabbat*. Jerusalem: Institute for Science and Halacha.

Ostow, Mortimer. 1980. The Jewish Response to Crisis. *Conservative Judaism* 33 (4): 3–25.

———. 1982. Judaism and Psychoanalysis. In *Judaism and Psychoanalysis*, Mortimer Ostow, ed., 3–44. New York: KTAV Publishing House.

Ostrov, Stewart. 1978. Sex Therapy with Orthodox Jewish Couples. *Journal of Sex and Marital Therapy* 4: 266–278.

"P," Mr. 1984. *The World's Best Yiddish Dirty Jokes*. New York: Castle.

Palatnik, Lori. 1994. *Friday Night and Beyond: The Shabbat Experience Step-by-Step*. Northvale, N.J.: Jason Aronson.

Pardes, Ilana. 2000. *The Biography of Ancient Israel: National Narratives In the Bible*. Berkeley: University of California Press.

Paschen, Wilfried. 1970. *Rein und Unrein: Untersuchung zur biblischen Wortgeschichte*. München: Kösel-Verlag.

Patai, Raphael. 1977. *The Jewish Mind*. New York: Charles Scribner's Sons.

Peli, Pinchas H. 1988. *Shabbat Shalom: A Renewed Encounter with the Sabbath*. Washington, D.C.: B'nai B'rith Books.

———. 1991. *The Jewish Sabbath*. New York: Schocken Books.

Phillips, Anthony. 1969. The Case of the Woodgatherer Reconsidered. *Vetus Testamentum* 19: 125–128.

Pick, Eli. 1998. *Guide to Sabbath Observance*. 2nd edition. Southfield, Mo.: Targum Press.

Pinches, Theophilus G. 1904. Sabattu, The Babylonian Sabbath. *Proceedings of the Society of Biblical Archaeology* 26: 51–56.

Pinker, Aron. 1994. The Number 40 in the Bible. *Jewish Bible Quarterly* 22: 163–172.

Plutarch. 1956a. Advice About Keeping Well. In *Plutarch's Moralia*, Vol. 2, pp. 214–293. Cambridge: Harvard University Press.

———. 1956b. Superstition. In *Plutarch's Moralia*, Vol. 2, pp. 453–495. Cambridge: Harvard University Press.

Poirier, John C. 1996. Why Did the Pharisees Wash their Hands? *Journal of Jewish Studies* 47: 217–233.

Pollack, Herman. 1971. *Jewish Folkways in Germanic Lands (1648–1806): Studies in Aspects of Daily Life*. Cambridge: MIT Press.

———. 1973. On Jewish Folkways in Germanic Lands. *Journal of American Folklore* 86: 293–294.

———. 1980. The "Minhag": Some Examples of Its Characteristics. In *Go and Study: Essays and Studies in Honor of Alfred Jospe*, Raphael Jospe and Samuel Z. Fishman, eds., 341–351. Washington, D.C.: B'nai B'rith Hillel Foundations.

Pollack, Simon R. 1979. *Jewish Wit for All Occasions*. New York: A & W Visual Library.

Pollak, Jerrold. 1987. Relationship of Obsessive-Compulsive Personality to Obsessive-Compulsive Disorder: A Review of the Literature. *Journal of Psychology* 12: 137–148.

Potok, Chaim. 1967. *The Chosen*. New York: Simon and Schuster.

Prange, Arthur J., and M. M. Vitols. 1990. Jokes Among Southern Negroes: The Revelation of Conflict. In *Mother Wit from the Laughing Barrel*, Alan Dundes, ed., 628–636. Jackson: University Press of Mississippi.

Precker, Michael. 1981. How to "Beat" and Obey Sabbath Halacha. *Jewish Digest* 26 (July): 72–74.

Pritchard, James B. 1969. *Ancient Near Eastern Texts Relating to the Old Testament*. 3rd ed. Princeton, N.J.: Princeton University Press.

Quinsey, Vernon L., T. C. Chaplin, and D. Upfold. 1989. Arsonists and Sexual Arousal to Fire Settings: Correlation Unsupported. *Journal of Behavior Therapy and Experimental Psychiatry* 20: 203–209.

Rabinowitz, Abraham Hirsch. 1996. *The Study of Talmud: Understanding the Halachic Mind*. Northvale, N.J.: Jason Aronson.

Rabinowitz, Daniel. 1997. Crockpots: Are They All They're Cracked Up to Be? *Journal of Halacha and Contemporary Society* 34 (Fall): 103–114.

Rabinowitz, Louis I. 1971. Shabbes Goy and Shabbes Jew: The Challenge to Jewish Law in Israel. *Conservative Judaism* 25 (Winter): 29–35.

Rank, Otto. 1922. *Psychoanalytische Beiträge zur Mythenforschung*. Leipzig: Internationaler Psychoanalytischer Verlag.

Raskin, Richard. 1991. God versus Man in a Classic Jewish Joke. *Judaism* 49: 39–51.

———. 1992. *Life Is Like a Glass of Tea: Studies of Classic Jewish Jokes*. Philadelphia: Jewish Publication Society.

Reinhart, A. Kevin. 1990. Impurity No Danger. *History of Religions* 30: 1–24.

Renteln, Alison Dundes, and Alan Dundes, eds. 1995. *Folk Law: Essays in the Theory and Practice of* Lex Non Scripta. 2 vols. Madison: University of Wisconsin Press.

Richter, Alan. 1995. *Sexual Slang*. New York: HarperCollins.

Riesenfeld, Harald. 1970. The Sabbath and the Lord's Day in Judaism, the Preaching of Jesus and Early Christianity. In *The Gospel Tradition*, Harald Riesenfeld, ed., 111–137. Philadelphia: Fortress Press.

Rindisbacher, Hans J. 1992. *The Smell of Books: A Cultural-Historical Study of Olfactory Perception in Literature*. Ann Arbor: University of Michigan Press.

Roback, A. A. 1957. *Freudiana*. Cambridge: Sci-Art Publishers.

Robinson, Gnana. 1980. The Idea of Rest in the Old Testament and the Search for the Basic Character of Sabbath. *Zeitschrift für die Alttestamentliche Wissenschaft* 92: 32–42.

Rosenberg, Bernard, and Gilbert Shapiro. 1958. Marginality and Jewish Humor. *Midstream* 4 (2): 70–80.

Rosenfeld, Azriel. 1966. On the Concept of Sabbath Work. *Proceedings of the Associations of Orthodox Jewish Scientists* 1: 53–60.

Rosenthal, Judah. 1961. The Sabbath Laws of the Qumranites or the Damascus Covenanters. *Biblical Research* 6: 10–17.

Rossi, William A. 1976. *The Sex Life of the Foot & Shoe*. New York: Ballantine Books.

Rosten, Leo. 1970. *The Joys of Yiddish*. New York: Pocket Books.

———. 1972. *Leo Rosten's Treasury of Jewish Quotations*. New York: McGraw Hill.

———. 1976. The Schnorrer: Piety and Paradox. In *Next Year in Jerusalem: Portaits of the Jew in the Twentieth Century*, Douglas Villiers, ed., 121–125. New York: Viking Press.

———. 1982. *Hooray for Yiddish!* New York: Simon and Schuster.

———. 1992. *The Joys of Yinglish*. New York: Signet.

Roth, Joel. 1986. *The Halakhic Process: A Systemic Analysis*. New York: The Jewish Theological Seminary of America.

Roth, Philip. 1967. *Portnoy's Complaint*. New York: Random House.

Rowland, C. 1982. A Summary of Sabbath Observance in Judaism at the Beginning of the Christian Era. In *From Sabbath to Lord's Day*, D. A. Carson, ed., 42–55. Grand Rapids, Mich.: Zondervan.

Rubenstein, Richard L. 1963. The Significance of Castration Anxiety in Rabbinic Mythology. *Psychoanalytic Review* 50: 289–312.

Rubinstein, Amnon. 1971. Law and Religion in Israel. In *Jewish Law in Ancient and Modern Israel*, Haim H. Cohn, ed., 190–224. New York: KTAV Publishing House.

Sadger, J. Isidor. 1910. Analerotik und Analcharakter. *Die Heilkunde*, 43–46.

Sanders, E. P. 1990. *Jewish Law from Jesus to the Mishnah*. London: SCM Press.

Sapir, Edward. 1931. Custom. *Encyclopaedia of the Social Sciences*. Vol. IV, 658–662. New York: Macmillan.

Sartori, Paul. 1894. Der Schuh im Volksglauben. *Zeitschrift des Vereins für Volkskunde* 4: 41–54.

Schachter, Hershel. 1983. The Laws of Eruvin—An Overview. In *Halacha and Contemporary Society*, Alfred S. Cohen, ed., 131–150. New York: KTAV Publishing House.

Schauss, Hayyim. 1962. *The Jewish Festivals: History & Observance*. New York: Schocken Books.

Schechter, Solomon. 1892. Legal Evasions of the Law. In *Lectures on the Growth and Origin of Religion*, C. G. Montefiore, ed., 557–563. London: Williams and Norgate.

Schlossberg, Eli W. 1996. *The World of Orthodox Judaism*. Northvale, N.J.: Jason Aronson.

Schlossman, Howard H. 1966. Circumcision as Defense: A Study in Psychoanalysis and Religion. *Psychoanalytic Quarterly* 35: 340–356.

Schultze-Gallera, Siegmar. 1909. *Fuss- und Schuhsymbolik und Erotik: Folkloristische und sexualwissenschaftliche Untersuchungen*. Leipzig: Deutsche Verlags-Aktien-Gesellschaft.

Schwartz, Gedalia Dov. 1990. Kashruth—Problems and Solutions. *Judaism* 39: 427–435.

Sharvit, Baruch. 1979. The Sabbath of the Judean Desert Sect. *Immanuel* 9: 42–48.

Shilo, Shmuel. 1982. Circumvention of the Law in Talmudic Literature. *Israel Law Review* 17: 151–168.

Siegel, Seymour. 1982. The Sabbath and Conservative Judaism. *Judaism* 31: 45–54.

Sigal, Phillip. 1966. Halakha in Crisis. *Jewish Spectator* 31 (April): 23–26.

———. 1982. Toward a Renewal of Sabbath Halakhah. *Judaism* 31: 75–86.

Simoons, Frederick J. 1961. *Eat Not This Flesh: Food Avoidances in the Old World*. Madison: University of Wisconsin Press.

Sion, Avi. 1997. *Judaic Logic: A Formal Analysis of Biblical, Talmudic and Rabbinic Logic*. Geneva: Editions Slatkine.

Sokol, Binyomin. 1986. *A Physician's Hospital Manual: Hilchot Shabbat*. Jerusalem: Regensberg Institute.

Smith, Anna Deavere. 1993. *Fires in the Mirror: Crown Heights, Brooklyn and Other Identities*. New York: Anchor Books.

Somogyi, Joseph de. 1958. An Arabic Monograph on the Number Seven. *Islamic Culture* 23: 245–249.

Spaulding, Henry D. 1969. *Encyclopedia of Jewish Humor*. New York: Jonathan David Publishers.

Spears, Richard. 1997. *Hip & Hot: A Dictionary of 10,000 American Slang Expressions*. New York: Gramercy Books.

Sperling, Abraham Isaac. 1968. *Reasons for Jewish Customs and Traditions*. New York: Bloch Publishing.

Spirn, Nahum. 1992. Carrying People on Shabbat. *Journal of Halacha and Contemporary Society* 24 (Fall): 108–120.

Steingroot, Ira. 1995. *Keeping Passover*. San Francisco: HarperCollins.

Strand, Kenneth A. 1978. From Sabbath to Sunday in the Early Christian Church: A Review of Some Recent Literature. *Andrews University Seminary Studies* 16: 333–342.

———. 1979. From Sabbath to Sunday in the Early Christian Church: A Review of Some Recent Literature. *Andrews University Seminary Studies* 17: 85–104.

Strean, Herbert. 1993. *Jokes: Their Purpose and Meaning*. Northvale, N.J.: Jason Aronson.

———. 1994. *Psychotherapy with the Orthodox Jew*. Northvale, N.J.: Jason Aronson.

Stroes, H. R. 1966. Does the Day Begin in the Evening or Morning? Some Biblical Observations. *Vetus Testamentum* 16: 460–475.

Tawil, Hayim. 1980. Azazel The Prince of the Steepe: A Comparative Study. *Zeitschrift für die Alttestamentliche Wissenschaft* 92: 43–59.

Telushkin, Joseph. 1992. *Jewish Humor*. New York: William Morrow.

Tendler, Moshe David. 1988. *Pardes Rimonim: A Manual for the Jewish Family*. Hoboken, N.J.: KTAV Publishing House.

Tendler, Moshe David, and Fred Rosner. 1987. Dental Emergencies on the Sabbath. *Journal of Halacha and Contemporary Society* 14 (Fall): 49–64.

Thompson, E. P. 1991. *Customs in Common*. New York: New Press.

Thompson, Stith. 1955–58. *Motif-Index of Folk-Literature*. 6 vols. Bloomington: Indiana University Press.

Toy, C. H. 1899. The Earliest Form of the Sabbath. *Journal of Biblical Literature* 18: 190–194.

Trepp, Leo. 1980. *The Complete Book of Jewish Observance*. New York: Behrman House.

Trillin, Calvin. 1994. Drawing the Line. *New Yorker* 70, no. 41 (12 December): 50–62.

Tsevat, Matitiahu. 1971. The Basic Meaning of the Biblical Sabbath. *Zeitschrift für die Alttestamentliche Wissenschaft* 84: 447–459.

Tuchman, Gaye, and Harry Gene Levine. 1993. New York Jews and Chinese Food: The Social Construction of an Ethnic Pattern. *Journal of Contemporary Ethnography* 22: 382–407.

———. 1996. Safe Treyf. *Brandeis Review* 16 (4): 24–31.

Van Baaren, Th. P. 1972. The Flexibility of Myth. *Studies in the History of Religions* 22: 199–206.

Van der Toorn, K. 1989. La Pureté Rituelle au Proche-Orient Ancien. *Revue de l'Histoire des Religions* 206: 339–356.

Vecsey, George. 1979. The Making of an Eruv. *Jewish Digest* 25 (October): 11–13.

Vermes, Geza. 1998. *The Complete Dead Sea Scrolls in English*. New York: Penguin Books.

Wax, Douglas, and Victor Haddox. 1974. Enuresis, Fire Setting, and Animal Cruelty in Male Adolescent Delinquents: A Triad Predictive of Violent Behavior. *Journal of Psychiatry and Law* 2: 45–71.

Waxman, Chaim I. 1982. The Sabbath as Dialectic: The Meaning and Role. *Judaism* 31: 37–44.

Webster, Hutton. 1916. *Rest Days: A Study in Early Law and Morality*. New York: Macmillan.

Weinberger, Theodore. 1991. The Case for Not Driving on Shabbat. *Jewish Spectator* 56 (1): 16–18.

Weingreen, J. 1966. The Case of the Woodgatherer (Numbers XV 32–36). *Vetus Testamentum* 16: 361–364.

Weiss, Avraham. 1987. The *Eruv*: A Microcosm of the Shabbat Spirit. *Tradition* 23 (1): 40–46.

Weiss, Herold. 1990. The Sabbath in the Synoptic Gospels. *Journal for the Study of the New Testament* 38: 13–27.

———. 1998. The Sabbath in the Writings of Josephus. *Journal for the Study of Judaism* 29: 363–390.

Weltman, Gershon, and Marvin S. Zuckerman. 1975. *Yiddish Sayings Mama Never Taught You*. Van Nuys, Calif.: Perivale Press.

Werfel, Franz. 1935. *The Forty Days of Musa Dagh*. New York: Viking Press.

White, J. Benton. 1993. *Taking the Bible Seriously*. Louisville: Westminster/John Knox Press.

Whitfield, Stephen J. 1978. Laughter in the Dark: Notes on American-Jewish Humor. *Midstream* 24 (2): 48–58.

Wiesel, Elie. 1979. *The Trial of God*. New York: Random House.

Williams, A. R. 1945. Seven. *Folk-Lore* 56: 257–259.

Wilson, Edward O. 1978. *On Human Nature*. Cambridge: Harvard University Press.

Wolfram, Richard. 1972. *Prinzipien und Probleme der Brauchtumsforschung*. Wien: Hermann Böhlaus.

Wolpe, David J. 1990. *The Healer of Shattered Hearts: A Jewish View of God*. New York: Henry Holt.

Woolf, M. 1945. Prohibitions Against the Simultaneous Consumption of Milk and Flesh in Orthodox Jewish Law. *International Journal of Psycho-Analysis* 26: 169–177.

Wortis, Joseph. 1963. *Fragments of an Analysis with Freud*. Indianapolis: Charter Books.

Wouk, Herman. 1959. *This Is My God*. Garden City, N.Y.: Doubleday.

Wright, David P. 1987. *The Disposal of Impurity: Elimination Rites in the Bible and in Hittite and Mesopotamian Literature*. Atlanta: Scholars Press.

Yadin, Yigael. 1985. *The Temple Scroll: The Hidden Law of the Dead Sea Sect*. New York: Random House.

———, ed. 1983. *The Temple Scroll*. Vol. 1. Jerusalem: Israel Exploration Society.

Yang, Yong-Eui. 1997. *Jesus and the Sabbath in Matthew's Gospel*. Sheffield: Sheffield Academic Press.

Zborowski, Mark, and Elizabeth Herzog. 1962. *Life Is With People*. New York: Schocken Books.

Zemer, Moshe. 1999. *Evolving Halakhah: A Progressive Approach to Traditional Jewish Law*. Woodstock, Vt.: Jewish Lights Publishing.

Zeplowitz, Irwin A. 1997. Jewish Law. *Journal of Dharma* 22: 379–395.

Ziv, Avner. 1986. *Jewish Humor*. Tel Aviv: Papyrus.

Zivotofsky, Ari Z. 1995. "Your Camp Shall be Holy": Halacha and Modern Plumbing. *Journal of Halacha and Contemporary Society* 29 (Spring): 89–128.

Index

About the Author

Alan Dundes is recognized as one of the world's leading authorities on folklore. He is author or editor of more than thirty books, and has also written over two hundred articles for professional journals. Books previously published by Rowman & Littlefield include *Two Tales of Crow and Sparrow: A Freudian Folkloristic Essay on Caste and Untouchability* (1997), *Holy Writ as Oral Lit: The Bible as Folklore* (1999), and *International Folkloristics: Classic Contributions by the Founders of Folklore* (1999). Dundes lives in Berkeley where he is professor of anthropology and folklore at the University of California.